Terrorism : Perspectives from Behavioral and Social Sciences

Terrorism : Perspectives from Behavioral and Social Sciences

Avinash Bharti

CYBER TECH PUBLICATIONS
4264/3, Ansari Road, Daryaganj, New Delhi-110002 (India)
Ph.: 011-23244078, 011-43559448 Fax: 011-23280028
E-Mail: cyberpublicationsdelhi@yahoo.com
Website: www.cybertechpublications.com

TERRORISM : PERSPECTIVES FROM BEHAVIORAL AND SOCIAL SCIENCES

Avinash Bharti

First Edition 2010

Published by :

G.S. Rawat for **Cyber Tech Publications**
4264/3, Ansari Road, Daryaganj, New Delhi-110002 (India)
Ph.: 011-23244078, 011-43559448 Fax: 011-23280028
E-Mail: cyberpublicationsdelhi@yahoo.com
Website: www.cybertechpublications.com

Printed at: Asian Offset Printers, Delhi-53

Preface

Terrorism involves the illegal use or threatened use of violence, is intended to coerce societies or governments by inducing fear in their populations, and typically involves ideological and political motives. The attacks on September 11, 2001, have made Americans acutely aware of the devastation of terrorism. As the nation engages in the "war on terrorism," the psychological health of the public must not be neglected.

Terrorism, whether in the form of a mass physical attack or a chemical, biological, radiological, or nuclear event, can be psychologically devastating. Psychological consequences include an array of emotional, behavioral, and cognitive reactions. People may experience insomnia, fear, anxiety, vulnerability, anger, increased alcohol consumption, or smoking, and a minority will develop psychiatric illnesses such as posttraumatic stress disorder or depression. The number of people affected and the severity of consequences will vary according to the type and intensity of the event. The broad nature of these consequences demands a full public health response.

The nation's mental health, public health, medical, and emergency response systems currently are not able to meet the psychological needs that result from terrorism. Gaps exist in the coordination of agencies and services, training and supervision of professionals, public communication and dissemination of information, financing, and knowledge- and evidence-based services.

Management of the psychological consequences of terrorism will require a range of interventions at multiple levels involving a variety of service providers. Interventions are needed for the pre-event, event, and post-event phases of a terrorist attack and will have to address affected individuals and populations, the broader social environment, and the terrorists who seek to harm. The committee offers an example for a public health strategy that may serve as a base from which plans to prevent and respond to the psychological consequences of a variety of terrorism events can be formulated. This approach is a strategic vision for assessing the completeness and effectiveness of plans, and to defining and addressing gaps in preparedness and response. It is hoped that lessons learned from preparing for the psychological consequences of terrorism may serve additional benefits by being applied to a variety of other violent events that affect the population. By comprehensively addressing the physical, psychological, and sociocultural needs of the population, the desired end result will be achieved—that is, the limitation of adverse psychological consequences, facilitation of growth and empowerment, minimization of disruptions to daily life, and enhancement of community cohesion.

—Author

CONTENTS

Preface

1. Terrorism 1
2. Terrorism in Pakistan 22
3. Terrorism—A Threat to Democracy 41
4. Social Impact of Terrorism on National Development 50
5. The War on Empiricism 75
6. Insurgency and Terrorism in Afghanistan 83
7. Terror, Terrorist, Terrorism 104
8. Capitalism and Terrorism 184
9. The Faces of Terrorism: Social and Psychological Dimensions 220
10. Suicide Terrorism as a Tool of Insurgency Campaigns 252

Bibliography 263

Index 264

1

TERRORISM

INTRODUCTION

The history of mankind is replete with tales of horror of some power-wielding humans going mad, while others have been the victims of their unimaginable brutalities. The perpetrators have ranged from individuals to armed groups to states. The systematic use of terror as a means to attain political objectives exists all over the world.

The attention we give to terrorism often seems disproportionate to its real importance. Terrorism incidents make superb copy for journalists, but kill and maim fewer people than road accidents. Nor is terrorism politically effective. Empires rise and fall according to the real determinants of politics – namely overwhelming force or strong popular support – not according to the bit of mayhem and pandemonium caused by isolated fanatics whom one would take seriously enough to vote for it. Indeed, the very variety of incidents that might be described as Terrorism has been such as to lead critics to suggest that no single subject for investigation exists at all. Might we not regard terrorism as a king of minor blotch on the skin of an industrial civilization whose very heart is filled with violent dreams and aspirations. Who would call in the dermatologist when the heart itself is sick?

But popular opinion takes Terrorism very seriously indeed and popular opinion is probably right. For the significance of Terrorism lies not only in the grotesque nastiness of terrorist outrages but also in the moral claims they imply. Terrorism is the most dramatic exemplification of the moral fault of blind willfulness. Terrorism is a solipsistic denial of the obligation of self-control we all must recognize when we lived in civilized communities.

Certainly the sovereign high road to misunderstanding Terrorism is the pseudo-scientific project of attempting to discover its causes. Terrorists themselves talk of the frustrations, which have supposedly necessitated their actions, but to transform these facile justifications into scientific hypothesis is to succumb to the terrorists' own fantasies. To kill and main people is a choice people make, and glib invocations of necessity are baseless. Other people living in the same situation see no such necessity at all.

HISTORY OF TERRORISM

Terrorism is not a recent phenomenon. The Zealots employed it against the Roman occupation in Palestine. The Assassins used it in eleventh and twelfth centuries in Persia and Syria. The Thugs in India used it for many centuries against innocent travelers to appease the bloodthirsty goddess Kali. Terrorism became an important feature of European politics during and after the French Revolution as different political groups comprising anarchists, nationalists and social revolutionaries practiced assassinations, bombings and various forms of violent seizure and destruction of property.

Terrorism has become the greatest evil in our worlds today. It is perpetrated by fanatics who are utterly indifferent to the sanctity of human life. Although the international community remains divided a universal definition of what is meant by terrorism, yet it remains committed to confront it through a variety of means.

WHAT IS TERRORISM?

In the present scenario, the terrorism is being successfully tackled by the United States and its allies who have declared War on Terrorism. If we ponder upon the word Terrorism, it's a relative term, which takes on a different meaning if we change its context. Terrorism has no absolute and globally accepted definition and its interpretation can easily be used or abused to suite particular needs. The adage that "one man's terrorist is another's freedom fighter" reveals the wide range of variations in its interpretation but, if simply stated, terror is extreme or intense fear. It is a psychological state, which combines the physical and mental efforts to create dread and insecurity. The matter of terrorism is complicated. The terrorist of yesterday is the hero of today and the hero of yesterday is the terrorist of today. This is serious matter of constantly changing world in which we have to keep our heads straight to know what is terrorism and what is not. But most importantly to know what causes it and how to stop it. The present terrorism scenario is very closely related with Islam.

GLOBALLY ACCEPTED DEFINITIONS

On December 6, 2001, Justice Ministers of the 25-member European Union adopted a new common definition of terrorism. It defined terrorism as:

"Acts committed with the aim of seriously intimidating a population, forcing a government or international organization to abstain from performing any act, or seriously destabilizing or destroying the fundamental political, constitutional, economic or social structures of a country or an international organization."

Bruce Hoffman, an expert on terrorism, defined it as:

"Ineluctably political aims and motives, violent, or equally important, threatening violence, designed to have far-reaching psychological repercussions beyond the immediate victim or target, conducted by an organization with an identifiable chain of command."

International Summit on Democracy, Terrorism and security held in Madrid on March 10, 2005. The panel calls for a definition, which would make it clear:

"Any action constitutes terrorism if it is intended to cause death or serious bodily harm to civilians with the purpose of intimidating a population or compelling a government or an international organization to do or abstain from doing any act."

THE RISE OF TERRORISM

"Most Muslims are not fundamentalists, and more fundamentalists are not terrorists, but more present day terrorists are Muslims and proudly identify themselves as such.", writes Bernard Lewis in 'The Crisis of Islam'.

Thanks to the rapid development of the media, and especially of television, the more recent forms of terrorism are aimed not at specific and limited enemy objectives but at world opinion. Their primary purpose is not to defeat or even to weaken the enemy militarily but not to gain publicity and to inspire fear – a psychological victory. The same kind of terrorism was practiced by a number of European groups, notably in Germany, Italy, Spain, and Ireland. Among the most successful and most enduring in this exercise has been the Palestine Liberation Organization (PLO).

The PLO was founded in 1964 but became important in the 1967, after the defeat of the combined Arab armies in the Six-Day War. Regular warfare had failed; it was time to try other methods. The targets in this form of armed struggle were not military or other government establishments, which are usually too well guarded, but public places and gatherings of any kind, which are overwhelmingly civilian and in which the victims do not necessarily have a connection to the declared enemy. Examples of this tactic include, in 1970, the hijacking of three aircrafts – one Swiss, one British, and one American – which were all taken to Amman. These and other operations by the PLO were remarkably successful in attaining their immediate objectives – the capture of the newspaper headlines and television screens. They also drew a great deal of support in sometimes-unexpected places, and raised their perpetrators to staring roles in the drama of international relations. Small wonder that others were encouraged to follow their example.

For a while freedom and independence were used as synonymous and interchangeable terms. The early experience of independence, however, revealed that this was a sad error. Independence and freedom are very different, and all too often the attainment of one meant the and of the other, and the replacement of foreign overlords by domestic tyrants, more adept, more intimate, and less constrained in their tyranny.

A new phase in religious mobilization began with the movement known in western languages as pan-Islamism. Launched in the 1860s and 1870s, it probably owed something to the examples of the Germans and the Italians in their successful struggles for national unification in those years. Their Muslim contemporaries and imitators inevitably identified their objectives in religious and communal rather than nationalist or patriotic terms, which at that time were still alien and unfamiliar. But with the spread of European influence and education, these ideas took root and for a while dominated both discourse and struggle in the Muslim lands. Yet the religious identity and loyalty were still deeply felt, and they found expression in several religious movements, notably the Muslim Brothers. With the resounding failure of secular ideologies, they acquired a new importance, and these movements took over the fight – and many of the fighters – from the failed nationalists.

A letter to America published in November 2002, and attributed to Usama Bin Ladin, enumerates in some detail various offences committed not just by the government but also by the people of the US and set forth, under seven headings, "what we are calling you to do, and what we want from you." The first is to embrace Islam; the second is to stop your oppressions, lies, immorality, and debauchery; the third, to discover and admit that America is a nation without principles or manners; the fourth, to stop supporting Israel in Palestine, the Indians in Kashmir, the Russians against the Chechens, and the Manila government against the Muslims in the southern Philippines; the fifth, to pack your luggage and get out of our lands. This is offered as advice for America's own goods, so do not force us to send you back as cargo in coffins. The sixth, to end your support of the corrupt leaders in our countries. Do not interfere in our politics and method of education. Leave us alone, or else expect us in New York and Washington; seventh, to deal and interact with the Muslims on the basis of mutual interests and benefits, rather than the policies of subjugation, theft and occupation. The document ends by telling the Americans that, if they reject this advice, they will be defeated like all the previous Crusaders, and their fate will be that of the Soviets who fled from Afghanistan to deal with their military defeat, political breakup, ideological downfall, and economic bankruptcy.

"If freedom fails and terror triumphs, the peoples of Islam will be the first and greatest victims. They will not be alone, and many others will suffer with them."

THE TROUBLE WITH TERRORISM

Charles Townshend writes in "Terrorism":

"Terrorism upsets people. It does so deliberately. That is its point, and that is why it has engrossed so mush of our attention in the early years of the 21st century. Insecurity can take many forms, but nothing else pays quite so sharply on our sense of vulnerability. After September 11 we found ourselves in an apparently open-ended and permanent state of emergency, a "war against terrorism", whose ramifications are as inscrutable as terrorism itself. Terrorism is never easy to understand, and least of all in the aftermath of a terrorist attack. When society feels under threat, attempts at rational analysis are often openly resisted as giving aid and comfort to, or even sympathizing with, the enemy. Yet without such analysis, combating Terrorism seems a baffling contest against an indefinite threat. Although Terrorism can sometimes took rational, more often it seems to go straight off the chart of common sense – to be not only unjustifiable, but atrocious, mad or mindless."

The Problem of Definition

"Both political and academic efforts to get to grips with terrorism have repeatedly been hung up on the issue of definition, of distinguishing terrorism from criminal violence or military action. In a word it is labeling because terrorist is a description that has almost never been voluntarily adopted by any individual group. It is applied to them by others, first and foremost by the governments of the states they attack. States have not been slow to brand violent opponents with this title, with its clear implications of inhumanity, criminality, and – perhaps most crucially – lack of real political support. Equally, states find it quite easy to produce definitions of Terrorism. The USA, for instance, defines it as ' the calculated use or threat of violence to inculcate fear, intended to coerce or intimidate governments or societies'; the UK as 'the use or threat, for the purpose of advancing a political, religious, or ideological course of action, of serious violence against any person or property'."

"In the states view, only the state has the right to use force – it has, as academics tend to say, a monopoly on the legitimate use of violence. But outsiders may wonder whether all use of violence by non-state actors is equally unjustifiable, even it is formally illegal. The very first revolutionary terrorists in the modern sense believed themselves justified in opposing with violence a repressive regime in which no freedom of political expression or organization was permitted."

"Thus arose a notorious adage that one person's terrorist is another's freedom fighter. This relativism is central to the impossibly of finding an uncontentious definition of Terrorism."

"Terrorism is a distinctive form of modern political agency, intended to threaten the ability of a state to ensure the security of its members' – and thus its claim to legitimacy. To get closer to a definition of Terrorism we need to unpick its political logic. For the core of nearly all definitions of Terrorism – the use of violence for the political ends – is too similar to the definition of war to be much of use."

Terrorism & War

"Clearly war and terrorism are intimately related. It is hard to imagine a war that did not generate extreme fear amongst many people, and sometimes this is more than a by-product of violence – it is a primary objective."

"The essence of Terrorism, by contrast, is surely the negation of combat. Its targets are attacked in a way that inhibits self-defence. But, of course, what marks Terrorism out in the public mind is its readiness to attack not just selected but also random targets; in the indiscriminate bombings of a street market, a store, or a bar, we see a deliberate flouting of the international law of war, and a refusal to accept as binding the prevailing moral distinctions – b/w belligerents and illegitimate targets. So the vital part of the US definition is the non-combatant targets against whom violence is perpetrated."

The Terror Process

I. Seizing attention: shock, horror, fear, or revulsion: this is certainly the most straightforward stage. The thirst for order and security impels societies to establish conventions and boundaries to regulate violent coercion: when these are transgressed, shock is generated.

II. Getting the message: what do terrorists want: by no means all-terrorist groups rush to claim responsibility for their actions, or if they do so, deliver a comprehensible rationale or demand. When terrorist acts are left unsigned - like 9/11 attacks – it is up to the onlookers to fill in the blanks. The results can be varied. George W. Bush assured his citizens that the 9/11 attacks were 'intended to frighten our nation into chaos and retreat'. But retreat from what, or where? American commentators, both official and unofficial, showed a marked reluctance to accept a surely well-established view that Usama bin Laden's primary motive against the US was the defilement of Saudi Arabia by the presence of US troops. Instead they preferred more abstract explanations of the attacks rooted in envy or hostility towards American prosperity and democracy.

III. Fight or flight? – The response: partly because the assessment of motives can be quirky, responses can be unpredictable or contradictory. If the demands are comprehensible and fulfillable, fear may drive people to comply. It is easy enough for people to fulfill minimal demands – to keep quiet and defuse to help the police, for instance; but bigger political demands can't usually be delivered directly. The people who are most likely to be intimidated or alarmed are the people who in most political structures are outside the decision-making sphere.

Strategies of Terror

T. P. Thornton proposed two basic varieties: enforcement and agitational terror. The function of the enforcement terror is likely to be limited, aimed at preserving the security of the rebel organization by deterring the public from giving information to the security forces. To succeed in this, the organization needs a sufficiently extensive surveillance system to persuade people that assisting the authorities will be detected: most terrorist groups are simply too small for this. Agitational terror is likely to grasp at mush extensive, longer-term goals: revolution of some kind, or 'national liberation'. Some of these goals are more feasible than others.

"Terrorist action may be auxiliary -one element of a larger military or guerilla strategy; it may be confined to limited goals; or it may be absolute – the pursuit of political goals through the systematic use of terror alone. It is this absolute, independent terror strategy, rather than terrorist action per se, that should properly be labeled terrorism. "Thus Terrorism properly so-called is not just the use of violence for political ends; not just outrageous violence; not just violence by the armed against the unarmed; it is conceived as a free-standing, sufficient, and decisive political strategy."

Terror & Politics

"Thinking about the terror process leads to the conclusion that the essential distinction b/w war and terrorism lies in their operational logic: war is ultimately coercive, terrorism is impressive. War is physical, terrorism is mental. Terrorism operates, therefore, through subjective psychological pressure.

Women & Terrorism

From Vera Zasulish, who carried out the first Narodnik armed attack when she shot the governor of St. Petersburg in 1878, to Waffa al-Edress, the first female Arab suicide bomber in Israel in January 2002, women have been frontline actors and, consequently, pioneer recasters of gender roles.

CRUSADERS & CONSPIRATORS

The Good Terrorist

Good terrorist are those whose actions are justified by the oppressiveness of the system they oppose.

Who becomes a terrorist? The answer is likely to be that it depends on the circumstances. Terrorist organizations differ markedly in how they recruit their members. Some will indeed require fanatics, ideologies, dreamers; others may be so embedded in their communities that recruitment resembles a rite of passage.

Freedom Fighters: that one man's terrorist is another man's freedom fighter – or one man's freedom fighter is another man's terrorist – is surely a commonplace of our times. There are some obvious grounds for relativism. Terrorism as a distinctive political concept got its name from the actions of the holders of the state power, perhaps the first modern regime – the French Convention of Year II of the French Revolution (1793-4). Since then, governments have been on any quantitative measure the most prolific users of terroristic violence. Yet there is not hint of this in the dominant official discourse, terrorism is used by extremists – rebels – against the established order – the state.

International Terrorism

"Communist states, especially Soviet Union and their surrogates, as well as other militant totalitarian regimes like Iran, Libya and Syria, are actively exporting terrorist and terror techniques into other countries. Their activity is a manifestation of transnational state-sponsored terrorism. They indoctrinate, fund, train, arm sub-state groups of diverse national origins to at as their tools, using psychological warfare and propaganda to create severe psycho-social conflict in contempoiary life."

US insistence on the central role of state-sponsorship has survived such cautionary advice, however; and several of the old 'rogue states' have been recently re-identified by President Bush as part of an axis of evil.

Super Terror

It has become clear over the last decade that we need to look into the future, to access the possibility of terrorists acquiring and using so-called 'WMDs' – chemical, biological and nuclear weapons. Although they did not involved such weapons, the unprecedented scale of 9/11 attacks seemed to bring the exponential expansion of destruction a big step closer.

THE REIGN OF TERROR

"Virtue without Terror is Powerless"

The French Revolution's ruthless and systematic use of violence created a model for the application of terrorizing force by the holders of state power over the next couple of centuries. A recent college textbook on terrorism identifies three functional levels of state terrorism: intimidation, coerced conversion; genocide – deliberate extermination of an entire class. Ethnic, or religious group. Although the prime exponents of terrorism from above were overtly repressive autocracies and despotisms, or radical revolutionary regimes like the Bolsheviks during the Russian civil war. The USA tolerated the persistent, systematic terrorization of the Southern Black community by the Ku Klux Klan, as well as the less dramatic use of intimidatory violence by employers against labour organizations.

NATIONALISM & TERROR

We need to understand the way in which different societies maintain their vision of their collective selves, and so produce different terrorisms and different terrorists. In other words, the framework for much modern terrorist action is ethnic or nationalist. Indeed, the emblematic terrorist act of the early 20th century – the assassination of Archduke Ferdinand, heir to the throne of Austria-hungry, at Sarajevo in June 1914 – was carried out by a Serbian nationalist. Nationalist movements have shown mush greater resilience and destructive capacity than the small and fissiparous left-wing revolutionary groups. They tend to be significantly bigger, for one thing, and to draw on a broader pool of recruitment; and though their cause – freeing or uniting the nation – is not necessarily more practicable than the revolutionary dream of total social transformation, nationalism has dominated modern politics precisely because it connects with a visceral, apparently natural force.

Terrorism may play a leading part in the attempt to preserve or reawaken the national spirit, and also in the accompanying struggle against a foreign or imperial government. But there is another and possibly more intractable problem: what all too often stands in the way of national liberation movements is not only the foreign government, but the fact that people of other ethnic groups live within the presumed national territory.

RELIGIOUS TERROR

"The fight in defence of religion and belief is a collective duty; there is no other duty after belief than fighting the enemy who is corrupting our life and our religion."

At the end of the 20th century the world faced a revival of religious fundamentalism, quite puzzling to many people who has assumed that the process of secularization was, although perhaps erratic, an irreversible one. The long standing liberal assumption that the rise of modern society and the decay of religion were two sides of the same coin was suddenly thrown into doubt; and the shock effect of this was soon registered in writing on terrorism, where religion has confidently been consigned to the margins of terrorist motivation.

One of the leading surveys in the late 1990s asserted that 'the religion imperatives for terrorism is the most important defining characteristic of terrorism today.' While the author of an American college textbook on terrorism put 'religious fanaticism' top of her list of terrorist motives. Official assessments reflect this too; for instance, the Canadian Security intelligence Service 2000 Public Report states that 'one of the prime motivators of contemporary terrorism is Islamic religious extremism'.

SUICIDE BOMBINGS & TERRORISM

The suicide bombing in Iraq, Afghanistan, Palestine even in London and other parts of the world including the Muslim countries as well is also referred by many philosophers, leaders etc. in the ambit of terrorism.

Recently, Robert Pape wrote a book "Dying to win: the Logic of Suicide Terrorism". Pape is an assistant professor at the university of Chicago. He had collected a storehouse of information on 462 suicide bombers who made headlines by their successful missions from 1980 to 2004. By analyzing demographic data, the psychology of the terrorists and their ideological and political motives, Pape had drawn interesting and valid conclusions.

The most important point stressed by the Pape is that "Islamic fundamentalism is not a closely associated with suicide terrorism as many people think."

In the Bruce Hoffman's Inside Terrorism, most of the part is devoted to religion. Pointing out that none of the identifiable terrorist groups that had been operating in 1968 could be classified as religion, Hoffman notes that the first modern religious terrorist groups did not appear until around 1980. By 1994, however, fully a third (16 out of 49) of known terrorist groups 'could be classified as religious in character and motivation', and thus proportion leapt again the following year to almost half (26 out of 56).

COUNTERING TERRORISM THROUGH TERRORISM

Although terrorism is an inevitable reality in the present scenario, when the whole world is in the cruel jaws of it, but this ineluctable reality cannot be curtailed through the more terrorism or on the same pace; as many countries of the present world are trying to do it in this way. The obvious example of Kashmir and Palestine tells otherwise. The relative term 'one man's terrorist is another man's freedom fighter' is also fully involved here. The freedom movements of Palestinians, Kashmiris and the Chechens have been branded through the Western media and also through diplomatic efforts the specific countries are doing on their best.

In the present scenario, countering terrorism has become more difficult for the countries in order to establish peace and stability in the world. As we discuss above, the definition of terrorism is still under the fog, and it would be under the fog until and unless the member countries of UNO would not adopt a universal definition of it; or until the US and its allies would not get their hidden motives under the umbrella of their 'war on terrorism'.

In order to counter terrorism countries are unilaterally adopting the same attitude (definition), which the US has set for them – pose the opposition as terrorists in front of the world and attack them unilaterally. Israel as well as India's state-terrorism falls in this scenario. As in the current imbroglio of Middle East Crisis, Israel's unilateral attack over Lebanon – just to search its two beloved and loyal soldiers – has further not only deteriorated the situation but also tell the whole world that "if you want to wipe off the terrorist from the surface of the world then kill the innocent civilians and change the cities into the graveyards", then you might be able to curtail terrorism and then peace, harmony and security can be established.

State-terrorism has become the order of the day. It is evident not only from Israel's unilateral attack over Lebanon but also in the case of India and Russia in Kashmir and Chechnya respectively.

COUNTERTERRORISM & DEMOCRACY

A world in which 80 per cent of terrorists were not Marxists but Muslims might present a totally different kind of issue. But the American response to September 11 showed that little had changed, except the roster of usual suspects: Afghanistan, Iraq and Sudan in place of the rogue states of the 1980s, Libya, Syria and Iran. The theory of state-sponsorship may be weakly developed but its practical significance is immense: it validates the direct retaliation, which has become an established American policy preference. A belief in the American deterrent effect of smart munitions has survived a surprising amount of contrary evidence.

Democracy against Terrorism

There can be no dispute that terrorism s undemocratic in that it ignores all conventional processes of representative politics. But does it go further than this? Is it inherently antidemocratic? And are democracies uniquely vulnerable to terrorism? We have already noted that democratic states may be more sensitive to the threat that terrorism is seen to present to public safety.

AMERICA'S 'WAR ON TERRORISM'

Prior to 9\11, whether this terrorism existed in this shape or not. Noam Chomsky, a Noble prizewinner, of USA defined terrorism:

"Its calculated use of violence or threat of violence to attain goals that are political, religious or ideological in nature through intimidation, coercion or instilling fear."

On Jan 2001, President Bush declared Iran, North Korea and Iraq-the axis of Evil. 9\11 provided them perfect logic. After 17th September 2002, USA sums up with her national security strategy. USA possesses the right of pre-emption strike. The United States has right for preemption strike against any measures that can crop up with fear. USA has attained unlimited military superiority of the world and there is no enemy of the United States except Terrorism. After 9\11, war started against the Muslims on the name of terrorism.

FBI defines terrorism, "The unlawful use of force or violence against persons or property to intimidate or coerce a government, the civilian population, or any segment thereof, in furtherance of political or social objectives."

Department of Defence (DoD), "The calculated use of violence or the threat of violence to inculcate fear, intended to coerce or intimidate governments or societies as to the pursuit of goals that are generally political, religious or ideological."

Department of State (DoS), "Premeditated, politically motivated violence perpetrated against noncombatant targets by subnational or clandestine agents, usually intended to influence an audience."

If we take a look of the above-mentioned definition, the following steps can be derived:

I. For political stability

II. Dialogue

III. Involvement of other forces as UNO etc.

IV. War

Interior Motives of US War on Terrorism

If we take a look of Political disputes like Bosnia, Iraq, Chechnya etc the Interior motives of war on terrorism are:

I. To get hold of world's natural resources to ensure sustained supply. This is the foremost motive of Europe and America. After the first Arab war, Europeans did not want the cut off the oil from Arab. They directed against those countries, which possess natural resources. If this is not the case, why this war on terrorism is in the Middle East.

II. To malign Muslim freedom struggles. Wherever in the world, there is bloody freedom movement going on such as in Kashmir, Xing yang, Chechnya, Palestine. It is not in the best interest of America that these would be successful. Because according to Domino theory, a movement leads to another movement.

III. To damage the ideologies of Islam specially Jihad. They are against the Jihadees not against the independence of practicing Muslims. For that purpose, they have started reforms in the Madressahs in Pakistan providing them computers etc.

IV. To stop the rise of orthodox Muslim governments. They are doing it in the name of democracy. They are changing the elected governments. e.g.; in Taliban's case. In Iran. It is being isolated. They are there to protect monarchies in Gulf States. These changes are just to protect Israel.

V. To spread its own culture. If a nation dies it's a national death but if a nation dies of cultural death, it's all over. The United States is permeated its culture in the countries on the name of terrorism. As in Iraq, they made dance clubs in the Green Zone. The uniform of new force of Iraq i.e. identical as it matched with USA.

CAUSES OF TERRORISM

I. Unresolved political disputes: In the hot disputes of the world, Muslims are involved. No effort has been made to resolve these issues. The cause is inherent in the disputes of one religion against the other politically. E.g.; Kashmir, Palestine, Chechnya.

II. Ineffectiveness of UNO: The world bode formed after the Second World War. "To avert any other international war. But it utterly fails in going that. The disputes if resolved in UNO, the terrorism was not prevailed as it is.

III. Globalization: It is suited to Western interests than the third world countries. It seeks the occupation of countries by multinational corporations (MNC's). This is spreading poverty and unemployment in the third world countries.

IV. Universal law of cause-and-effect: "like cause will produce like effects". If the go about combating terrorism with terrorism, it will produce obviously terrorism.

V. Double standards of the West: On one hand, previously when Afghan Jihad was going on- they were projected as heroes and then became terrorists. These are the pure double standards towards democracy. They are motivating the third world or least developed countries to increase their defence budget. As Pakistan is buying 75 Jets at the cost of $ 3.2 billion from America. Debt traps have been orchestrated.

WHAT TERRORISM HAS DONE?

It started after 9\11. Bush administration had got chance "to become world more safer". But it did in opposite manner;

I. Unilateralist approach of USA. It gave up the approach of bilateralism and multilateralism. "This terrorism is a threat to entire world community". The United States has decided to go it alone to combat terrorism.

II. The United Nations was sidelined. The prestige attached to UNO was ended.

III. The Muslim country's nuclear ambitions were strictly checked. As in Iran. As in Dr. AQ Khan's case.

IV. Calls were being made to challenge American superiority. No matter how we dislike this sole super power element. It does not have any vested interest.

V. Huntington's Clash of the Civilizations. This theory came to be true. " The battle line would be drawn on tenets lines of civilization." There is going to be war wherever a civilization ended. As Jews v/s Muslims, Hindus v/s Muslims, Islam and the West etc.

EFFECTS ON PAKISTAN

Pakistan has adversely affected by terrorism than any other country of the world. No country in the world has suffered in wake of terrorism than Pakistan. Although, Pakistan is a victim of terrorism is being labeled as a state sponsoring terrorism. The emergence of terrorism in Pakistan was the consequence of its direct involvement in Afghanistan war. Pakistan has learned the lesson "the hard way" but it is imperative that we must not forget it. Lot of time and energy of Pakistan is being consumed to make world understand that Pakistan is not the sponsor of terrorism but it's a victim, and while doing so it is being forced to make compromises on its vital interests. Even the friendly countries like China, Iran, Indonesia started looking towards Pakistan with suspicion. In a nutshell, terrorism has formed Pakistan to go on a back foot and became more defensive on this issue. It has become more important for Pakistan to clean its image tinted with terrorism and take rightful place amongst the community of nations.

Steps Taken By Pakistan:

I. Intimation of war on terrorism: First motive was to clean its image in the eyes of international community.

   President Musharraf took various steps to clean it. He visited many countries of the world, which were never being visited by any leader of Pakistan.

II. U-turn on its foreign policy: Pakistan had taken drastic u-turn after 9\11. It wanted to show international community that we are not fundamentalists. Pakistan took u-turn on its Kashmir and Afghan policy.

III. Ban on Jihadee organizations: Government of Pakistan banned almost all Jihadee organizations on 12th January 2002.

COUNTERTERRORISM STRATEGY BY DR MALEEHA LODHI:

"There is no silver bullet that can address global terrorism in all its complexity," writes Dr Maleeha Lodhi in "The Threats of all Threats". "In a globalised world of interconnected threats and challenges," she further writes, "terrorism poses a clear and present danger to peace and security, more menacing than ever in the past. This threat has grown more urgent since 9/11; the attacks on the United States dramatised the increased lethality of terrorism and marked a watershed in the history of terrorism. Every continent has seen acts of terrorism. Perpetrators belong to diverse backgrounds, ethnicities and faiths. Since 1968, there have been at least 8,000 serious incidents of terrorism across the world. About 70 countries have been affected by the activities of as many as an estimated 100 terrorist entities.

She proposed a broad-gauge counter-terrorism strategy based on nine 'Cs':

(1) Comprehensiveness: A comprehensive, multifaceted strategy is needed that encompasses law enforcement, political, social, cultural, financial and diplomatic measures.

(2) Consensus at the global level is required on a strategy. incorporating both short- and long-term measures that work in tandem.

(3) Causes and conditions that breed, encourage and contribute to terrorism must be objectively identified and addressed.

(4) Confusion between explanation and justification must be removed. Trying to understand a phenomenon does not mean giving in to terrorism.

(5) Capabilities must be improved and national capacities strengthened across the spectrum to pursue terrorists and prevent terrorist activities.

(6) Cooperative rather than coercive national and international strategies should be pursued so that the reaction to counter-terrorism measures does not compound the problem.

(7) Civil liberties and principles of good governance must be upheld in the fight against terror, because real security can only be achieved through respect for human rights.

(8) Civilisational and cultural: dialogue and understanding including engaging in the battle for the hearts and minds, must become an integral part of global consensus-building to evolve a joint strategy. Such a dialogue must be premised on the understanding that the root cause of friction between civilisations are not primarily religious differences, but mainly issues of power, competing political and economic interests, policies and misunderstandings.

(9) Conference at the summit level must be called to craft and coordinate an approach based on these elements.

CONCLUDING REMARKS

- Today terrorism is hybrid and complex in nature and scope, even across the continents by non-state actors. Countering this multi-headed phenomenon requires a multi-pronged, multinational, and sustained policy by the governments across the globe.

- One of the characteristics of the prevailing environment is that deprivation and an unjust political and socio-economic dispensation rapidly give rise to frustration. The consequent perception of helplessness is sufficient to motivate individuals and groups to adopt violence as an expression of their anger.
- Many decades ago, Dr. Martin Luther King Jr. said: "Injustice anywhere is a threat to justice everywhere." And time has proved how much right he was.
- The remedy lies in a tolerant and democratic society. Man's capacity for justice makes democracy possible but man's inclination to injustice makes democracy absolutely necessary. However to enable the United Nations to evolve an effective strategy for this purpose it is imperative to define terrorism that may be acceptable globally. Also make a distinction between terrorism and legitimate struggle for freedom and right of self-determination, the denial of which can breed terrorism and a threat to "peaceful co-existence".

2

TERRORISM IN PAKISTAN

INTRODUCTION

Terrorism has emerged as the most ominous threat to the global peace and security. Transcending of the geographical boundaries, this growing menace has directly or in-directly affected most of the countries with having varying degrees of terror, havoc, destabilization and devastation.

Pakistan is the major victim and worst hit owing to its contiguity with the epicenter of terrorism i.e. Afghanistan. It has posed an extremely serious threat to the integrity, stability, progress and internal security of the country. Besides our internal vulnerability, competing interest, intrigues and nefarious designs of external players in the region have profoundly compounded the milieu. We have, therefore, no option but to thwart the heinous design of the internal and external enemies by facing this challenge squarely.

The phenomenon of extremism and terrorism is extremely complex, fraught with awesome socio – economic, politico-religious and military implications. It is politically destabilizing, economically crippling and militarily devastating. Having fathomed the perils of this menace for the integrity of Pakistan, our government has taken a bold and principled stand to root out terrorism from our soil.

In pursuance of our national policy and resolve to combat terrorism with all our might, a large number of army formations and troops are engaged in war against particularly in FATA, Swat,

Baluchistan and some other areas neighboring of Afghanistan. Pakistan is front line state in war against global terrorism. Pakistan Army has played a key role in breaking the back of Al-Qaeda and foreign Taliban by killing and apprehending most of the militant leaders, busting their bases and destroying their sanctuaries. In the accomplishment of this noble and sacred task, army has made unprecedented sacrifices.

While our operational preparedness and battle worthiness attained through sustained training our the year for conventional operations have stood us in good stead in undertaking myriad operations successfully in the war against terror, we have also suffered heavy causalities in some of the operation due to the inadequate training in LIC. In order to minimize our losses in life, weapons/ equipment, to rejuvenate our traditional fighting spirit and successfully combat terrorism. Our grey areas on LIC training and conduct of counter terrorism operations need to be addressed at priority.

Historical Perspective of Terrorism

Terrorism is often understood as new form of warfare and relatively a modern technique to operational engagement. In fact it was documented 2000 years ago by a Jewish sect known as Zealots:-

a. Terrorism appears in the Bible's Old Testament, and there were frequent incident of political murder, even systematic assassination, e.g. the murder of 'Julius Caeser'

b. During 8 century, the group of assassins called Fida'I led by Hassan Bin Sabbah, a pronounced pioneer of suicide terrorism, perpetrated the killing of governors, prefects, caliphs and crusader king of Jerusalem.

c. Terrorism continued to be active right from the Middle Ages up to the Modern Times wars of Thirty years (1618-1648) including the Napoleonic Wars (1799-1815)

d. Between 14 and 17 centuries, the Peasant Revolution spread throughout Europe particularly in Britain and Germany. In early 19 century (1808-1813), the first major guerrilla band appeared in Spain against the French rulers. This movement introduced the term 'guerilla'.

e. The high tide of terrorism rose toward the end of the 19 century. Among the main active groups were the Irish Rebels, the Russian Socialist Revolutionaries and assorted anarchists all over Europe and North America. But secret societies were also actively spreading terrorism in Egypt as well as in India and China, aiming at national liberation.

f. The violence of 19 century terrorist's was noteworthy; they killed a Russian Tzar (Alexander II), American president (William McKinley in 1901 and before him in 1881, James Garfield) and King Umberto of Italy.

g. One particular terrorist act, the assassination of Austrian Archduke and heir to the throne, Francis Ferdinand and his wife Sophia on 28 June 1914 perhaps altered the course of world history, resulting in death of millions of people, leading to the fall of four imperial dynasties (German, Russian, Austro-Hungarian and Ottomans).

h. Post World War II historical perspective reveals a world with high potentials for violent conflicts. Since then there have been 160 or more armed conflicts around the world, of those, perhaps three quarters have been of so-called "low Intensity nature".

Terrorism Acts in Pakistan

Numerous terrorist acts also took place in Pakistan some of them are as under:-

a. In Pakistan, sporadic acts of terrorism can be traced back from the assassination of Mr. Liaqat Ali Khan.

b. Indian sponsored "Mukhti Bahni" in East Pakistan can also be termed one of the organized terrorist movements resulting in creation of Bangladesh. Insurgency in Baluchistan was yet another event involving Pakistan Army to such an environment

c. Pakistan was subjected to foreign sponsored terrorism for its moral support to afghan Mujahedeen against Russian Intervention.

d. The activities of RAW in collaboration with other anti Pakistan elements/ agencies worked on Afghan refugees in particular to create harassment and lawlessness in various parts of the country.

e. Recently the assassination of the Benzair Bhutto is one of the brutal act of terrorism in Pakistan

Post 9/11 Environment

After 9/11 the direction of terrorism in the world changed its face some salient aspects are:-

a. The environment of 9/11 was a direct confrontation between America and the Forces against America/ America interests. Non state actors mainly Al Qaeda worked as a magnet for all those who were In search of an allying point/ base. This was future compound by direct onslaught of Americans forces in Afghanistan. Iraq and Afghanistan played major role in dragging Pakistan onto this quagmire. Interests of extra regional forces compounded the situation further. Subsequent event drew Pakistan into international lime light due to its geographical location bordering Afghanistan and Iran.

b. Since Taliban who were Pashto speaking residing mostly in southern part of Afghanistan adjacent to FATA, were the target of American forces, hence on Pakistan side of Pak Afghan border, Sympathies with them rose to the highest point among the locals. Afghan militants were welcomed and assisted by locals. However, international environment were against this nexus. American President remarked on the rubbles of World Trade Center "America today is on the bended knee in prayers for people whose lives were lost here…. The rest of the world hears you. And the people, who knocked these buildings down, will hear all of us soon". They declared Taliban responsible for the tragedy because Al Qaeda's main leadership in Afghanistan, which according to USA was organizing, planning and initiating anti American activities from the soil state ruled by Taliban.

c. Pakistan, due to its own compulsions, having recognized Taliban regime was justifying its stance at various international forums. However 9/11 surprised the whole world including Pakistan and this blatant act of terrorism could not be justified. Pakistan principally condemns terrorism in all its forum and manifestations. It was the need of the hour to work with international community to rid the world of this peril.

d. The government of Pakistan took a considered decision to support Global War against Terrorism, safeguarding own national interests. Revenging attack on World Trade Center, USA retaliated and because of its operation in Afghanistan (Tora Bora), Pakistan Army was deployed on the western border to seal it and prevent influx of militants into Pakistan. It was a golden opportunity to open "No Go areas" in FATA and bring it par with the rest of the country.

Pakistan Internal Security and Terrorism

In the new literature on national security, internal factors are equally and sometimes more important than the traditional factors. The state of Pakistan at the moment has a stronger challenge to its security from the internal factors as compared to external. Pakistan faces multi forms of terrorism, no other country in the world is entangled in this problem as the Pakistan of today. Ethnic terrorism which led to the dismemberment of Pakistan in 1971 resurfaced again on the question of linguistic differences in the some parts of the country but has been brought under control with the mainstreaming of ethnic political parties. Nationalist terrorism has mainly been witnessed in province of Baluchistan at regular intervals and mainly revolves around the issues of exploitation of resources and threat to the political identity and culture of minorities sub-nationalities. Sectarianism in Pakistan was an extended version of rivalries between Northern Alliance and certain Sunni factions in Afghanistan and an aftermath of Iran & Iraq War, Jehadi terrorism which emerged in the post 9/11 scenario is by far the most serious threat to Pakistan so far because of its role as the front line state in war against terrorism. The tension between ultra conservative and moderate followers of Islam is mounting and weakening the sate structure. It is beyond the capacity of a single person or a one time effort to eradicate the deep rooted problem from the society. An institutional mechanism with wide ranging participation on regular and permanent basis is the only way to fight this menace.

No doubt for century's national security has been the basic and paramount concern of the nation states. While achieving enduring security has remained to be the most cherish able reward for states, over the years the concept of security has developed and considerably changed. Since its inception, Pakistan has been facing the challenge of national security. Traditionally, the threat to Pakistan's security has been external. However, today it can be arguably asserted that the major threat to national security in Pakistan emanates more from internal sources rather than external. The most serious threat facing Pakistan at the moment is posed by terrorism and the focus of our national efforts to ensure lasting security should be addressed to these internal factors.

Comparative Levels of Violence in Pakistan, 2003-2007

Year	Civilians	Security Force Personnel	Terrorist	Total
2003	140	24	25	189
2004	435	184	244	863
2005	430	81	137	648
2006	608	325	538	1471
2007	1523	597	1479	3599

Source: Institute for Conflict Management Database

Kind of Threats Faced By Pakistan

Pakistan is facing the menace of terrorism in multiple forms. Pakistan at present is facing the most unique, difficult and gruesome faces of terrorism. No other country in the world is so deeply entangled in this problem as the Pakistan of today. All text book categories of terrorism confront Pakistan.

a. Ethnic threat. Pakistan had the first taste of ethnicity in the very early period of its being when the whole eastern wing agitated on the question of one national language – Urdu. The discontent established itself into a political movement and led ultimately to the unfortunate events of 1971 resulting in dismemberment of the state. The political struggle organized on ethnic lines gave a harrowing display of ethnic terrorism when militant organization like Mukti Bahni started eliminating West Pakistanis and specially the Punjabis. In the recent history of 'New' Pakistan, ethnicity emerged again in the wake of language riots. This time in the province of Sindh where Urdu speaking urbanites of Karachi and Hyderabad clashed with native Sindhis. The quest of Mohajirs – migrants in the wake of partition – for a parallel political identity as the fifth sub nationality along with the native Punjabi, Sindhi, Pashtuns and Balochs lead to large scale bloodshed and terrorist activities. The ethnic terrorism took hold of major urban cities for nearly a decade in late 80s and 90s but it has subsided for the time being partly due to rejuvenated economic activity and mainstreaming of the ethnic groups but mostly due to political stability giving enough economic and political space to the major players. Sub nationalists who like to call themselves nationalists have been fighting for a proper identity and recognition within the federation. Their main fears and apprehensions emanate from the pre-dominant role of Punjab in military and civil bureaucracy. They are frustrated by the prospects of facing permanently the majority of one province. They feel threatened about their value system traditions and culture.

They also agitate against the use of their resources by other regions at cheaper costs. The poverty around them frustrates them and the advantaged amongst them successfully point their fingers to the other provinces to turn their gaze that way. The centre and its power corridor on the other hand take this insistence on rights as a kind of revolt against the centre and the rejection of federation. These strained relations have led the extremists amongst the nationalists/sub nationalists to take up arm against the centre quite regularly and sometimes against the state itself. The sub nationalist's terrorism has been emerging intermittently since military operations in Pakistan in 1960s.Governments of the day have been pointing at the external backing of both these types of terrorism. Pakistan on the whole has done fairly well to withstand the ethnic and sub nationalist terrorism even when fanned by external hands and the state structures have been able to work regularly and formally even in the face of these threats.

b. Sectarian Thereat. Another major form of terrorist threat facing Pakistan emanates from the sectarian terrorism. Since long, Pakistan has been a victim of the violence by sectarian motives, the recent years have witnessed a high rise in both the frequency and lethality of the sectarian violence. "Domestic terrorism in Pakistan, much of it associated with Islamist sectarianism, has become an increasingly serious problem affecting major Pakistan's cities". Sectarian terrorism in Pakistan has been an off shoot of some historical and some regional rivalries. There are four different schools of thought in Muslims of Pakistan i.e. Brailvi, Deobandi, Ahle Hadith and Shias. The first three are commonly grouped as Sunni but their thinking and its expressions are wide apart. The differences between Sunni and Shia thinking and intra Sunni faction have been historical but they have generally co-existed peacefully. The prolonged Iraq-Iran war and then post Afghan Jehad rivalries between Northern Alliance, predominantly Shia and orthodox Sunni backed by Saudi Arabia and Pakistan, had adverse impact on sectarian harmony in Pakistan. The main source of recruitment for Jehad in Afghanistan had been Deo Bund and Ahle Hadith madrasas which got undue patronage from Zia govt. and finances from Saudi Arabia and some international agencies. These two groups aligned themselves with anti Shia forces in Afghanistan in late 1980s, and all along in 1990s. The battle in Afghanistan raged in the towns of Pakistan as well when there was pointless and ruthless killings of Shia's and then by Shias in large number. The country virtually had a blood bath on this account during the period 1985-1990. Sectarian terrorism has affected all parts of the country in varying degrees at different points in time. The northern areas and southern Punjab were the worst sufferers with sporadic strikes in major urban centers as well. The decade of 1990s has been the worst on this account. It did pose a serious threat to the internal security of the country but it has lost its sting due to two major reasons; one the people of Pakistan refused to get divided on sectarian lines and the fissure remained restricted to the fanatics and the extremists with the vast majority remaining detached, unsympathetic and rather antagonist to this approach. Secondly, the emergence of a far grave phenomenon of Jehadi terrorism overshadowed rather watering down the sectarian terrorism. Taking it as a national security concern the government of Pakistan need to overcome and address the genuine grievances of these sectarian groups. The groups involved in terrorist activities should be banned by the government, other groups to be brought into dialogue with government. It is the emergence of Jehadi terrorism, which is posing a real threat to the national security of Pakistan. The epicenter of Jehadi terrorism is Afghanistan. Initially, it was directed towards infidels and occupation forces but gradually it had to turn towards Pakistan, because of its alliance with the West in the War on Terrorism. The Jehad of 1980s, against the Soviet occupation of Afghanistan degenerated first into in fighting on ethnic lines and ethnic terrorism and then to sectarian terrorism with the arrival of Taliban on the scene. The Taliban took upon themselves the so called divine duty of enforcing Islamic order with the force of arms. Their narrow, myopic and ultra orthodox view of Islam is a force of regression and decadence. When the resistance moment against American occupation of Afghanistan started engulfing Pakistan also, the perpetrators of Jehadi terrorism were out to chastise the Muslims of Pakistan. The march of Jehadi terrorism towards Pakistan has refueled the sectarian terrorism as well and we have been witnessing the most lethal combination of these two evil forces. "The scene in Pakistan resembled a jungle in which every one was fighting at times everyone else. The terrorists were making money by drug trafficking and gun running, so they were heavily armed. Their operations endangered the very existence of the state, and no one put an estimate even remotely how many people were killed in this fighting". Military means cannot be the only solution to eradicate terrorism as causes of terrorism can be social, political and economic. The roots of Jehadi terrorism can also be found in social, economic and political factors. Looking at the present economic, social and political conditions in Pakistan it is inconceivable that there are going to be no Jehadi elements in the country. The Jehadi terrorism and its combination is threatening the national security of Pakistan on both the external and internal fronts. 'The acquisition of nuclear war heads by India and Pakistan threatened to make their resolved conflict over Kashmir go ballistic'. On the external front the vital freedom movement in Kashmir has been undermined. Though the freedom movement in Kashmir is essentially different from the Jehadi terrorism as it is against the occupation forces of India and not to enforce a particular doctrine, but Indians have got a golden chance to malign it by drawing analogies with the Jehadi terrorism. Resultantly forcing Pakistan to be more flexible than it is due on the issue of Kashmir.

Sectarian Violence in Pakistan, 2007

Month	Incidents	Killed	Injured
January	3	5	21
February	0	0	0
March	9	8	1
April	72	121	119
May	2	3	1
June	0	0	0
July	0	0	0
August	2	2	0
September	0	0	0
October	0	0	0
November	118	181	314
December	135	121	174
Total	341	441	630

Source: Institute for Conflict Management database

c. Islamic Militancy. Today the most challenging issue emanates from the Islamic militancy. Pakistan has become a hot bed of various militant organizations, resorting to violence in the name of religion. Since the Afghan jihad against the Soviet Union, the militant Islamic organizations have flourished and have been supported by the governments in Pakistan. Therefore their growth was not controlled. One of the most major damages of the 1980s United States – Afghan War was the support provided to anti modern, extremist and intolerant forces of this region. To defeat the Soviet, the US and Pakistan government provided official support to militant and fundamentalist Islamic groups, which eventually led to religious extremism and sectarianism. This religious radicalism spread out in the other parts of the world also. Those forces became influential which rejected tolerance and secularism. With the changed regional and global environment, Pakistan drastically needs to change its approach towards the militant organizations. 'Sponsoring terrorism is like riding a tiger. Pakistan has to pay a heavy price for its support for Taliban. Even though Musharraf demonstrated wisdom by supporting US war on Terror against Taliban in neighboring Afghanistan, the country continues to be caught in a very complex web of terrorist activity, with greater radicalization of extremists groups'. The bases of this militant challenge operates in the Tribal areas of west of Pakistan and North West Frontier Province and Federally Administered Tribal Area (FATA). These areas mostly comprise of the Pushtuns and ethnic groups which are conservative, have close religious and tribal links with Pushtoon in Afghanistan and anti western. 'The Pushtun tribal areas have long been a heaven for displaced Afghans and refugees'. The hilly and difficult terrain of this region has turned out to be a heaven for militant organizations both foreign and national. The foreign militants over here mainly are Uzbek, Chechens and Pushtun Afghanis.

d. Ethno-Nationalist Threat. In Pakistan, minority and separatist movements are common. In the south west of Pakistan is the province of Balochistan which is mostly a tribal area, over there, intermittent gorilla war has been a feature since last two decades.10 This is another major form of terrorist threat to Pakistan which is of the separatist nature. The largest but the most underdeveloped area of Balochistan currently is the centre of this threat. It is the ethno-nationalist conflict between the government and the separatists for long that these separatists comprising of tribal militants have been indulged in violent acts for more political and economic authority in Balochistan. In Balochistan the various insurgents have adopted various violent tactics to sabotage the system. This problem if not resolved in time has the potential to challenge the national integrity of the state.

e. Threat To Creating State Within The State. Another new form of terrorism which has started to challenge the state is the takeover by the students, of religious seminaries in the capital city Islamabad of a children's library. The students and administration of madrasa lately took over law in their hands abducting women, police men and Chinese nationals on various charges thus creating state within the state. This brought great embarrassment to the government at both national and international level.

External factors for Terrorism in Pakistan

Identifying and dealing with internal factors are just one aspect of solving Pakistan's terrorism puzzle. External factors cannot be ignored either. It is clear that the governments of other countries, or groups from there with vested interests, have used Pakistan for their causes.

a. Indian Role

(1) While other countries did not have any ill will against Pakistan, India has been a long time sponsor of separatist movements in the country. Indian funding of Sindhi and Pashtun separatists has been an open secret in Pakistan. This author once visited a neighbor who came back injured from a fight in a Karachi college. Upon asking how students can get so many arms to fight each other, he revealed which classmates were getting the arms and support from India which were being used in those ethnic fights.

(2) India, with which it has fought three wars over the issue of Kashmir, is probably among the most active external elements to create violence and terror in Pakistan. Knowing that the country supports the Kashmiris' resurgence, India has supported and financed terrorist attacks in Pakistan, sometimes burning train stations, other times providing arms in ethnic conflicts. Or it engages in random shootings through agent provocateurs or supports criminal elements.

(3) Sometimes it seems that Pakistanis and Indian agencies settle scores between themselves through terrorist activities. In the early 1980s, seven Pakistani train stations in Sindh were burned down. But the interesting thing was that those processions were far away from the train stations. Some Indian agents were arrested and then there was silence in the media until suddenly one day 27 Indian train stations in the state of Punjab were burned down. That was also followed by a curious silence in the Indian media about who did it.

b. Russian Factor

(1) Remember the "Hathora" (hammer) groups of the 1980s? These terrorists would attack innocent civilians as they slept, crushing their heads with hammers. After a series of these terrifying incidents, law enforcement discovered that the vicious culprits were from the Soviet bloc, teaching a lesson to Pakistan for its pro-Afghanistan policy.

(2) Another was the phenomena of shootings in Masjids, now commonly associated with the Shia-Sunni conflict in Pakistan. Curiously, this method of terrorism was not a response to particular grievances. Rather, it was very obviously an attempt to ignite violence, hatred and dissension between groups that had a potential for conflict.

(3) For instance, my son was once standing outside a Pakistani Masjid after prayers when suddenly, two terrorists on a motorcycle with their faces covered appeared. Facing the mosque's gate, one of the terrorist sprayed it with bullets and drove off. This was a well-known multi-ethnic mosque in a city that was ethnically divided. This meant that the terrorist attacker probably didn't know the ethnically diverse nature of the worshippers. The attack failed to ignite a conflict between

any groups because those killed and injured were part of all communities.

(4) On other occasions, these terrorists, however, were successful in starting ethnic or sectarian violence because they targeted one specific group. The February 26, 2002 attack on a Shia mosque in Rawalpindi which killed ten people was conducted in exactly the same manner. This attack, because it targeted a predominantly Shia mosque, could serve as an incentive to Shia gangs to retaliate against Sunni mosques. Most religious leaders believe that although now there are well-known armed groups on both sides. Initially this conflict was engineered by others.

(5) Pakistan needs to strengthen checks on diplomats in the country by not allowing them to use their position to foment internal destruction and dissension. Pakistan must take a strong stand in ensuring that they do not go beyond promoting legitimate public relations for their countries by cultivating a sectarian clientele, be it ethnic or religious.

(6) Because of the Kashmir issue, it is unlikely that India will reduce its support to dissent and subversion in Pakistan any time soon. Therefore, it is important for Pakistan to enhance its counter-intelligence operations within the country to reduce the subversive support to terrorism within its borders.

Role of Law Enforcing Agencies In Controlling Terrorism

After 9/11 incident and also when Pakistan Govt. realized the gravity of the threat posed by the uncontrolled militant elements, the govt. decided to establish the writ of the state in these areas. Pakistan military initiated operations against these forces and had to face stiff resistance. Wana operation which was started by the military became very controversial and has brought about heavy losses to the government forces and has also resulted in heavy criticism of the government. But still the Pakistan Army Along With other law enforcing agencies is playing its role in troubled areas of Pakistan to control terrorist activities in Pakistan

Possible Solutions to these Internal and External Problems

Some of the possible solution of the problems that are been faced by Pakistan are as under:-

a. Formal Education Needs to be Enhanced with the Message of Tolerance: The first effort should be on the educational front. Pakistan has made significant improvement in its literacy rate in the last ten years. There is a popular national consensus about the importance of education. It is important to develop the curricula and syllabi of the first twelve years of education and to rewrite books on Islamic studies, social studies, history, Urdu, and English for all school levels to strengthen the elements which deal with pluralism, the rights of others, tolerance, justice and love. These books need to develop a unique mix which relies on Pakistan's Islamic heritage but also benefits from the content and techniques developed for the multicultural education movement in America and inner-city educational experiments.

b. Dialog Between Shias and Sunnis: An ongoing dialog between the leaders of the two groups at a national as well as at the city level is important. Many times, culprits of the violence between the two groups have been unknown gunmen who have killed at either Sunni or Shia Masjids with no one claiming any responsibility. Most leaders from both sides are not involved in the violence. Most Masjids do not preach violence against any group. Then who starts these fights? If leaders from both sides engage each other in dialog, there is a good chance that they will be able to help save lives on both sides. If, for 1,000 years, with little exception, Shias and Sunnis have lived together peacefully, there is no reason for this extraordinary surge in violence of the last decade.

c. Regular Conference Between Ethnic Groups in Karachi: Karachi has seen the most ethnic violence and still it manifests the resilience of Pakistanis by continuing to be the most multi-ethnic city of Pakistan. At the height of ethnic violence, Dr. Akhtar Hameed Khan developed a dialog between two warring factions and was able to develop an island of peace. If the civil leadership facilitates a dialog at the city level and puts the Muhalla (neighborhood leadership) in contact with each other, many of the incidents could be averted as they work together on a common agenda in their neighborhoods.

d. Dialog between Muslims and non-Muslims: Most Pakistanis rarely meet a non-Muslim considering it is Muslim majority country. Muslim leadership in civil society needs to take the initiative to develop a positive relationship with the minorities living in their midst. Muslims must understand and properly deal with the concerns of Christians, Hindus and Qadianis in Pakistan. A dialog between people of different faiths will reduce tension and enhance the chances for peace.

e. A Drug Jihad is Needed: A major Jihad against drugs is overdue for Pakistani society. One cannot think of winning the safety and security of Pakistani citizens unless a massive educational movement is unleashed. It should accompany rehabilitation programs. Masjids and Islamic organizations can be enlisted in the fight against drugs both as instruments of mass education and centers for rehabilitation programs. Since crime and terrorism in Pakistan are linked with drug trafficking and drug abuse, it will not be possible to deal with the issue of security without dealing with the issue of drugs.

f. Education of Police: Pakistani police need better education, better training and refresher courses on an ongoing basis. So that they can come up to the standards of new era.

g. Better Arms and Equipment is Needed: Pakistan makes the type of equipment which can help the police. But equipment does not mean only weapons. It includes computers, databases, detection gear, testing equipment and DNA technologies.

h. Electronic Surveillance Equipment to Fight High-Tech Criminals: Cell phones and emails are being used by criminals along with other citizens. However, in the absence of electronic monitoring systems, the police resorts to funny things like banning all cell phone usage which has been done more than once in Karachi. This of course doesn't stop the criminals, but it hinders business and the average Pakistani who can afford it an important tool whereby he can quickly access safety in a dangerous situation. Electronic monitoring systems are very much needed in the urban terrorist culture of Pakistan.

i. A Research and Analysis Wing of the Police Academy: Pakistan needs to start learning from criminals while trying to fight crime. There should be surveys of those in prison and crime statistics. We need to learn about criminals, trends in crime statistics and criminology. This is not the traditional Pakistan. The crime's Pakistan is facing is a fairly new ball game.

j. Empowering Citizenry: While Pakistan is working on coming up with systemic change and processes which can enhance internal security for Pakistan, citizens need to be empowered to safeguard themselves.

k. Independent Security Companies: In response to the lack of adequate police protection, civil society has given birth to an enterprising private security business. Many Pakistanis have turned to these companies. This phenomenon has helped businesses and factories start operating again. It will be good if in the private sector there is an association of these companies that can work on standardization, licensing, and a defined and open relationship with police, a training program and a grievance board.

l. Better Law Schools: There is a need to enhance the criminology portion of law schools' curriculum. Bar exams should also be stricter so that the quality of law education can be improved.

m. Citizens' Task Force on Law & Order: The author proposes a task force in civil society which can study, recommend and supervise the whole law and order situation in Pakistan. It should issue its quarterly report and act as a watchdog group as well as a semi-think tank for law and order. The leading scholar/lawyer Khalid Ishaq can be requested to take the lead in this field. Other participants can also be people of insight and scholarship.

CONCLUSION

President Musharaf has on a number of occasions reteriated that serious efforts are required to 'combat this modern day evil, which threatens to destabilize our societies'. Unlike terrorist groups in other countries, the groups in Pakistan involved in terrorist activities and violence are also active in political arena in Pakistan. Internally, the latest ultra orthodox combine preaches a distorted, tri ballistic, ritualistic and dark version of Islam with no light of tolerance, peaceful co-existence, human rights and finer things of life. This deadly combine seeks to impose their version with the use of arms. The most dangerous part is that they can allure the law, befool the young, hoodwink the questioner, and over the skeptic in the garb of divine authority. They are against every institution and manifesto of modern age. Their special focus and victims are the women. They want them to be frightened within home: good only for domestic chores and child rearing. They are moving forward as they see a real chance of seizing power in this country and with their march the whole process of development, all institutions of the country, the way of life, religious beliefs and the state structure are under threat, forcing us to think what else constitutes the national security.

3

Terrorism—A Threat to Democracy

The terrorism according to United Nations can be defined as:-

"Any action that is intended to cause death or serious bodily harm to civilians or non-combatants, when the purpose of such an act, by its nature or context, is to intimidate a population, or to compel a Government or an international organization to do or to abstain from doing any act.

"Terrorism" is an ambiguous term whose definition implies a political act. Over the years, the term has been used more frequently, and today it often seems to be synonymous with "evil". Generally speaking, the term "terrorism" can be used to describe a "systematic use or threat of violence in order to achieve political goals". But this definition does not address some of the problematic aspects of the phenomenon, and does not differentiate between terrorism and other forms of political violence, such as revolution, uprising and guerrilla warfare. Terrorism is subjective. One person's terrorist is another's revolutionary crusader. Terrorism in its modern interpretation is a new word for cruel criminal acts. Terror can be committed in the name of Good – but basically it is a way to fight for political goals in a criminal manner. Indeed, disputing the claim that it is important to define terrorism in order to effectively battle it, some argue that clearly defining terrorism and making it a singular criminal offense may serve to authorize the deprivation of the human rights of the suspects. Regardless of the definition of terrorism, democracies must be beware of the danger of transforming the war on terrorism from a means of defending democracy to one that undermines its foundations.

Terrorists have killed people of all nationalities, faiths and backgrounds. Terrorists aim to achieve objectives through intimidation and fear. They assert that "end justify means", no matter what the cost in human life and suffering.

Since past, we have encountered several main types of terrorism:

1. Acts of terrorism committed by the state against internal or external opposition.
2. Acts of terrorism committed in order to oppose the state or in order to promote national independence.
3. Acts of fundamentalist terrorism, which is an expression of a struggle between religions or cultures.

Some examples of terrorist acts involve:

- The use of explosive devices and suicide bombers
- The assassination of political, military or media figures
- Hostage taking
- The hijacking of airplanes or other vehicles
- The destruction of infrastructure and communications
- The use of chemical, biological and nuclear weapons

Their methods, too, are different. Because they recognize no common bonds with people who have different beliefs, they are prepared to kill indiscriminately. Indeed, mass murder is their explicit objective, their measure of success in their terms, and their methods of recruitment bear more comparison with self-destructive cults than political movements.

Democracy lies in the hearts and minds of people. It permeates those hearts and minds, so that no one allows them to be usurped by force or in any other way. Democracy is a condition in which the vast numbers of people who comprise a nation — and ultimately the world — submit themselves to institutions of law of their own making, and in which they care about each other and the planet on which they live. Democracy is not only an idea; it is also a set of values (freedom, equality and brotherhood) and a way of governing."Terror" in the sense of a "terror-regime" is originally another way of governing - without democratic values. It is a thread against democracy which is not threaded as criminal acts but as something, that can suspend democratic rights in societies.

Democracy is not a form of government but a set of principles that guide how we govern ourselves. Terrorism is merely a method of utilizing fear as a means to an end. Therefore, Terrorism cannot destroy the principles of democracy. Terrorist can and indeed are attempting to cause us to ignore those principles as we cater to our fears that terrorism brings. It is when we abandon the principles, even in the short term that will bring the ultimate demise of Democracy. So we should not allow ourselves to publically fear terrorism but instead, we should discipline ourselves to allow the principles of Democracy and peace to prevail. I believe that even a terrorist desires peace. The question is who gets to lead the peace, the people or the terrorist?

Terrorism poses a direct and indirect threat to democracy. The direct threat is a result of terrorism's capability to undermine the fundamental security that nations and international organizations are supposed to provide their citizens, which is the foundation of the legitimacy of a government. Terrorism also poses a direct threat to the basic human rights of life and property. But the indirect threat to democracy is by far the most dangerous. The war on terrorism challenges the democratic institutions of the nations and their ability to ensure the security of their citizens without harming innocent people. The terrorist attacks signal a turning point not only in the intensity of global terrorism, but also a warning to any enlightened democracy that wishes to combat the threat of terrorism.

Democracy is traditionally seen as a panacea to provide security and civil liberties to citizens and avoid political extremism or terrorism provoked by un-redressed grievances. The oft-cited theory of democratic peace holds that democracies do not wage war against each other. Democracy is in crisis; insecurity is on the rise and the threat of terrorism is equally menacing in newly democratizing and long-democratic countries.

Terrorism, and equally the fight against terrorism, pose a dual challenge to recent and long-established democracies: terrorism undermines a cherished goal and objective of democracy, that of providing citizens with security and the rule of law; and in responding to terrorism, democracies risk undermining the values of democracy such as the rule of law and human rights that are central to their existence and legitimacy.

Terrorism's greatest power lies in the arbitrary nature of its victims and in the large amount of coverage it receives in the media. Today, in addition to "conventional" terrorism, there are also the risks of the use of weapons of mass destruction and cyber-terrorism. The ability to use diverse methods in order to wreak havoc indicates that although terrorism has not yet become an existential world threat, if we didn't wake up then, that day is not far-off.

In my views, Terrorism can both destroy and build democracy. Throughout past, the oppressed and abused have used such means as were available to them to strive to attain social justice and gain individual dignity based on liberty, freedom and full access to democratic rights of citizenship. The means have often been inhumane but the character of the struggle is as much determined by the resistance of those in power as the selected means of the terrorist. In Zimbabwe the threats of the Zanu-PF thugs against all opposition voters destroyed the validity of the last two- three elections there. But making the most inspiring sights in the modern world for democracy to be seen, the peoples rose above the threats of terrorists and millions queued patiently to cast their ballots despite the physical perils involved in going to polling stations. This happened in Afghanistan after the fall of the Taliban and of course then again in Iraq in December 2005.

While Islamic fundamentalist terrorists see an undemocratic religious state as the fulfillment of their earthly goals, this is one type of terrorism. Other types of terrorism can create democracy - for example, the African National Congress had an armed wing, led by Nelson Mandela, which easily falls under the category of terrorist. Indeed, 'Free Nelson Mandela' records and T-shirts could fall under the category of glorification of terrorism. Yet this very organization and this very terrorist leader were responsible for leading South Africa to democracy.

In Sri Lanka, the ongoing war between the Tamil Tigers and the Colombo administration is in danger of undermining the nation's fragile democracy. Similarly, in the Gaza strip, Algeria and most obviously Pakistan, terror and the threat of terror are a serious impediment to nurturing a viable, democratic state. By contrast, the voters of Spain responded to the Madrid train bombings with a bravura display of popular sovereignty. And in Northern Ireland it was the ballot box and not the Armalite that brought the struggle to an end.

We cannot rely exclusively on military power to assure our long-term security. Lasting peace is gained as justice and democracy advance. In democratic and successful societies, men and women do not swear allegiance to malcontents and murderers; they turn their hearts and labor to building better lives. And democratic governments do not shelter terrorist camps or attack their peaceful neighbors; they honor the aspirations and dignity of their own people. In our conflict with terror and tyranny, we have an unmatched advantage, a power that cannot be resisted, and that is the appeal of freedom to all mankind."

Freedom of speech, freedom of the press, and the right to peaceably assemble, serve to empower citizens, legitimize debate, and provide alternatives to violence. The fair and independent judicial systems present in liberal democracies play a similar role. A truly independent judiciary is a vital check on executive power and a protector of those exercising their rights to free expression. Ensuring that no group is above the law also gives average citizens a greater stake in their political systems. Absent these democratic attributes, we find conditions that in some instances give rise to sympathy for terrorism. This is especially true in nations where demagogues who preach the language of hate under the guise of religion are the only alternatives to corrupt or brutal elite. Today, the danger to us comes not exclusively from dictators who make war directly upon us, our allies, and our interests — it also Proceed from dictators who create an atmosphere so poisonous and so brutal that evil sprouts and motivates a small but radicalized cadre to terrorism.

To counter terrorism, we seek genuine representative government that brings liberty and democracy to all of a country's citizens, including those who often have been excluded — especially women. Women have a critical role to play in democracy, in civil society, and in ensuring that democratic ideals are instilled in future generations. Our long-term strategy is to strike at the heart of terrorism by depriving it of its shelter, its recruitment grounds, and its foot soldiers. We will do this in no small measure through the avid promotion of democracy and freedom. I believe that this can be achieved because we have developed a highly successful model of integration which enables people of all backgrounds and faiths to prosper and live together within the safeguard of common values. Our society is itself an affront, and a reproach, to the ideologues who believe that only their way of living life is the right one. And make no mistake: The threat we face is ideological. It is not driven by poverty, or by social exclusion, or by racial hatred. Those who attacked London in July, those who have been engaged in terrorist networks elsewhere in the world, and those who attacked New York in 2001 were not the poor and dispossessed. They were, for the most part, well educated and prosperous.

Unlike the liberation movements of the post-World War II era, these are not political ideas like national independence from colonial rule, or equality for all citizens without regard for race or creed, or freedom of expression without totalitarian repression. Such ambitions are, at least in principle, in many cases have actually been negotiated. However, there can be no negotiation about the re-creation of the Caliphate; there can be no negotiation about the imposition of

Sharia law; there can be no negotiation about the suppression of equality between the sexes; there can be no negotiation about the ending of free speech. These values are fundamental to our civilization and are simply not up for negotiation. It is equally wrong to claim, as some do, that the motivation of terrorists and their allies is driven by some desire to seek justice in the Middle East—the part of the world where progress has been most difficult to achieve in the past 30 years. I do not accept this in any respect.

I suggest that the best way to contest this threat is by building and strengthening the democracy of our society, by isolating extremism in its various manifestations, by strengthening the legal framework within which we contest terrorism, and by developing more effective means to protect our democracy.

First, in each of our societies, we need to strengthen our democracy. That means promoting a society which is based upon the true respect of one individual for another, one culture for another, one faith for another, one race for another. It means promoting the view that democracy is the means of making change in our societies, and it means working to strengthen our democracy so that young people from all communities can see the ways in which their engagement in our societies can bring about democratic change and reduce the alienation which can make individuals prey to those who seek to destroy us.

Second, we need to take steps to isolate extremist organizations and those individuals who promote extremism. In so doing, it is essential for us to work closely with the mainstream faith communities and to understand their preoccupations. In our country, we need legislation which outlaws incitement to religious or race hatred and makes it clear that glorification of terrorism is not a legitimate political expression of view. We wish to encourage faiths to pursue their faith openly and directly. We should intend to attack the foci of extremist organization, whether they are in training camps, in prisons, in bookshops, or in places of worship. We should, work with international allies where appropriate, to identify the networks and individuals who are promoting extremism, and use legal power to disrupt and weaken them. We should intend to remove from the India those foreign citizens who are using their time in our country to promote extremism, though this course is not legally straightforward. All of these measures will further isolate and weaken those extremists who wish to promote terrorism as an appropriate form of activity.

Third, we need to strengthen the legal framework within which we can address these issues. I assert throughout all this the need to retrain and strengthen our human rights and the values which underlie them. But I say at the same time that the right to be protected from the death and destruction caused by indiscriminate terrorism is at least as important as the right of the terrorist to be protected from torture and ill-treatment. I believe that our peoples expect not only the protection of individual rights, but also the protection of democratic values such as safety and security under the law. We need a legal framework which seeks to address the difficult balance in these rights. We cannot properly fight terrorism with one legal hand tied behind our back, or give terrorists the unfettered right to defend themselves as they promote and prepare violent attacks on our society. For that reason, we should propose legal changes in our country which outlaw acts preparatory to terrorism and terrorist training.

Fourth, we need to strengthen our ability to control our borders. That means doing our best to harmonize the biometric data on passports, visas, ID cards where they exist, and perhaps even driving licenses. This is a substantial agenda to contest the threats we face, but I believe it to be essential for us.

Democracy is the strongest form of society and the most resilient. It is the aspiration of peoples throughout the world. Through democracy, extremist terrorism will be defeated. As we face the challenge of terrorist attack, most recently in Delhi again last Saturday, it is our duty to analyze and then determine the means by which this threat can be best contested. We have to clarify the values and society which we are defending; identify the threat with which we have to deal; and set out the central means by which we need both to contest those who seek to destroy us and to build the solidarity and determination which we need to succeed.

The most important conclusion to draw from this analysis is that there is not some particular government policy decision, or even some overall policy stance, which we could change and thus somehow remove our society from the terrorist firing line. Their nihilism means that our societies would only cease to be a target if we were to give up all those values of freedom and liberty which we have fought to extend over so many years.

We all know that our society, based on these values, will continue to evolve and develop. But we also know that the achievements we do have are based on centuries of struggle. The societies which we have built, with the values which they embody, are not slight or passing. They are deeply rooted and profound. However, it is the case that these are absolutely enormous changes in one generation, which proves that change for the good can happen and, moreover, that it can happen in very many cases without violence or bloodshed. And the fight for democracy is at the core of this change.

It can be lastly concluded that terrorism can not be a threat to democracy but democracy can be a weapon to fight against terrorism. I assert that the single most important weapon that we have in defending the societies from which we come is our determination and our solidarity.

4

SOCIAL IMPACT OF TERRORISM ON NATIONAL DEVELOPMENT

DEFINITIONS

In order to understand the Topic first we'll divide it into three main parts.

- Social Impact
- Terrorism
- National Development

SOCIAL IMPACT

Definition

The word social Impact in this topic tells us about the Society, In order to understand it first we'll discuss the definition of society.

"An extended social group having a distinctive cultural and economic organization"

Or

"A formal association of people with similar interests"

As the definition shows, a society is a grouping of individuals, which is characterized by common interest and may have distinctive culture and institutions. In a society members can be from a different ethnic group. A "Society" may refer to a particular people such as Pakistani, or to a broader cultural group, such as Western society. Society can also be explained as an organized group of people associated together for religious, benevolent, cultural, scientific, political, patriotic, or other purposes.

The English word society emerged in the 15th century and is derived from the French "société". The French word, in turn, had its origin in the Latin "societas", a "friendly association with others," from "socius" meaning "companion, associate, and comrade or business partner." Implicit in the meaning of society is that its members share some mutual concern or interest, a common objective or common characteristics.

TERRORISM

The word Terrorism can best be defined as

"The calculated use of violence (or threat of violence) against civilians in order to attain goals that are political or religious or ideological in nature; this is done through intimidation or coercion or instilling fear"

Or

"Terrorism is the use of threats and violence to frighten or alarm people."

Terrorism is a term used to describe violence or other harmful acts committed (or threatened) against civilians by groups or persons for political or ideological goals. Most definitions of terrorism include only those acts which are intended to create fear or "terror", are perpetrated for an ideological goal (as opposed to a "madman" attack), and deliberately target "non-combatants".

As a form of unconventional warfare, terrorism is sometimes used when attempting to force political change by: convincing a government or population to agree to demands to avoid future harm or fear of harm, destabilization of an existing government, motivating a disgruntled population to join an uprising, escalating a conflict in the hopes of disrupting the status quo, expressing the severity of a grievance, or drawing attention to a neglected cause.

The terms "terrorism" and "terrorist" (someone who engages in terrorism) carry a strong negative connotation. These terms are often used as political labels to condemn violence or threat of violence by certain actors as immoral, indiscriminate, or unjustified. Those labeled "terrorists" rarely identify themselves as such, and typically use other generic terms or terms specific to their situation, such as: separatist, freedom fighter, liberator, revolutionary, vigilante, militant, paramilitary, guerrilla, rebel, jihadi or mujahidin, or fedayeen, or any similar-meaning word in other languages.

National Development

To understand the concept of National Development we will go through certain definitions of National Development.

"Act of improving a nation by expanding or enlarging or refining"

Or

"The act of making some area of land or water more profitable or productive or useful"

Or

"National development is a sustainable increase in living standards that implies increased per capita income, better education and health as well as environmental protection."

National Development (in general) - it is a dynamic process of improvement, which implies a change, an evolution, growth and advancement. Development as a phenomenon suggests that people are able to control their future and can improve their condition in the world (living conditions, capacity to feed, education level, life length, etc.) through process towards something better.

National development encompasses a number of techniques designed to grow an economic enterprise. Such techniques include, but are not limited to, assessments of marketing opportunities and target markets, intelligence gathering on customers and competitors, generating leads for possible sales, follow up sales activity, formal proposal writing and business model design. National development involves evaluating a Nation and then realizing its full potential, using such tools as marketing, sales, information management. For a sound Nation able to withstand competitors, National development never stops but is an ongoing process.

Explanation

Now as we know what the topic is about, now I will explain what the "Social Impact of Terrorism on National Development". The Social Impact of Terrorism on National Development means how people or the nation suffers due to Terrorism. Nowadays in the world everyday you come to know about the effects of terrorism on the people of a country like economic effects, psychological effects & etc.

Almost every nation in the world including Pakistan is facing bad social impact & hurdles in national development.

Proofs about Bad Impact on National Development & Socialization Due To Terrorism

It is a matter of everyday now that we hear; there was a terrorist attack somewhere in the world & due to which the Economy of that country was affected in a negative manner & people of that country stopped investing etc. Now these terrorist attacks jolt the economy of the country from its roots, from Government to a small school going child everyone is affected because of Terrorist attacks.

Major Terrorist Attacks & Their Effects

The Major Terrorist attacks which occurred in the world & there effects with respect to our topic are given below.

SEPTEMBER 11, 2001 TERRORIST ATTACKS

Scenario

The September 11, 2001 attacks (often referred to as 9/11—pronounced "nine eleven") consisted of a series of coordinated terrorist suicide attacks by Islamic extremists on the United States on September 11, 2001. The victims were predominantly civilians.

On the morning of September 11, 2001, nineteen terrorists affiliated with al-Qaeda hijacked four commercial passenger jet airliners. Each team of hijackers included a trained pilot. The hijackers intentionally crashed two of the airliners (United Airlines Flight 175 and American Airlines Flight 11) into the World Trade Center in New York City, New York, one plane into each tower (1 WTC and 2 WTC), resulting in the collapse of both buildings soon afterward and irreparable damage to nearby buildings. The hijackers crashed a third airliner (American Airlines Flight 77) into the Pentagon in Arlington County, Virginia, near Washington D.C. Passengers and members of the flight crew on the fourth aircraft (United Airlines Flight 93) attempted to retake control of their plane from the hijackers; that plane crashed into a field near the town of Shanks Ville in rural Somerset County, Pennsylvania. In addition to the 19 hijackers, 2,973 people died; another 24 are missing and presumed dead.

- Social Effects: The 9/11 attacks had immediate and overwhelming effects upon the United States population. Gratitude toward uniformed public-safety workers (dubbed "first responders"), and especially toward firefighters, was widely expressed in light of both the drama of the risks taken on the scene and the high death toll among the workers. Many police officers and rescue workers elsewhere in the country took leaves of absence to travel to New York City to assist in the grim process of recovering bodies from the twisted remnants of the Twin Towers. Blood donations also saw a surge in the weeks after 9/11.

Numerous incidents of harassment and hate crimes were reported against Middle Easterners and other "Middle Eastern-looking" people, particularly Sikhs, due to the fact that Sikh males usually wear turbans, which are stereotypically associated with Muslims in the United States. There were reports of verbal abuse, attacks on mosques and other religious buildings (including the firebombing of a Hindu temple) and assaults on people, including one murder; Balbir Singh Sodhi was fatally shot on September 15. He, like others, was a Sikh who was mistaken for a Muslim. Apart from this, many children & people started felling unsecured about there life's. There were numerous news about the people suspecting Asian's, Middle East people as terrorists. Muslims basically started facing a lot of problems after the 9/11 attacks.

- National Development Effects: The opening of the New York Stock Exchange (NYSE) was delayed after the first plane crashed into the World Trade Center's north tower, and trading for the day cancelled after the second plane crashed into the South Tower. NASDAQ also cancelled trading. The London Stock Exchange and other stock exchanges were also evacuated. The New York Stock exchanges remained closed until the following Monday. This was the third time in history that the NYSE experienced prolonged closure, and first time since March 1933. The NYSE also shut down for a few months at the beginning of World War I.

Trading on the United States bond market ceased, with the leading government bond trader, Cantor Fitzgerald based in the World Trade Center.

The Federal Reserve issued a statement, saying it was "open and operating. The discount window is available to meet liquidity needs." Federal Reserve Governor Roger Ferguson, the only Governor in Washington DC on the day of the attacks, has described in detail this and the other actions that the Fed undertook to maintain a stable economy and offset potential disruptions arising in the financial system

Gold prices spiked upwards, from $215.50 to $287 an ounce in London trading. Oil prices also spiked upwards. Gas prices in the United States also briefly shot up.

Currency trading continued, with the United States dollar falling sharply against the Euro, British pound, and Japanese yen. The next day, European stock markets fell sharply, including a 4.6% decline in Spain and 8.5% decline in Germany. Stocks in the Latin American markets also plunged, with a 9.2% drop in Brazil, 5.2% drop in Argentina, and 5.6% decline in Mexico, before trading was halted.

War in Afghanistan

The War in Afghanistan (2001–present) started in October 2001, in the wake of the September 11, 2001 attacks on the United States, marking the beginning of its War on Terrorism campaign, seeking to oust the Taliban and find al-Qaeda leader Osama bin Laden. The Afghan Northern Alliance provided the majority of ground forces, while the U.S. and fellow NATO members provided support. The U.S. military name of the conflict was Operation Enduring Freedom (OEF).The officially-stated purpose of the invasion was to destroy al-Qaeda and deny them sanctuary and freedom of movement within Afghanistan and to remove the Taliban regime.

- Social Effects: Due to this attack people of Afghanistan suffered a lot, previously due to the attack of former USSR (Russia) they faced many problems. The ratio of crimes, drug use etc was very common in the Afghan society after the attack. Afghan National's starting leaving there country due to non availability of security, good life etc. The Afghan Society is nowadays called as the most troubled nation in the world.
- National Development Effects: It is estimated that in Afghanistan there are 1.5 million suffering from immediate starvation, as well as 7.5 million suffering as a result of the country's dire situation - the combination of civil war, drought-related famine, and, to a large extent, the Taliban's oppressive regime and the U.S.-led invasion.

Afghanistan is an extremely impoverished country, one of the world's poorest and least developed nations. Two-thirds of the population lives on less than 2 US dollars a day. The economy has suffered greatly from the recent political and military unrest since the 1979 Soviet invasion and subsequent conflicts, while severe drought added to the nation's difficulties in 1998-2001.

The economically active population in 2002 was about 11 million (out of a total of an estimated 29 million). While there are no official unemployment rate estimates available, it is evident that it is high. The number of non-skilled young people is estimated at 3 million, which is likely to increase by some 300,000 per annum.

Inflation had been a major problem until 2002. However, the depreciation of the Afghani in 2002 after the introduction of the new notes (which replaced 1,000 old Afghani by 1 new Afghani) coupled with the relative stability compared to previous periods has helped prices to stabilize and even decrease between December 2002 and February 2003, reflecting the turnaround appreciation of the new Afghani currency. Since then, the index has indicated stability, with a moderate increase toward late 2003.

LONDON BOMBINGS, 2005

The 7 July 2005 London bombings were a series of coordinated terrorist bomb blasts that hit London's public transport system during the morning rush hour. At 8:50 a.m., three bombs exploded within fifty seconds of each other on three London Underground trains. A fourth bomb exploded on a bus nearly an hour later at 9:47 a.m. in Tavistock Square. The bombings killed 52 commuters and the four suicide bombers, injured 700, and caused a severe day-long disruption of the city's transport and mobile telecommunications infrastructure.

- Social Effects: Although there were security alerts at many locations, no other terrorist incidents occurred outside central London. Suspicious packages were destroyed in controlled explosions in Edinburgh, Brighton, Coventry, and Darlington. Security across the UK was raised to the highest alert level.

Many other countries raised their own terror alert status (for example: Canada, United States, France, and Germany), especially for public transport. For a time US commanders ordered troops based in the UK to avoid London.

Police sniper units were reported to be following as many as a dozen Al Qaeda suspects in Britain. The covert armed teams were under orders to shoot to kill if surveillance suggested that a terror suspect was carrying a bomb and he refused to surrender if challenged. It was initially rumored, incorrectly, that a man was found in Canary Wharf (London) armed with a bomb but he was shot down by a sniper before he could carry out any attack.

For most of the days after the attack, central London's public transport system was effectively crippled because of the complete closure of the underground system, the closure of the Zone 1 bus networks, and the evacuation of Russell Square. Bus services restarted at 4 p.m. the same day, and most mainline train stations reopened shortly after. Tourist river vessels were pressed into service to provide a free alternative to the overcrowded trains and buses. Thousands of people chose to walk home or make their way to the nearest Zone 2 bus or train station. Most of the Underground apart from the affected stations restarted the next morning, though some commuters chose to stay at home.

- National Development Effects: There were limited immediate reactions to the attack in the world economy as measured by financial market and exchange rate activity. The pound fell 0.89 cents to a 19-month low against the U.S. dollar. The FTSE 100 Index fell by about 200 points in the two hours after the first attack. This was its biggest fall since the start of the war in Iraq, and it triggered the stock market's special measures, restricting panic selling and aimed at ensuring market stability. However, by the time the market closed it had recovered to only 71.3 points (1.36%) down on the previous day's three-year closing high. Markets in France, Germany, the Netherlands and Spain also closed about 1% down on the day.

US market indexes rose slightly, in part because the dollar index rose sharply against the pound and the euro. The Dow Jones Industrial Average gained 31.61 to 10,302.29. The Nasdaq Composite Index rose 7.01 to 2075.66. The S&P 500 rose 2.93 points to 1197.87 after declining up to 1%. Every benchmark gained 0.3%.The markets picked up again on 8 July as it became clear that the damage caused by the bombings was not as great as initially thought. By close of trading the market had fully recovered to above its level at start of trading on 7 July. Insurers in the UK tend to re-insure their terrorist liabilities in excess of the first £75,000,000 with Pool Re, a mutual insurer set up by the government with leading insurers. Pool Re has substantial reserves and newspaper reports indicated that claims would easily be covered.

On 9 July, the Bank of England, HM Treasury and the Financial Services Authority revealed that they had instigated contingency plans immediately after the attacks to ensure that the UK financial markets could keep trading. This involved the activation of a "secret chat room" on the British Government's Financial Sector Continuity website, which allowed the institutions to communicate with the country's banks and market dealers.

PAKISTAN'S CASE

Pakistan has been a victim of Terrorism from its very Independence. The Social & National Development effects which Pakistan faced due to terrorism are given below.

War Of 1965, 1971, 1999

The Indo-Pakistani War of 1965, also known as the Second Kashmir War, was the culmination of a series of skirmishes that occurred between April 1965 and September 1965 between India and Pakistan. The war was the second fought between India and Pakistan over the region of Kashmir, the first having been fought in 1947.

The war lasted five weeks, resulted in thousands of casualties on both sides and ended in a United Nations (UN) mandated ceasefire. It is generally accepted that the war began following the failure of Pakistan's Operation Gibraltar which was designed to infiltrate and invade Jammu and Kashmir.

The Bangladesh Liberation War (Mukti Judhho in Bangla), incorporating the Indo-Pakistani War of 1971, was an armed conflict between West Pakistan (now Pakistan) and East Pakistan (now

Bangladesh) that lasted for roughly nine months, from 26 March until 16 December 1971. The war resulted in Bangladesh's independence from Pakistan.

The Kargil War, also known as the Kargil conflict, was an armed conflict between India and Pakistan that took place between May and July 1999 in the Kargil district of Kashmir.

The cause of the war was the infiltration of Pakistani soldiers and Kashmiri militants into positions on the Indian side of the Line of Control, which serves as the de facto border between the two nations.

Directly after the war, Pakistan blamed the fighting entirely on independent Kashmiri insurgents; however, documents left behind by casualties and later statements by Pakistan's Prime Minister and Chief of Army Staff showed involvement of Pakistani paramilitary forces. The Indian Army, supported by the Indian Air Force, attacked the Pakistani positions and, with international diplomatic support, eventually forced a Pakistani withdrawal across the Line of Control.

- Social Effects: Social effects of war of between Pakistan & include harsh emotions for India's. The war of 1965 & 1999 as won by Pakistan left a small amount of social problems for Pakistani people, but the major social problems arose due to the War of 1971 when West Pakistan bore independence due to political problems in the west wing. Pakistan lost this War & many people lost their Bengali brothers as a result to this war. People after this war were shocked & traumatized.

Before the starting of the war & after it a group called "MUKTI BANI" were involved in numerous crimes like robberies, martyring innocent people from East Pakistan. Socially the East Pakistan at that time was not a great place to live because of increasing rate of crime there.

- National Development Effects: Following table shows the Development effects faced by Pakistan due to these wars.

Year	Gross Domestic Product	US Dollar Exchange	Inflation Index (2000=100)
1960	20,058	4.76 Pakistani Rupees	-
1965	31,740	4.76 Pakistani Rupees	-
1970	51,355	4.76 Pakistani Rupees	-
1975	131,330	9.91 Pakistani Rupees	-
1980	283,460	9.90 Pakistani Rupees	21
1985	569,114	16.28 Pakistani Rupees	30
1990	1,029,093	21.41 Pakistani Rupees	41
1995	2,268,461	30.62 Pakistani Rupees	68
2000	3,826,111	51.64 Pakistani Rupees	100
2005	6,581,103	59.30 Pakistani Rupees	126

Now in the above table you can see that the Currency level with respect to Dollar & the Inflation increased due to these wars & terror. People stopped investing because of being unsure about the future; no foreign investment was made during the years of conflict. Due to this the process of development stopped & Pakistan is facing difficulties up till this day.

Soviet Invasion & Pakistan

The Soviet war in Afghanistan was a nine-year conflict involving Soviet forces supporting Afghanistan's Marxist People's Democratic Party of Afghanistan (PDPA) government against the Mujahedeen insurgents that were fighting to overthrow Communist rule. The Soviet Union supported the government while the rebels found support from a variety of sources including the United States, Pakistan and other Muslim nations in the context of the Cold War. The conflict, concurrent to the 1979 Iranian Revolution and the Iran-Iraq War, was also seminal in the rise of Mujahedeen's in central Asia.

- Social & Development Effects: The Soviet Invasion is a darkest chapter in the history of Pakistan. The Social effect of this war includes "Kalashnikov Culture" meaning it was the first step or the stone breaking ceremony for terrorist organizations. Social evils like drug abuse etc became common in the Pakistan society which came here from Afghanistan. Crime rates increased due to increasing number of refuges.

As the above given economic chart shows that Pakistan's economy contently faced troubles after 1979 this was because of large number of Refuges which crossed the border & came to Pakistan. This act increased inflation & GDP of the company fell. The Development process was stopped due to this Soviet Invasion.

- Terrorist Groups: More over now after so many years, the Afghan and foreign Mujahedeen which took part in the Soviet War afterwards starting misusing their powers by using them in terrorist activities, nowadays in Pakistan 100% terrorist attacks are carried out by these Terrorist groups a detail of which is given below.

Lashkar-e-Omar is a terrorist organization which is believed to have its members derived from 3 organizations, Harkat-ul-Jihad-i-Islami (HuJI), Lashkar-e-Jhangvi (LeJ) and Jaish-e-Mohammed The main terrorist activities for which it has been accused are:

"Attack on a church in Bahawalpur in Punjab on October 28, 2002, resulting in 18 deaths and 9 injuries"

"March 17, 2002 grenade attack on a church in the heavily guarded diplomatic enclave in Islamabad in which five persons, including a US diplomat's wife and daughter, were killed and 41 others injured"

"Involved in the suicide bombing outside the Sheraton Hotel in Karachi on May 8, 2002 and the June 14th attack on the US consulate in Karachi, in which 10 persons, including five women, were killed and 51 others injured."

Sipah-e-Sahaba Pakistan

Previously known as Anjuman Sipah-e-Sahaba (ASS), this group is thought to be behind most of the attacks on Shiites. It came into prominence following the Iranian Revolution in 1980s. Incidents thought to be caused by this group are:

"October 7, 2004 bomb blasts in Multan that killed 40 people"

"September 21, 2004: Suspected SSP members gunned down at least three members of a Shia family in a sectarian attack in Dera Ismail Khan"

"March 2, 2004 More than 45 people killed and over 100 wounded in an attack on Shi'a Muslims in Quetta"

"It has also been involved in assassinating Iranian diplomats with the most severe being the killing of five Iranian Air Force cadets in Rawalpindi in 1997"

Apart from these attacks Pakistan numerous other attacks have taken place which cost human life's, Social Problems & Development challenges for Pakistan.

THE ROLE OF THE NEWS MEDIA IN THE WAR ON TERRORISM: REPORTING ON HUMAN RIGHTS VIOLATIONS

The twenty first century allows media to play a major role in shaping the viewer's understanding. A main example of this is the crucial role the media plays in the "war on terrorism". The way in which media represent this conflict is part of the conflict itself. Media coverage has effects not simply on the audience, understood to be passive bystanders, but on those actually and potentially involved in the war on terrorism. This is responsible for shaping the perceptions of opponents, supporters and neutral groups influences whether they will become involved and how they will participate. Mobilizing information and persuasion are two integral factors that help shape, or conduct, the war against terrorism .The result explains and attempt to shape is that attempting to shape the representation of terrorism conflict becomes more important for the belligerents even as it become harder to do (Brown, R., 2003, P 85).

Conversely, after the start of war against terrorism, international anti-terrorism efforts reviewing the complex issue of media and terrorism. Nations engage in conventional and new types of warfare to combat terrorism and resolve conflicts, accurate information and analysis are needed. For antagonists and protagonists alike, media are important because they generate information, symbols, impressions and ideas that are critical in the battle for the hearts and minds of nations and people. Since 11 September 2001, the international press freedom landscape has become very complex. Journalism itself has become a battleground as governments on all sides seek to influence media coverage to suit their own political and strategic interests. At the same time, journalists and media workers have taken tragic risks to report and to disseminate news and information about terrorism and the various efforts to deal with it (Waheed A. Khan, 2003, P IX).

However, under the importance of media and war against terrorism, this essay will carry its intentions in two-fold: first to understand theoretical dimensions of media coverage on war against terrorism; and second, it will mainly analysis the relationship between media and counter terrorism war in the concretive framework of human rights abuses ,which were reported during this anti-terrorism war.

Though, presently terrorism has quite precarious relationship with media. The interplay between media reporting and the use of violence by extremists and terrorists movements has always been an interesting field of study. It has been observed that violent extremists and terrorists understand the capacity of the present day media network to disseminate information through satellite and digital technology and to present the events 'live' and / or graphically and to cater to the global audience. This instantaneous media exposure brings forward their grievances and facilitates them in garnering larger audience. Keeping in view the media point, they have their 'own incentives to report-major terrorist incidents' (Martin, G., 2003, P 279). While, the world's most published and media debatable terrorist attack was plotted by Al-Qaeda in USA on September 11,2001. That resulted in catastrophic losses of more than 3000 lives and many more injured. "The attacks on the World Trade Center in New York and on the Pentagon near Washington, D.C. were shocking global media events that dominated public attention and provoked reams of discourse, reflection, and writing" (Kellner, D., April 2004, P 42), for example Seventy-nine(79) million Americans were watching news on broadcast and cable television during prime time on Sept. 11, 2001.Three days later, 39.4 million viewers tuned in to television news coverage (William, A. H., 2005, P xviii).According to a study by Jupiter Media Metrix, an authoritative source of online demographics, an average of 11.7 million Americans visited online news sites on each day in the week after the Sept. 11 attacks — nearly double the 6 million who had visited news sites in the week before the attack (Glass, J.A. ,2001, P 3).On the same time, major news web sites, which normally take between 2.5 and 3.5 seconds to access a Web page, the access time proved to be between 20 and 40 seconds. Even, some of the Internet's foremost news sites — including MSNBC, CNN and ABC — were unavailable nearly three hours after the 9/11 attack because their primary servers had been destroyed in the collapse of the World Trade Center towers (Glass, J.A., 2003, P 51).

After 11 September, "USA President George W. Bush compared the attack to one on freedom itself and vowed that the nation's freedom will be defended. The United States has responded to these attacks in different ways. Since then, the whole gamut of the debate on terrorism has undergone tremendous change. The declaration of a 'war on terrorism' by the US in response to 9/11 attacks have provided increased attention to the problem of terrorism worldwide and it has since then become a matter of grave global concern(Sharma, K.S., 2006, P 7)" specially in US and UK, where propaganda machines have been cranked up to levels not seen outside the 1939-45 war (Miller, D.,2004).From the days and week after following 9/11 ,till the United States attacked on Afghanistan in October 2001 and Iraq in March 2003,US broad cast media have managed to maintain a sustained level of patriotism fanning the public mood to keep the United States safe by whatever means possible. Television channel logos since 9/11 carry blurbs ranging from "America under attack" to "America strikes back "America at war" "America's new war" (Peter van der veer and Munshi, S., 2005, P 50 and 51). News coverage of the Sept. 11 events was dramatic enough, especially with the added dimension that the events were real. After the attacks, the media constantly depicted further terrorist acts as possible, if not likely. Given those circumstances, it is reasonable to assume that (US) people would feel unsafe and fearful: "television's mean and dangerous world tends to cultivate a sense of relative danger, mistrust, insecurity, vulnerability, alienation and gloom (Rubi Ala M., Paul M.H. and others, 2003, P 128).

While, on September 11,2001 the first time in history, the vast vertical integration of America's mass media came out of hiding ,as parent companies simulcast their news flagships sister cable networks, CBC news coverage was carried on Viacom owned MTV and VH1.AOL-Time Warner broadcast CNN news coverage on TNT,TNN and Courts TV. Even ESPN was taken over ABC News broadcasts, "America's new war" to "Operation Ending Freedom" and "Operation Iraqi Freedom" (Peter and Munshi, S., 2004, P 49 and 51). But on the other hand, Arab, South and Southeast Asia televisions were showing a vastly different war than the one presented on Fox, CNN, NBC etc. US broadcast media labeled Iraq war "Operation Iraqi Freedom" while Canadian CBC and Arab networks labeled it "War on Iraq" and referred to the war in terms of 'occupation' or 'invasion' (Peter and Munshi, S., 2004, P 56).Further more, the language used by Arab media to describe the violent acts in Iraq, they use the term "suicidal attacks" to describe any acts where suicide bombers kill either Iraqis or Americans. Arab media outlets also use loaded terms like "Iraqi resistance" when troops from the coalition forces are killed. However, when Iraqi civilians or Iraqi policemen are killed, the Arab media refer to the perpetrators as "unidentified armed men." Moreover, the Arab media refer to the American troops as "occupying forces" or "invaders" rather than "coalition forces" (El-Nawawy, M., 2004, P 7).

However, shortly after September 11, 2001, when USA launched an attack on Afghanistan dated October 7, 2001 in the reflection of 9/11 attacks with the significant support of media specially with its own media. Many estimate that more civilians were killed during

USA's bombardment on Afghanistan than died in the September 11 strikes (Zacharias, U., 2003, P 123). Likewise, "USA started "Operation Iraqi Freedom" on March 20, 2003.United States, United Kingdom, Australian and Polish troops invaded on Iraq with this allegation that Iraq possess and had been actively developing Weapons of Mass Destruction (WMD).USA reasoned that these Nuclear and Biological Chemical (NBC) weapons provide a grave threat to them.

But then, Mohamed El-Baradei the United Nation Chief inspector and Director General of the International Atomic Energy (IAEA) March 7, 2003 report clearly shows that they never found any WMDs in Iraq before US and its allies attacked . It is said in his report "we have to date found no evidence or plausible indication of the revival of a nuclear programme in Iraq" (Krista, H. and Kim Rygiel, 2006, P 7).Same as the Ex. UN Secretary General Kofia Annan, interviewed by BBC bluntly called the Iraq war "illegal" (Rick, F. and R Hinnebusch, 2006, P 15).However, during the heavy bombardment, number of Iraqi civilians died. The UN human rights report, issued in January 2007, said that 34,452 Iraqi civilians were killed and more than 36,000 wounded in year 2006(Human Rights Watch, April 2007). According to BBC, 15 October 2006 total number of reported civilian dead at 41,744 to 46,668 and the number of police dead at 2,578 (BBC News, 23 October 2006).

However, during the war against terrorism, the media (print and electronic) was keeping an eye on the number of civilian, terrorist, coalition forces deaths. Alongside that, they were also working closely with International Non Governmental Organizations (INGOS) and reporting any human rights abuses ,like ,according to Universal Declaration of Human Rights (UDHR) article 12"No one shall be subjected to arbitrary interference with his privacy, family, home or correspondence, nor to attacks upon his honor and reputation". But in Iraq and Afghanistan, American army entered houses usually after dark, breaking doors, yelling orders, forcing family men into room under military guards while searching the rest of the house ,breaking doors, cabinets and other property. Sometimes they arrest all adult males present in a house including elderly, handicapped or sick people (Danner, M., 2004, P 256). Moreover, according to UDHR (Article 10) which says "Everyone is entitled in full equality to a fair and public hearing by an independent and impartial tribunal". But during this war people being arrested by allied forces has become a daily routine. According to Kenton Keith the former US ambassador in Qatar "The situation changes almost by the hour, but I believe the latest number of prisoners to be around 7,000 in total, in Afghanistan" (BBC News, 21 December, 2001).In October 2001, for the deliverance of members of al-Qaeda and the Taliban, US dropped leaflets announcing high rewards from $50 to $5000 while 35-40,000 people had been arrested, majority of those by the Northern Alliance in Afghanistan (world Can't Wait) .Same as, in January 2004, according to Human Rights Watch (HRW), there were 10 enemy prisoner of war camps in Iraq detaining approximately 9,000 prisoners. The total number of detainees whose names appeared on the database on January 24, 2004 was 8,968 (Human Rights Watch , May 2004).Former UN Secretary General Kofi Annan repeatedly called attention to the Coalition's policies of arbitrary imprisonment, referring in 2005 to "the detention of thousands of persons without due process".

In context of the war against terrorism, US has gradually built a network of secret and semisecret prison centers in Bagram, Kandahar (Afghanistan),Guantanamo (Cuba);Qatar and Diego Garcia, Abu Ghraib, Camp Cropper (Iraq). National and international media always tried to report human rights violations in these centers. But they were restricted in many ways by the U.S. Army. December 12, 2001, The New York Times reported that in Afghanistan, 43 prisoners had died in half a dozen containers on the way, either from injuries or asphyxiation. The deaths occurred as the prisoners, many of them foreign fighters for the Taliban, were brought from the town of Kunduz to the prison here, a journey that took two or three days for some (Gall, C. , The New York Times, December 11, 2001).The prisoners were crammed at gunpoint into large, oblong freight containers. When no more could be squeezed in, the metal doors were shut tight. Slowly they began to suffocate. By the time the containers were opened two days later - at the end of the journey from Kunduz to Sheberghan - many were dead." There was no oxygen," said Maqsood Khan, a 26-year-old Pakistani from Rawalpindi. "We drank the sweat off our own bodies and off the dead men. Some drank their urine. Of 400, half were dead by the time we arrived" (Telegraph, 18 Mar, 2002).

Media have focus especially on Guantanamo and Abu Ghraib prison centers. USA leased Guantanamo bay for use as a coaly (fueling) station from Cuba. But since 2002 under the leadership of Joint Task Force (JTF) Guantanamo has become a military prison and interrogation camp. At the end of 2006, approximately 395 detainees of around 30 nationalities continued to be held without charge or trial at the US naval base in Guantánamo. Some had been held there for nearly five years (Amnesty International, Annual Report 2007, P 274).Many Guantanamo detainees conformed that they tortured in prison like Ibrahim Ahmed Mahmoud al Qosi of Sudan said "with an Israeli flag draped around him, loud music being played and a strobe light flashing". Moazzam Begg, a British detainee "He said he witnessed two detainees die after U.S. military personnel had beaten them". British detainee Martin Mubanga, one of Mickum's clients, wrote his sister that the American military police were treating him like a "rent boy"(Leonnig, D.C., Washingtonpost , December 26, 2004) .

While, all of these prison centers and torture activities are open violation of Universal Declaration of Human Rights (UDHR) article 10,11and third Geneva convention article 4,5,27,31,32 and 33. Besides this, the US president George W. Bush clearly refused Geneva convention in a memorandum (paragraph,2,d) dated February 7,2002 " based on the fact supplied by the Department of Defense and the recommendation of the Department of Justice, I determine that the Taliban detainees are unlawful combatants and therefore ,do not qualify as prisoners of war under the article 4 of Geneva .I note that, because Geneva dose not apply to our conflict with Al Qaeda, Al Qaeda detainees also do not qualify as prisoners"(Danner, M., 2004, P 391).

On April 28,2004, "60 Minutes II" CBS news magazine television program broke the news first time with graphic picture showing American military personals in act of abusing prisoners in Abu Ghraib (CBC News , February 18, 2005). However, many pictures and videotapes of the Abu Ghraib detainees released later, on different print and electronic media. Most published photographs taken during last three months of year 2003. In many of these photographs, detainees were naked, showing dogs snarling at cowering prisoners, Iraqi women forced to expose their breasts, and naked prisoners forced to have sex with each other, handcuffed, hooded prisoners tortured with electric shocked, abuse from dogs and being beaten. Like wise, in many of the pictures, US soldiers making the victory signs on dead and naked prisoners (Danner, M., 2004, P 217 and 224) .

Throughout this war on terror, media gets many reports on physical and sexual abuses on war detainees especially on Abu Ghraib prisoners. According to The Fay-Jones investigation report on Abu Ghraib "The abuses spanned from direct physical assault, such as delivering head blows rendering detainees unconscious, to sexual posing and forced participation in group masturbation. At the extremes were the death of a detainee in Other Government Agencies (OGA) custody, an alleged rape committed by a US translator and observed by a female soldier, and the alleged sexual assault of a female detainee. These abuses are, without question, are criminal act. They were perpetrated or witnessed by individuals or small groups. Such abuse can not be directly tied to a systemic US approach to torture or approved treatment of detainees" (MG George R. Fay, August 2004, P 71). While, according to international law, under the General Assembly resolution 39/46 of (10 December 1984) is "any act by which severe pain or suffering, whether physical or mental, is intentionally inflicted on a person for such purposes as obtaining from him or a third person information or a confession, punishing him for an act he or a third person has committed or is suspected of having committed, or intimidating or coercing him or a third person, or for any reason based on discrimination of any kind, when such pain or suffering is inflicted by or at the investigation of or with the consent or acquiescence of a public official or other person acting in an official capacity is 'torture'"(*Office of the High Commissioner for Human Rights*) .Media reports on Abu Ghraib and Abu Ghraib detainees pictures clearly described that It was torture and violation of laws of Geneva Convention and UDHR.

Since the beginning of the U.S. Occupation in Iraq, there has been a dramatic increase in sexual abuse, harassment and rape against Iraqi women by US forces. Many women have been taken hostage, tortured and sexually abused by them. According to Human Rights Watch Survey,2003, at least 400 women and girls as young as eight were reported to have been raped in Baghdad during or after the war, since April 2003 (Ellen, August 2005,P 2).On May 2, 2004 - (ACN) The release, by CBS News, of the photographs showing the heinous sexual abuse and torture of Iraqi prisoners of war at the notorious Abu Ghraib, later new photographs were sent by "La Voz de Aztlan " from confidential sources depicting the shocking rapes of two Iraqi women by US Military men (Cienfuegos, E., May 2004) .Like wise, on March 12, 2006, Four US armed soldiers with AK-47s rifles took Abeer Qassim Hamza family her mother, Fikhriya Taha; her father, Qassim Hamza; and her 5-year-old sister, Hadeel Qassim Hamza into a bedroom and killed them. He came out ….trying saying, according to sources the victim was seen to have blood on him clothes, bragging about what he'd just done. Then he and another soldier took turns raping Abeer 14 year's old girl. When they were done, they shot and killed her. Then they set fire to her body **(Revolutionary Communist Party,** July 2006 and Ghaith Abdul-Ahad ,The Guardian ,October 20 2006).

In short, in all above mentioned human rights abuses, Western mainstream media, led by the Washington Post, The New York Times, The Christian Science Monitor, CNN in the U.S. and The Guardian, Daily Telegraph, Daily Mirror, Sky TV and BBC in Britain, have abortive reporting on these horrific and sexual crimes than local and International Non Governmental Organizations (NGOs). But timely, awareness of human rights abuses around the world increased. The spread of news reportage and television documentaries are crucial, but so too is massive extension of international organizations such as Amnesty International, Human Rights Watch, The United Nations Children's Fund (UNICEF) and Red Cross have more human rights abuses reports on their record than which international media presented (Webster, F., 2003, P 65).

However, on the other hand, "freedom of expression, and of the media, has suffered in a number of ways since the war against terrorism began. Official actors have taken steps which both directly limit freedom of expression and information and which indirectly have a chilling effect on freedom of expression. Equally important is the serious climate of media self censorship and bias in many countries, which leads to a denial of the public's right to know. Restricting human rights in the aftermath of a terrorist attack somehow represents a victory for the terrorists who seek to undermine our way of life, including democracy and human rights. Furthermore, restricting freedom of expression is likely to undermine, rather than enhance, long-term strategies to address the problem of terrorism" (Mendel, T., 2003, P 49) for example in Arab media, Al-Jazeera television network popularity is increasing very fast since 2001.Because this is only one in world ,who broadcast the Al Qaeda leaders including Osama Bin Ladin audio and video massages several time during the USA war against terrorism. Its reporters make different documentaries and reports on Al Qaeda and Taliban fighters. Al Jazeera is the sole source to know the terrorist point of view, What they want? Why they attack on someone and become suicide bombers, apart from western point of view. However, US and UK government always try to control or ban Al Jazeera satellite transmissions. "On November 29, 2005, David Keogh and Leo O'Connor, appeared in the Bow Street Magistrates' Court in London. The charges against the pair relate to the alleged leak of a document containing what purports to be a discussion between Tony Blair and George W. Bush at one point. It is alleged this document shows that Blair had to dissuade Bush from bombing Al-Jazeera in Qatar" (Norton-Taylor, R., The Guardian, November 29, 2005).

Following that, in November 2001 US military seemed to have deliberately bombed Al Jazeera Kabul office and in the same month the channel's correspondent in Washington Muhammad Al-Alami was detained as he was on his way to cover the Russian- American summit in Texas (US) (Miladi, N., 2003, P 158 and 159).Likely, Tuesday, 8 April, 2003,. US hit a missile on Al Jazeera office in Baghdad. One member of staff (Tarek Ayoub) died and wounded other (BBC News, 8 April, 2003). The wife of Tarek Ayoub comments published in the Guardian on October 4,2003, she wrote "the US bombed al-Jazeera because it was angered by reports that did not confirm its one-sided picture of the war. For the past five years, Al-Jazeera and other Arab stations have been gaining credibility and fame not only in the Arab countries but also in the west, competing with international networks such as the BBC and CNN. Al-Jazeera in particular became very popular during the American war in Afghanistan. The channel aired voice recordings of al-Qaida and Taliban leaders as well as the speeches of President Bush and allied leaders. This decision to broadcast both sides was in keeping with its motto - "The opinion and the counter-opinion" - but the Americans could not allow such freedom of expression to prevail" (Tahboub, T.D., The Guardian , October 4, 2003).Above mentioned facts shows that US and its allies never been followed the UDHR article 19 and European Convention on Human Rights (ECHR) Article 10 during war against terrorism which gives the freedom of expression.

To sum up, after analysis the relevant sources, pre going discussion summarizes that the countries like United States, United Kingdom and their allies using the exaggeration power during the war against terrorism. They don't care the 'international war and human rights laws during this anti-terrorism war'. There are lowest estimates that at least 687,079 people have been killed, and 1,318,163 seriously injured in this terror war" (Unknown News, September 5, 2008) . Unfortunately deaths counting and injures still in row. Although, media already reported, number of illegal arresting, detainees torture, sexual abused, civilian's harassment and rape cases during this war. Afghanistan and Iraqi economic and social structure completely destroyed by US and its allies forces. In media, Press freedom ranking 2006 shows the statistics that US and UK media have 56 and 28 position in the world with 13,00 and 6,50 points respectively(Reporters With Out Borders, 2006) .Same as the governments of these countries always trying to control anti state media like Al Jazeera.

Conversely, on the summarization of the role of news media in the war against terrorism, I should say that, international media playing a very important role during this war against terrorism, especially in developed countries (USA, UK) electronic media like CNN, ABC, NBC, CBS, BBC, SKY and ITV which produced hundreds of pro and anti pro reports and debates on war against terrorism. Likewise, in leading print media e.g. Washington post, The New York Time, News Week, USA Today, The Post, Christian Science Monitor, The Guardian, Daily Telegraph and Daily Mirror creating a large number of reports and articles on war against terrorism since 2001.But on the other hand, affected countries with war on terrorism like Afghanistan and Iraq independent print or electronic media have no sound in the world. So argue is that, most of people in the world have so far been influenced with Western mainstream media rather than local country media inflicted with terror war. Now, it is responsibility of international political and Human Rights organizations to promote the local media in these countries because in my point of view "this war against terrorism is also a test for journalism; a test of its claim to guarantee free, accurate and plural information-gathering which allows citizens to choose and helps those who govern to avoid mistakes; and a test, also, of its capacity to demonstrate that human rights in general and freedom of the press in particular are the most effective weapons in the fight against terrorism and for the protection of our societies" (Paul, J.M. , 2003, P 56).

5

The War on Empiricism

DANGERS OF THE CONFIRMATION BIAS IN THE POLICING OF TERRORISM

The human brain is a phenomenal supercomputer. Neurons and cells relentlessly absorb and connect the details of a chaotic outside world to make sense and derive some order out of the chaos. As a result, the mind is constantly looking to impart an excessive amount of value to confirmatory information - favourable beliefs and theories - as it is 'easier to deal with cognitively'. While perhaps a necessary tool for sanity and survival, this *confirmation bias* has profound negative implications in the world of psychological profiling, especially in the field of the prevention and investigation of terrorist acts. In order to best illustrate its negative influence in this area, an examination of the mechanics of this cognitive bias is necessary before a shift in focus onto its effects. Past examples of the bias at work and the sheer power of its manipulations will be put to the reader to provide a wider 'historical' context. Following this, the essay will then examine the impact of the confirmation bias on the modern day investigative techniques and profiling methods used in policing terrorism. Also, the negative consequences of these profile biases on ethnic and minority groups in the larger context of western society will be canvassed.

The confirmation bias is an unfortunate part of the human condition and there are demonstrated examples throughout history of its power to warp the fields of inquiry usually reserved for rational empiricism, reason and logic. The negative effect of a steadfast adherence to a widely held belief can be found as far back as the 17th century. The practice of witch hunts in Western Europe and the estimated deaths of over 40,000 people 'is a particularly horrific case of the confirmation bias functioning in an extreme way at the societal level'. Even the legal system was besieged by irrational and fervent beliefs that abandoned rational thought and logic. Bodinus, a 17th-century French legal authority, had this to say about the conditions of the legal system at the time; 'The trial of this offense must not be conducted like other crimes. Whoever adheres to the ordinary course of justice perverts the spirit of the law, both divine and human. He who is accused of sorcery should never be acquitted, unless the malice of the prosecutor be clearer than the sun; for it is so difficult to bring full proof of this secret crime, *that out of a million witches not one would be convicted if the usual course were followed!'*

The conformation bias has the definite power to distort a society's legal system, but its effects can also be measured at a policy and governmental level. To take a modern example; the justification of the policy decision that drew the United States into the Vietnam War for over 15 years against 'countless evidences that it was a lost cause from the beginning' is a clear example of the bias in effect. According to Nickerson quoting Tuchman;'Once a policy has been adopted and implemented, all subsequent activity becomes an effort to justify it'. He also argued that after a policy is implemented by a government, the subsequent decisions and considerations become focused on the continued justification of that policy.

Even in the world of science, the confirmation bias infects. Within the proper practice of empirical analysis, there is an inbuilt resistance to bias and this is one of the ways in which scientific thinking is different from ordinary thinking. However, human cognitive weakness often outweighs this empirical approach and this has profoundly negative effects in investigative procedure;

'When Robert Millikan published the experimental work on determining the electric charge of a single electron, for which he won the Nobel prize in physics, he reported only slightly more than half (58) of his (107) observations, omitting from publication those that did not fit his hypothesis'

However, the field of science has an important safety mechanism that could prove useful to police investigative procedure;

'It is not so much the critical attitude that individual scientists have taken with respect to their own ideas that has given science the success it has enjoyed as a method for making new discoveries, but more the fact that individual scientists have been highly motivated to demonstrate that hypotheses that are held by some other scientist(s) are false. The insistence of science *as an institution* has ensured its relative independence from the biases of its practitioners'.

The above examples illustrate the dangerous impact that transgressions of the scientific requirement of empiricism can have. In moving to an examination of the effects that the confirmation bias has on the sphere of profiling terrorists however, it is important to discuss the psychological nature of both the bias and the practices of police investigation.

Integral to an understanding of the conformation bias is an examination of the concept of 'the need for cognitive closure – a term that connotes the desire for a clear cut opinion on a judgemental topic and an avoidance of confusion and ambiguity'. According to Ask and Granhag, the confirmation bias manifests itself into two distinct manipulative areas. Firstly, '*the selective information search'* is a danger in the investigative sphere when the actions of the police 'become too focused on incriminating (i.e. confirming) evidence against a prime suspect without any consideration in finding disconfirming information'. Secondly, '*biased interpretation*' takes this selective information and then interprets it in a way that is further 'partial towards an existing belief'. In terms of profiling, these two measurable factors become paramount influencers as the human need for cognitive closure is the driving force behind this kind of investigation; 'the logic of NFC thus predicts that investigators working under a need for closure become motivated to see that their suspicions against suspects are correct'.

Unlike science which is a 'self correcting institution', NFC inhibits and makes self correction impossible in the institution of criminal investigation.

To further illustrate the quest for 'closure', police investigators will structure both their profiles and decision making faculties around 'causal explanations of the situation at hand'. The human mind in general 'spontaneously constructs causal theories to make sense of the massive flow of information from the environment'. The limitations of an investigator's approach to their work, is astutely explained by Ask and Granhag when they add to their explanation of the confirmation bias; 'criminal investigation is a theory driven activity. That is, investigators are guided in their search for and evaluation of evidence by their preliminary theories or hypotheses regarding how and by whom a crime was committed.

...in taking a piece of evidence to support their working hypothesis, investigators may fail to realise that the very same evidence could be equally consistent with an alternative hypothesis'.

Therefore there is a problem in the investigation of any criminal activity - including terrorism - because the directional goals and theories inherent in police work involve an 'increase of the likelihood of a conformational bias'. Preconceived ideas and beliefs can clash with empirical investigative procedures, short-circuiting correct evidence gathering techniques and in effect, allowing prejudices to govern police decision making and influence terrorism profiles.

This illustration of the weakness in the investigative decision making process, signals the resulting negative and inefficient methods of profiling terrorists used today. Preconceived ideas and conformational biases manifest themselves in the controversial methods of *racial profiling* - a practice detrimental to traditional empirical investigative procedure. In the post September 11 world there has been a documented increase in western societal suspicion of people of 'Arab' and Middle Eastern appearance, perpetuating itself into profiling procedure. There is a simple, colloquial phrase that has in effect become 'profiling policy' in both Australia and in the United States; 'Not all Arabs are terrorists, but all terrorists are Arabs'

As a result, there has been not only been unfortunate social and moral transgressions (that will be discussed further in the essay) but also documented mistakes and inefficiencies because of this crude assumption. For example, the inefficiency of the current post September 11 policy of targeting 'only Arab looking individuals' is demonstrated by these statistics; 'as of May 2003, only three of the 1200 suspected terrorists arrested in the first seven weeks, and none of the nearly 4000 more foreign nationals arrested under related anti-terrorism initiatives turned out to warrant even *a charge* of terrorist-related criminal activity'.

Examples of cognitive bias creating havoc on police profiles existed well before the September 11 attacks. The 1995 Oklahoma City bombing in the USA saw the law enforcement establishment hunt for evidence pertaining to; 'suspected Arab and/or Muslim involvement... prompting them to post bulletins around the city describing their suspicions... Ultimately the bombers turned out to be two former army, Anglo-American Christians'.

In this case, police work was hampered by a non-empirically based idea – a bias that propelled a useless stereotype into the minds of the police, stalled the investigation and propagated a false idea into the community that people of Middle Eastern appearance were the culprits.

There is a good criticism to be made about the practice of profiling in general, not just in the sphere of combating terrorism. As psychological profiling is used as a means to narrow search parameters based on hypotheses, some critics argue the practice's merit as an 'empirical' scientific method of criminal investigation. In October 2002 during the infamous sniper killings in Washington DC, the traditional model for the serial killer; a disaffected white male of lower to middle class proved to be of no correlation with the actual killer; two black males. It is also mentioned by Swiney quoting Oliver Revell (a former FBI Director of Intelligence) that profiling 'can have [police] chasing a stereotype while the real culprit slips away' and 'in the end it was old fashioned dogged police work and cooperation from the public and media that cracked the case.

In the wider social context, the interference of the conformational bias to scientific investigative procedure is not the only negative aspect. Prejudicial treatment of various ethnic groups in western society, predominantly of people with Middle Eastern or Muslim backgrounds is an unfortunate consequence of the post September 11 world. Also unfortunate is the increasing popularity of racial profiling inside organisational and business policy. The Israeli airline El Al is quick to point out that it has been free of terrorism and hijacking for over thirty years in spite of its unstable Middle East location. Its policy of aggressive searching and screening of males of Middle Eastern appearance that 'fit the profile', appears to be effective on its face. However in this situation, this attitude towards racial profiling could well be a form of conformational bias itself, as the effectiveness of this method of airport enforcement 'flies in the face of existing empirical research'. According to evidence garnered by the anti-profiling initiatives of the US Customs Service, a remarkable increase in efficiency was gained in 'hit rates' after their policy of racial profiling was abandoned, leaving officers to profile and 'focus on specific behaviours such as nervousness and inconsistencies in passenger behaviour'. El Al in conjunction with the Israeli Intelligence Service (The Mossad) has demonstrated superior intelligence capabilities in the modern world, as well as highly trained security personnel that could have contributed to their hijack-free environment. The effectiveness of racial profiling as a law enforcement profiling tool increasingly lacks credibility as without a racial profile, investigators are free to use 'more refined techniques such as behavioural cues and suspect or crime-specific descriptions'. They are in effect free to use more empirical methods of profiling and detection.

In the wider context of society, these conformational biases and racial 'terrorism' profiles have lead to abhorrent instances of discrimination and unfair treatment concerning ethnic and minority groups. While in Australia there has been a flux of racially motivated violence towards Middle Eastern population (cf; The December 11, 2005 Cronulla Riots) there is far more significant documented evidence in the United States concerning different types of discrimination post September 11. According to Swiney, three months after the attacks, 'roughly fifty eight percent of American Muslims reported having been the victim of discrimination'. Also '700 incidents of murder, physical beatings and threats of death were reported in the first nine weeks after the attacks'. There is also evidence of governmental discrimination on its citizens with a blanket approach of preventative detention; 'federal agents raided Arab, Muslim and South Asian neighbourhoods "snatching men from sidewalks, as well as their homes, workplaces and mosques"...no one has been charged to date with links to terrorism'.

The 'terrorist' racial profile has a negative impact on the proper functioning of society as well as producing insignificant results to justify its use. 'Chasing the stereotype' and following racial profiles looks to be a fruitless and harmful exercise.

The stakes are high, but there are possible ways to combat the weakness of human cognition in the practice of psychologically profiling terrorists. Research is needed to examine the effectiveness of training police investigators more intensively in empirical law enforcement procedure, as it could be the most effective way to encourage police to 'resist the confirmation bias' - like *true* scientists. Relying less on profiling and gathering evidence in a more balanced way while raising 'awareness of a prevalent bias toward confirmation, even under relatively ideal conditions of evidence evaluation' could improve overall investigative technique. Also, an elimination of racial profiling in the fight against terrorism may increase efficiency and productivity in similar ways to the US Customs Service - where a focus on behavioural cues etc, has sparked improvement. In order to combat the negative effects of racial profiles and the confirmation bias on a societal level, studies are needed as to whether a basic level of cognitive psychological education about confirmation bias and the harmfulness of racial stereotypes would be effective. Teaching ordinary people about the fundamental weakness in their human perception could well be the best method in addressing injustice on a large scale.

In purely pragmatic terms, psychological profiling and police investigation is concerned with identifying suspects, making arrests and the systematic gathering of evidence for the prosecution to use in the courtroom. The mind's tendency to ignore empirical evidence and justify faulty premises and preconceptions is a weakness that must be addressed, especially in preventing and investigation of terrorist acts. The demonstrated fact that directional goals and a motivated 'need for cognitive closure' increases the likelihood of biased outcomes, is a testament to the fact that simplistic racial profiles are ineffective. Knowledge of the confirmation bias and its effect on empirical methods of investigation is vital for any profiler or policeman, in order to avoid the mistakes made in the past. Overall, education and a renewed *empirical approach* to profiling; a focus on behavioural cues, suspect and crime specific psychological descriptions, will ensure a more efficient fighting and investigative force in combating terrorism.

6

Insurgency and Terrorism in Afghanistan

COMPONENTS OF THE INSURGENCY: FOUR SEGMENTS

Hardcore Extremists

- Categorically reject elected government and western presence
- Directing campaign against Afghan security forces/coalition from Pakistan
- Seek to show Afghan government unable to provide basic security or services
- Can only be dealt with by military or police action

Cross-border Fighters

- Recruited primarily from within Afghan refugee community
- Joined by Pakistani and some foreign fighters linked to madrassas
- Trained within Pakistan in combat, communications, IEDs and suicide ops
- Heavily indoctrinated; some may reconcile, others require military/police action

Internal Fighters

- Jobless and landless youth from Afghanistan's Pashtun belt

- Foot soldiers of the insurgency; killed this year in larger numbers
- Little or no indoctrination; fighting for cash, coercion or tribal honour
- Will abandon insurgency in return for jobs and education

Alienated Tribal and Religious Groups

- Marginalized for various reasons in post-Bonn era
- Not opposed to government in principle, but enter tactical alliance with Taliban
- View government as corrupt and education system as un-Islamic
- Can be reconciled by intense outreach and consultation and economic progress

Contributing Factors

Political opportunists/criminals: Allied with insurgents for influence or monetary gain

Drug trafficking networks: formation of alliance of convenience to protect harvest or trafficking routes

Both require improved policing/interdiction and more robust justice system.

INTRODUCTION

The need to determine who is involved in the fighting in Afghanistan and why, was put to the international community by President Karzai in late June 2006. There has been much speculation over the past months as the intensity of fighting increased, especially in the south and east, as to who was responsible. Besides this quantitative change, a qualitative change, especially in the coordination of fighting, has also been detected. The term "Taliban" is often casually used when the actual perpetrators of violence may not be linked at all to that group. The same is true of Al Qaeda, Haqqani, HiG and the like. In order to best determine how to stabilize, and thereafter turn the state of instability around, it is necessary to fully understand who is involved, and why.

An understanding of the nature of the fighting is also important in trying to determine who is involved. Many observers use the term "insurgency" which may be interpreted in various ways. For the purposes of this paper, "insurgency" means the strategy of attempting to overthrow the present government of Afghanistan through violent means. It attacks the security forces of Afghanistan and its foreign military allies while simultaneously attacking all symbols of governance and development.

These elements are present in Afghanistan and as such, the conflict is an insurgency in the classical sense. The primary perpetrators of violence have been categorized in four Segments and in addition, a number of peripheral actors to the fighting have been identified. The Segments may, or may not be, ideologically linked, and base their cooperation on perceived common ground. All contribute to the current state of instability for different motives. The possible solution to each is also different, and ranges from concerted military and police action to political and social interventions.

AIM

The aim of this chapter is to identify in broad terms who is fighting against the legitimate government of Afghanistan and why, and to suggest appropriate broad strategies against them.

ASSUMPTIONS AND DEFINITIONS

Insurgents. Organizations motivated by ideology and who have expressed no desire to negotiate a settlement. The fighters themselves are primarily Afghan and may be resident within the country or infiltrate from over the borders, primarily from Pakistan. Assistance may also be provided by foreigners who are ideologically aligned to the Afghan groups. They are overtly, or through coercion, supported by an internal population base, in this case centered on the Pashtun areas of Afghanistan.

Terrorism. Besides direct military action against the statutory, uniformed, forces of the government and its foreign allies, the insurgent fighters use acts of terror against the population, government institutions and officials to achieve their ideological aims. In this sense they are terrorists employing a type of warfare known as terrorism.

Anti-Government Elements. As not all involved are directly connected to acts of terror, or personally linked to insurgency, collectively the perpetrators and supporters of violence are termed Anti-Government Elements or AGEs.

SCOPE

The paper is laid out in the four identified Segments followed by a summary and recommendations. A main conclusion is presented at the end.

SEGMENTS

Segment 1 : Hardcore Extremists

Hardcore extremists are defined for the purpose of this paper as both Afghan and other nationals either living in Afghanistan or externally whose goal in the main is the creation of a pure Islamic Emirate in Afghanistan. The goal of the extremists is expanded to include the rejection of the democratically elected Government of Afghanistan (GoA) and the installation of an alternative regime, as well as the expulsion of westerners from Afghanistan. Most importantly the position of the hardcore extremists is unalterable as they are fanatically dedicated to the attainment of their goal. This group cannot be induced to join the democratic process and will remain permanently outside; they are spoilers.

The hardcore extremist fighters belong to a variety of groups including al-Qaeda, the Taliban and the Hezb-e Islami Gulbuddin (HiG). Identification of the key members of these groups is by no means complete but media interviews, particularly through al Jazeera, provide information on the names and locations of their hierarchy.

The Taliban is led by Mullah Muhammad Omar who has made his views clear and they are summarized in the following quotation: "We will not accept a government of wrong-doers. We prefer death than to be part of an evil government." Mullah Omar has assembled a ten man advisory council, or shura, and has allocated appointments such as to Mullah Dadullah Akhund, who is responsible for military operations in central Afghanistan as well as recruitment. Other notable extremists include: Mullah Obaidullah, Mullah Berader, Mullah Osmani, Jalaluddin and Serajuddin Haqqani, Mullah Mansour, Hafiz Abdul Majid and Abdul Wahid Rais Baghrani. The location of these individuals is uncertain but Obiadullah, Hqqqani, Mansour and Berader have been identified in Pakistan while Osmani, and Dadullah-Lang have been mentioned as being present both in Afghanistan and Pakistan.

A second group, the HiG, and their leader Gulbuddin Hekmatyar have declared their willingness to fight under the banner of al Qaeda.

The links between the three primary groups are difficult to unravel and coupled with this is the further complication that AGEs are characterized by internecine quarrels and the subsequent shifts in allegiance among the tribes that these produce. This fluidity in the nature of the groups makes any analysis of the command and control structure difficult to precisely ascertain, however the presence of a significant number of the key extremist figures in Pakistan suggests that this is an important focal point.

Additionally, the fact that some key extremist figures are identified on both sides of the border suggests that close linkages exist and that the direction of operations is from Pakistan. However the existence of a loose relationship between the HiG, Taleban and al-Qaeda should not be considered a strengthening factor but quite the opposite, it is a weakness because of the tensions and rivalries engendered.

One of the effects of current Coalition Forces (CF) and Afghan National Security Forces (ANSF) operations such as Mountain Thrust is that they have forced AGEs to improve their capability to operate effectively on both sides of the border. This is necessary to protect the senior leadership and withdraw high value assets into Pakistan when necessary. CF operations inevitably have degraded the Taliban's operational ability especially with the removal of key personnel. Prior to this AGEs had the opportunity to build up their forces because of the safe havens in Pakistan and the lower military focus on the South.

Hardcore extremists are fighting toward the fulfillment of their strategic vision of an extremist Islamist government for Afghanistan, including the expulsion of western military forces. In order to achieve their objectives, they are conducting a deliberate campaign to undermine the credibility of the GoA both domestically and internationally. The ANSF are targeted to demonstrate that the extremists have the ability to disrupt daily life in Afghanistan and that the Afghan National Army (ANA) and Afghan National Police (ANP) are not able to counter AGE actions. This targeting has been effective as the security forces are in a developmental stage in terms of training and acquisition of equipment. Government officials are also targeted as they seek to deny the GoA the ability to extend the influence of state authority throughout Afghanistan. By paralyzing the security services and local government officials, hardcore extremists prepare the ground to persuade the general population that the GoA is not able to provide basic security, without which no other government services are able to follow.

Once the perception is accepted that the GoA is unable to deliver basic services, particularly to areas where traditionally there has been little government presence or amenities, the population is more likely to accept the vision of these hardcore extremists as the only alternative. AGEs are also able to quickly move back into areas temporarily occupied by CF and International Security Assistance Forces (ISAF) thus proving that their presence is the more enduring. The extremists are in a delicate position in regard to their relationship with the local population in sensitive regional and tribal areas, as they must maintain a level of support whether it is tacit or gained through coercion. If the balance is skewed too far towards coercive measures such as the brutal excesses utilized in the past, extremists will alienate the population despite still requiring their support. Another motivation of hardcore extremists is to demonstrate that they have the ability to inflict casualties on both the nascent ANSF as well as the CF and ISAF forces. Internationally, the insurgents can prove that they remain a force to be reckoned with as they are unafraid of engaging with foreign military forces present in Afghanistan. The approach of the hardcore extremists is long-term as a result of their ability to endure the pressure of military operations because the options exist to either withdraw to Pakistan or decrease the operational tempo in Afghanistan until more favorable circumstances arise. Extremists will deliberately target the ISAF countries whose public are less tolerant of casualties in the knowledge that Governments will withdraw forces from Afghanistan.

Conclusion: Hardcore extremists are located on both sides of the Pakistan/Afghanistan border, and they are so committed to their cause that inclusion in the political process cannot be considered a viable option. Links between the various extremist groups and their command and control relationships remain shrouded. Media and other reports however have identified by name and function several of Mullah Omar's shura as well as the fact that some individuals have been located on both sides of the border. This suggests Pakistan is an important location from where members of the extremist hierarchy have the ability to direct operations, and also a convenient sanctuary for high value personnel and equipment should the military situation in Afghanistan become temporarily untenable. The extremists are fighting to attain their goal of removing the current GoA and installing their regime. Their strategy is to discredit the GoA by targeting the security forces and local government officials to demonstrate that the current Government is not capable of providing security or other services to the population.

Solutions: In dealing with hardcore extremists the following solutions are worth consideration:

1. Severance of the link between the Pakistan based hierarchy and the less motivated AGEs in Afghanistan. As it is extremely

unlikely that the extremists will participate in government, they must addressed using military and police action.

2. The creation of an environment which is unfavorable to extremist influence, by improving the security situation to allow for the extension of state authority and services, as well as humanitarian services.
3. The continued capacity building of the ANSF.

SEGMENT 2 : CROSS-BORDER FIGHTERS

This group of fighters is primarily composed of Afghan refugees (and their families) and some foreign nationals recruited from madrassas or the camps themselves. This segment also includes mid-level commanders who frequently travel back and forth from Pakistan. The foreign nationals are predominantly Pakistani and include Arabs, Chechens and recently Turks. They are predominantly young, indoctrinated, ideologically motivated, and have a very narrow world-view. The group is rooted in remaining Afghan refugee communities in Pakistan, with the bulk originating from Quetta. As many are refugees, they remain unintegrated into the host society, and the majority are, notwithstanding their country of residence, "Afghans". Their activities have expanded from short-term cross-border infiltration to the establishment of a semi-permanent presence in Afghanistan.

A further group of cross-border fighters is the displaced. These are committed fighters who have either been driven out of Afghanistan by Coalition Forces or Government of Afghanistan Forces, or because their support structure within Afghanistan has been destroyed.

A third group of cross-border fighters exists because they feel more able to operate freely across the border in Pakistan. This group, which includes Haqqani and HiG fighters and supporters, utilize the porous borders and informal security structures that exist in the Federally Administered Tribal areas and the North West Frontier Province in particular. These cross-border fighters are able to maintain their status within their own community, recruit new impressionable young fighters and live the life of a feudal benevolent warlord whilst simultaneously exploiting the vulnerable and impressionable young men who flock to be their followers.

Due to their refugee status, this group is, and remains vulnerable, to ideological indoctrination. Any education they have received is most likely limited to religious education. Many Segment 2 fighters (including non Afghans) are educated in radical madrassas in Pakistan where the brand of teaching leans towards radicalism and as such is a motivation to join the insurgency. The fact that no jobs are available to them means that they are looking for a sense of purpose; being a fighter gives them status, in some cases money, and a cause to follow. Like young men everywhere, they crave excitement and danger; the life of the "fighter" provides this.

For those who are unconvinced of this path, peer pressure and propaganda (from radical preachers, newspapers, radio broadcasts, and the internet) serves as impetus. Once indoctrinated and trained, they have little or no fear of being killed - this makes them a very dangerous enemy.

This group is capable of a wide range of anti-Government activity, from suicide bombing, communications, bomb-making and normal foot soldier skills. The cross-border fighters are a disparate group. A mix of hardcore leaders, experienced fighters and young idealists. This mix is the most dangerous. The elder fighters with experience, authority and credibility are producing a steady throughput of fighters for the insurgency. It is these groupings that are reinforcing medium value targets (primarily from Segment 1) across the South and East. Their camps are production lines for young fighters and specialist training in operational security, IED construction and emplacement and suicide training are becoming more common.

Elements of the HiG network and Taliban Medium Level commanders are good examples of this grouping. These medium level commanders train fighters for a fee, transport fighters into Afghanistan and provide the support and logistic network required for the insurgency. Their cross-border operations and support mechanisms will only be defeated by military operations.

Recommendations. This group requires a twin-tracked approach. The experienced dedicated fighters and leaders are unlikely to participate in the Peace Through Strength (PTS) program or reconcile. The key trainers, who indoctrinate young men and send them into battle to be killed/ or captured by Government Forces or Coalition Forces need to be dealt with by military or police power.

A second, less attractive, option would be capture, as many radicals or dedicated insurgents would still continue their activities in preaching intolerance within prisons.

However the military/police solution to this segment is not automatic. There is potential, now and in the future, to attempt to include fighters and even mid-level commanders from this segment in a reconciliation/re-education programme.

To counter the steady throughput of young impressionable fighters, it is necessary to provide an attractive alternative to the life of the insurgent. This means employment (of sufficient status) and education/re-education. Given that many of this group has been involved in fighting for most of their lives, it may not be possible to reconcile all of them to peaceful employment. With economic benefits in limited supply and with no viable employment prospects, this group is expected to continue growing for the foreseeable future.

Segment 3 : Internal Fighters

The internal fighters make up the majority of the foot soldiers in the insurgency. They are the poor youth of the Afghan rural areas, predominantly in the Pashtun Belt. This group of fighters has been created in the recent past and is a result of the insurgency, not the cause of the insurgency.

The recent deterioration in many districts in the South has affected the traditional tribal way of life, to a great extent the result of AGE action. The AGEs have disrupted the authority of the

Elders and have demonstrated to many young men the impotence of the Tribal Shura and Tribal Elders. The authority in many areas now stems from the AGE commanders and thus, as the position of the elders deteriorates, the AGEs impose more direction and structure over the rural communities, and the recruitment of the young becomes easier.

This group may have little or no ideological motivation, as they have not received the indoctrination of the cross-border fighters. That said, their lack of employment prospects, poor or non-existent education and lack of a credible alternative, makes them become fighters. However, they are less likely to want to die "for the cause".

Money is a motivator for some fighters. ISI operatives (from Pakistan) reportedly pay a significant number of Taliban (or wavering/ former Taliban) living/operating in both Pakistan and Afghanistan to fight.

Some fight because of coercion. A large number of those fighting are doing so under duress as a result of pressure from ISI or Taliban operatives. Reporting indicates that Taliban fighters are canvassing villages for new recruits, threatening to kill entire families unless one able-bodied male agrees to fight with the Taliban against the Coalition Forces or the Government Forces. A small number fight for revenge. Some of those fighting have lost family and loved ones in fighting with the Afghan Government forces or the Coalition Forces and wish to avenge their deaths. A number of traditional Afghans seek tribal retribution as a form of simple justice in a society where the Government's justice system is lacking.

Disenfranchisement also causes some Afghans to fight. The Taliban were given no place in the Afghan Government under the Bonn Agreement, and are unable to live in Afghanistan freely as they did in the past. While PTS is reportedly working in some parts of the country, there are indications that more fighters would PTS if they could see more tangible benefits of doing so.

Tribal rivalry is also a factor why people fight. Harassment of tribal rivals by those fortunate enough to be part of the Government has served to create conflict in Northern Helmand Province, in parts of Uruzgan province, and to a lesser degree in Kandahar Province.

Growing frustration with the Government is often cited as a reason for driving some people to assist, if not actually join, the Taliban. Tribal harassment is also linked with other issues such as competition for control over resources, land and water.

For many in this group, their future is most likely as a foot soldier (or low-level criminal). They have no viable future and the gains from involvement in the insurgency will always outweigh the gains from legal employment. Many have no focus, no initiative and no knowledge of the wider world. They remain ripe for exploitation. Many of the underlying factors are the same as for the cross-border foot soldiers.

Recent reporting from western Afghanistan indicates that it is small numbers of foot soldiers that are willing to PTS. These are most likely local fighters who now wish to give up the fight. Many of these internal fighters no longer wish to be associated with the Taliban, but they see no viable alternative.

There is little incentive to PTS, there are few economic opportunities and some are waiting to see what assistance will be offered by the Government to help them rebuild their lives. The benefits of being a Taliban foot soldier are few, but many will continue to reluctantly take part in operations in return for modest payments.

Recommendations. The key to removing this group from the fight is, again, to provide credible alternatives to the life of a fighter. They are less well motivated, and so simple alternatives are all that is required to end their involvement in the insurgency.

A steady living, peaceful environment and some prospects for their future may be all that they need to desist from fighting. A stronger Afghan government, more visible and credible security and improved employment prospects would reduce the recruitment and retention of these fighters.

Segment 4 : Tribal and Religious Groups

While not definitionally linked to the insurgency, tribal and religious groups can play a large role in determining its continued viability or resolution.

The estrangement of such groups from the state underlies much of the AGE activity in the Pashtun belt. Achieving a rapprochement with them, principally by engaging their leadership and addressing their major grievances, is therefore a critical element in curbing the insurgency.

Reconciling Estranged Tribal Groups. Ensuring that individual Pashtun tribes and sub-tribes are fairly represented in district and provincial administrations – by persons who enjoy their confidence – is no less important for stability than providing for ethnic balance at the national level.

Even in the most detribalized Pashtun areas, tribal identity is closely linked to an individual's perceptions of economic and physical security: opportunities for employment, access to public services, and protection from criminal violence are all seen as flowing from having fellow tribesmen in positions of authority.

There have nevertheless been significant disparities in tribal representation since the formation of the Interim Administration, most acutely in the southern provinces. A few examples follow:

1. The perceived dominance of the Popalzai tribe in Uruzgan can be attributed to the prolonged governorship of Jan Mohammad and his selective appointment of fellow tribesmen to posts in the provincial administration. A local elder who is broadly pro-government said in May that "instability in Uruzgan is made by the authorities there" and accused the former governor of trying "to eliminate certain tribes' role in the province."
2. Many of the men recently fighting against the government in Kandahar's Panjwai, Maiwand, and Zherai districts were Noorzai, Alizai, and Ishaqzai tribesmen who had long-standing, unaddressed grievances against the Barakzai-

dominated administration of former governor Gul Agha Sherzai.

3. In Nangarhar, many Khogiani tribesmen have interpreted the removal of the Khogiani district manager and the deputy provincial governor as an attempt to restrict their tribe's power. Some Khogiani tribal leaders have responded by sheltering AGEs and have so far rebuffed overtures by a provincial governor whom they distrust as a result of the removals.

In some areas, the central government has inherited political alignments between individual tribes and rejectionist armed factions.

1. Zadran tribal territory has been a conspicuous center of AGE activity in Paktya provinces. As a recent study points out, commander Jalaluddin Haqqani built "a new network of traditionalist madrassahs in areas under his influence, thus creating the conditions for strong Taleban support to emerge." The UNAMA-assisted Zadran Arc Stabilization Initiative attempts to reconcile these areas to the government through a combination of incentives and sanctions; it conditions the delivery of development assistance packages, agreed upon in consultation with Zadran tribal councils, on security guarantees by those councils.
2. The areas of Zurmat in Paktya and Shahjoy in Zabul had high-ranking representatives in the Taliban regime and have seen their power wane with the arrest and continued detention of those officials. But the comparative weakness of tribal structures in these areas limits the ability of their tribal councils to enforce agreements reached with the state. At the same time, the strength of Deobandi religious networks is likely to provide a continued source of support for the Taliban. It may therefore be necessary to combine an incentives-based strategy with increased political representation of the local tribes.

Influential elders across the Pashtun belt say the role that they could play in building support for the government and serving as a channel for voicing popular grievances and concerns has been neglected.

To an extent, they are represented in the Wolesi Jirga and the provincial councils, but the elections to these institutions – particularly the Wolesi Jirga – also tended to reflect and reinforce the post-Bonn distribution of power in individual provinces. Consequently, regular, possibly formalized, meetings between provincial officials and tribal councils, consultation with elders on appointments, and – in areas where direct delivery of services is prevented by the insurgency – direct channeling of assistance through elders with a proviso of accountability, could all help reinforce the prestige of elders in tribal and detribalized areas alike.

Religious Alienation: Evidence suggests that alienation from the state's religious, moral, and social values is a critical factor behind the current insurgency.

A hadith frequently cited in propaganda in the southeast relates directly to the sins of corruption and bribery, both of which are associated by much of the population with the current government.

Similar concerns were recently voiced by Islamic leaders in Herat; who criticized the provincial police for unprofessional conduct and corruption, and called its performance a leading cause of dissatisfaction with the government.

Religious alienation also takes a wider range of targets into its embrace, not all of which can be harmonized with the government's obligations under international law and the Afghan constitution. The content of television programming, for example, is a common grievance among religious conservatives. Such discontent finds its most forceful expression among Salafists, adherents of a doctrine that seeks to respond to the political and cultural challenge of the West by returning to the values of the first three generations of Muslims.

In areas with a strong tradition of Deobandi influence, including much of the southern Ghilzai tribal territory, students have traveled for generations to the Indian subcontinent for training in madrassas. Migration to Pakistan for religious instruction in the present context, however, carries the risk that students will return radicalized by their environment and the content of preaching in their seminaries. Anecdotal evidence also suggests that lay preachers, or *tablighis*, affiliated with a Pakistani political party have this year increased their activity in central and eastern Farah, and are covertly recruiting young men for training camps in Pakistan.

One possible response, proposed by some independent observers as well as mullahs in the Pashtun belt and north alike, is the establishment of madrassas in Afghanistan to deter the migration of religious students to Pakistan.

1. Such an approach would allow the government to more readily regulate the content of religious instruction, a key element in reclaiming ownership of religious discourse within its borders.
2. It would also require careful planning and management to ensure that the institutions are not co-opted by religious networks that already provide ideological support for religiously motivated AGEs and instead mirror the diversity of religious thought in Afghanistan as well as in recognized centers of Islamic scholarship. Mullahs would have to meet strict criteria for employment and agree to the use of standardized, government-approved curricula.
3. Even with these precautions in place, however, it is likely that a significant degree of migration by religious students will continue, both because of the prestige now attached to some Deobandi institutions in Pakistan as well as the stipends and free board provided to students there.

Other Contributing Elements. The following other contributing elements have been identified. These are not seen as Segments in their own right:

Political Opportunists. These are politicians and government officials, former jihadi leaders and commanders whose criminal and self-enhancing actions weaken the State's authority and credibility, thereby inadvertently assisting to create an environment of instability which can be used to best advantage by insurgents.

Their actions mostly fall within the scope of severe corruption and crime where own gain is placed above the common good of the people and the State.

In the case of government officials, their abuse of power and resultant neglect of their responsibilities, diminishes their ability to focus on the real threat and provides propaganda for AGEs. The best solution to them will be to encourage the application of their considerable influence, power and resources towards the common good within the democratic system. This is a political leadership problem.

Concerted effort should be applied to identify who they are and through public exposure and the justice system, enforce compliance. Accelerated development of the ANP will also help towards a solution.

Low-level Criminals. This group is present in all societies, but thrives in Afghanistan due to the lack of professional policing and the absence of a robust rule of law and justice system.

They act with seeming impunity and contribute greatly to the climate of insecurity.

In this sense they undermine the ability of the statutory forces to address the main issue, i.e. insurgency, as military and police attention is divided between AGEs and criminal activities. There is also evidence that this group may be directly linked to AGEs in a symbiotic relationship.

The criminals may not be ideologically aligned to AGEs, but offer their services in the planting of IEDs, abductions etc on behalf of AGEs for own monetary gain. The only solution to this group is police action and the justice system.

Narcotics Actors. Narcotics play a significant role in the insecurity present in Afghanistan. Illicit crops, primarily poppy, are worth a significant amount of money; the estimated export value of the poppy crop in 2005 is $2.7 billion.

Estimates of drug profits that are used to fund the insurgency range from less than 1% to 20%. AGEs and major drug traffickers may engage in short term, mutually beneficial alliances at the local level.

Farmers have been known to pay local AGEs a poppy growing tax and/or a fee for protection. AGEs can also monopolize on the conflict created by the GoA's eradication policy for short term gains by providing protection to farmers in return for active or passive support of their own operations.

The actual effect or success of such protection agreements provided to farmers by AGEs in the face of eradication remains debatable. It is estimated that 120,000 itinerant workers were required in 2005 to assist farmers in lancing poppy crops.

Of those, roughly 15,000, or 12%, came from across the border. Harvesters tend to be extremely poor day labourers who move south to north with the crop calendar.

The movement of such a large number of workers provides an opportunity for AGE infiltration into areas throughout the country.

It also provides a short term opportunity to disguise the movement of cross-border fighters into the country, primarily from Pakistan. Additionally, farmers, who through bad weather conditions, market price fluctuations, eradication, or other factors, do not produce enough opium paste to pay their debts, as well as harvesters, are susceptible to recruitment into the insurgency.

This is not because they are involved in illegal narcotics or share a common ideology; but rather because of their need for survival. As such, they fall under the group outlined in Segment 3 of this paper.

SUMMARY AND RECOMMENDATIONS

Table below, summarizes the segments and other groups responsible for violence in Afghanistan. The motivation and recommendations as indicated are extracted from the text above.

	WHO	WHY	RECOMMEN-DATIONS
Segment 1: Hardcore Extremists	Various nationalities and groups. Primarily Afghan. Taliban, HiG, Haqqani, Al Qaeda, others. Primarily leaders and planners but also provide fighters	Ideologically motivated: Overthrow of current government by violent means; creation of a pure/extremist Islamic Emirate in Afghanistan according to their definition, under their own control	Military/Police Option only viable means of defeat. Will not negotiate on terms other than their own. Although an Afghan problem, foreign military support will be required for the short to medium term
Segment 2: Cross-Border Fighters	Primarily Afghan refugees (but includes other nationalities) who infiltrate from outside of Afghanistan, primarily Pakistan. Some mid-level commanders are also present. Main area of operations is south and east and belong to any of the Segment 1 groups above	Combination of ideology (inculcated mainly in madrassas in Pakistan), economic need, lust for status, revenge (against perceived government wrongdoing to self or family), peer pressure, propaganda	1. Military/Police action 2. Imprisonment with an aim to eventually reintegrate into society 3. Employment and Education
Segment 3: Internal Fighters	Predominantly young male Afghans recruited, trained and equipped internally. Operate under the direction of Segments 1 or 2	1. Disillusionment with current government and/or state of development 2. Lack of other viable employment prospects 3. Coercion 4. Survival needs	1. Military/Police option over short term 2. Combination of economically viable employment options, improved delivery of development, and improved GoA communication with citizens outlining realistic but positive expectations over medium to long term

Segment 4: Tribal and Religious Groups	Tribal elders and mullahs	1. Perceived loss of influence due to government abandonment 2. Perceived immoral nature of current society	Focused reengagement of shuras and ulemas by GoA and in particular personal involvement of the President. Most likely to be central to the solution
Other Contributing Elements: Political Opportunists	Corrupt and self-serving politicians, government officials, former jihadi leaders and commanders. Peripheral support directly or indirectly to insurgency	Personal financial gain and influence	Public exposure and punishment through improved rule of law and justice system
Other Contributing Elements: Low Level Criminals	Criminal elements as present in all societies. Can support insurgency through proxy acts	Personal gain	Improved rule of law and justice system, further development of ANP capabilities, economically viable employment options
Other Contributing Elements: Narcotics Actors	Farmers, Harvesters, and Traffickers. Overt or tacit support to the insurgency	Personal financial gain and self preservation	Improved rule of law and justice system, further development of ANP capabilities, economically viable employment options

Table. Summary and Recommendations

CONCLUSION

The combined assessment of the foreign community involved in the development of this paper is:

1. The conflict is an insurgency with the aim to overthrow the current Afghan government through violent means.
2. Those responsible for the fighting are conducting a simultaneous assault on the Afghan security forces and their foreign allies as well as all symbols of governance and development.
3. The leaders of the various AGEs involved are Afghan (with the exception of Al Qaeda), and as such, the problem is an

Afghan one, although a degree of foreign fundamentalist interests are present.

4. The fighters are predominantly Afghan, made up of idealists trained and recruited in Pakistan, young recruits with no viable economic alternatives both from Pakistan and Afghanistan, and opportunists primarily motivated by monetary gain.
5. The problem is exacerbated by unscrupulous elements within the society such as corrupt politicians and officials, and by criminals.

The insurgency cannot survive without its sanctuary in Pakistan which provides freedom of movement, safe havens, logistic and training facilities, a base for recruitment, communications for command and control, and a secure environment for collaboration with foreign extremist groups. The sanctuary of Pakistan provides a seemingly endless supply of potential new recruits for the insurgency due to the high number of Afghan refugees there, and a large base of ideologically motivated Pakistani Pashtuns. An important step in this process will be to facilitate the return of Afghan refugees from Pakistan as soon as possible, within realistic security constraints. A solution on a strategic, political and military level to address the Pakistan link to the insurgency in Afghanistan is vital to success.

The solution to the problem is both a military/police and a political/social one. The military/police option should focus primarily on Segments 1 and 2, while political and social interventions are required to address elements of Segment 2 and Segments 3 and 4. Due to the ideological nature of some of the perpetrators and their stated aim to overthrow the government, a military/police option is essential and for the short to medium term, will have to involve foreign military forces to augment the ANA and ANP. The political and social response must be perceived as Afghan, but for the short to medium term, will require considerable foreign assistance and impetus. Winning the trust of the population and showing visible proof of a viable economic and secure future is the key to defeating the insurgency.

7

Terror, Terrorist, Terrorism

INTRODUCTION

An atmosphere of fear and panic grew when, In 2001, four passengers' planes were crashed into the World Trade Center, Pentagon, and one plane that had destination to Dominican Republic injuring and killing thousands. In the days following, these attacks—totally unexpected in their timing and method, aimed at the world's only superpower—the world began debating the concept of terrorism that lay behind them, especially in the United States. But that didn't last long: Soon the entire world began wondering how best to combat terrorism. No longer could any country stand apart from the fight against terrorism and declare, "Those attacks weren't aimed at us." Citizens of every nation realized that the dark face of terrorism could confront them at any time, whether asleep in their beds, while watching television, taking their children to the park, or at work in the office.

The terrorists' aim, they realized, was to paralyze society, making civilians reluctant to venture into the street, much less use public transport or go shopping—in short, to create a permanent climate of fear. As soon as America recovered from the hypocrite shock of 9/11, it joined with a large number of other countries to launch a worldwide war on terrorism. Right from the start, however, officials of this powerful coalition declared openly that it wouldn't be enough for them to fight on the military field alone.

You will have noticed that, I gave reference of Dominican Republic, when I referred to terrorist act of September 11. Most of the journalistic from middle east and far east, has certainty that the airplane that took of few days after the aforementioned act from JFK, of New York City destination towards Dominican Republic, taking hundreds of people which explode in the air, leaving hundreds of dead persons. It was another attempt of terrorism, implemented by the same who directed the murders attempted against Word Trade Center and the Pentagon.

The journalists sustain the argue of aforementioned information, that this was the another terrorist act as a reprisal against Dominican Republic due to the words exteriorized by the Dominican president of that period on which he visited the zone zero (Place where WTC buildings were located). According to those journalists, the words was " I would kill them with my hands" making a direct reference to those person who attributed on the aforementioned acts.

If we take these information certain which attributed to have told by the Dominican mandatory, and if we took as a point of reference the fanatism, that characterize who implement these type of acts in the name of Allah and the silence of he North American authorities relation to this particular act of terrorism where they have not given a convincing explanation, at least publically, reason of which we do not have another alternative but to share the aforementioned information.

I have done this reference, in order to warn the world, of the danger that represents the Terrorism, of susceptibility and fanaticism that characterize and is necessary to reformulate the methods to combat. It is necessary for us to make good use of the Word of God, without misinterpretations, and then if we all thought so, these acts would not take place.

How should be the struggle against terrorism be pursued? To answer that question, we need to identify terrorism's roots. To do so, we must examine the course of the past century, during which terrorism first emerged as a major threat.

The 20th century's two World Wars, along with many regional conflicts and various acts of local violence, made it the bloodiest century ever. In addition to that, toward the end of the millennium, constant technological advances only helped terrorists widen their reach. Now, just one touch of a button could kill hundreds of innocents. High-tech terrorism could inflict billions of dollars in damage to any nation's economy and shape world politics without ever emerging into the daylight. Clearly, after the attacks on New York and Washington D. C. in the United States—the world's greatest technological power—no other country can consider itself safe from terrorism or beyond its deadly grasp. Worse still, if the necessary countermeasures aren't taken, the 21st-century terrorism will grow even more powerful, until one single chemical, biological, or even nuclear attack can slaughter tens of thousands.

THE TERRORISM

With terrorism dominating the world's agenda, the definitions of terror, terrorist, and terrorism assume a whole new importance. Many countries define terrorism, draw up terrorist profiles, and publish lists of terrorist organizations in the light of their own national interests. "Terrorist organizations" to some countries like Afghanistan, Pakistan, Iran, Iraq, India, Siria, Saudi Arabia are freedom fighters to others. What one country sees as "terrorist nations," mentioned countries welcomes as "loyal allies." Therefore, who defines terrorism? Who decides—and how do they decide—what a terrorist is? To establish a criterion, one can point out two distinct characteristics of terrorism:

Any occupied country has the right to resist an army occupying its territory. But if that resistance includes attacks on civilian targets, any justification ceases to apply, and terrorism begins. As we'll see later on in this book, this definition is entirely in accord with Islamic rules on war. The Prophet Muhammad (May God bless him and grant him peace) commanded his followers to do battle against those who declared war on them. But he also ordered them to never regard civilians as targets. On the contrary, every Muslim was ordered —

and still obliged — to take great care to ensure the safety of non-combatants.

If no state of war exists, then terrorism can also include attacks on military or official targets. Attacks intended to break down peaceful relations between countries or communities are acts of terrorism, even when aimed at military targets.

All attacks that threaten peace, or that are aimed at civilian targets, even in a state of war, are terrorism. There can be no question of defending, approving or justifying such attacks. However, such violence is very widespread in the modern world. That's why any war on terrorism needs to be wide-ranging. Its every stage should be carefully planned, with its final aim the total eradication of the entire concept. That, in turn, requires individuals in every nation to totally distance themselves from terrorism. Every form of terrorism must be unequivocally condemned—whatever its causes or aims, no matter what its targets, where it arises, or how it is carried out. Similarly, anyone sincerely opposed to terrorism should show the same empathy for the thousands of innocent victims it has slaughtered—not only at the World Trade Center, but in attacks in Japan, Spain, United Kingdom, in East Turkestan, Pakistan, India and Indonesia, in the massacre of more than half a million Hutus in Rwanda, in the murder of defenseless people in Palestine, Israel, and all across the globe.

Once every form of terrorism is fiercely condemned, then no longer will its perpetrators receive support from any country, or be allowed to seek shelter inside its borders, quite literally, terrorists will have nowhere to hide.

There is an urgent need to condemned the American foreign policies about terrorism. First USA must finish their own state terrorism which they apply to the third world countries, specially the Arab, far east and middle east countries. United State of America is an modern face of a beggar, who want to grow their country's wealth by taking power on small countries by means of arms, terror, or economically.

USA must need to review their foreign policy or the terrorist will make him do it by any means.

In another hand, third world countries also need to bring some change on its own home policies where the human rights are suffering enormous declination, therefore ; the religious countries specially where the Islam is dominated religion have a wrong use of Madarsas, located in Muslim countries specifically in Pakistan, Afghanistan and India. Those Madarsas trained Afghan Mujahedeen to be a freedom fighter and formed a group to whom they gave name "Taliban" means group of student. That group spread all over in Afghanistan in the decades of 80's, and 90's, later left their branches in Pakistan, India, Iran, Siria, Iraq, United Kingdom, and Dominican Republic, with whom the countries, especially my country Pakistan; still suffering series of terrorist acts killing, important people of the nation in all levels, like; politician, religious leaders and innocent citizens.

These Jamea or Madarsa's are places of teaching Qur'an-ul-Kareem to memorized by hard, and regular studies, but teaching wrong concept of Jihad, preparing innocent children, teenagers and young generation to kill others and kill himself in the name of Allah which is not promoted by Islam neither written anywhere in Quran-ul-Kareem. The book to whom I trust and follow. Islam is a religion of peace that teach love, submission, hospitality, forgive and forget, kindness, scarification for others, and consideration, But the Jamea's and Madarsas are supporting the Taliban in Afghanistan ,South and North Waziristan conceded that, students of these seminaries had joined the Taliban. "No doubt, their students are joining Jihadists because they are teaching jihad to fight against USA, in Afghanistan, Pakistan and in UK's Soil, which they called "Islamic Revolution"

Jamia Faridia and Jamia Hafsa in-charge Maulana Abdul Aziz told on his speech, they would not stop enforcing Shariat even if the government of Pakistan withdrew its decision to demolish mosques in the federal capital. He said "There were only six Taliban who enforced the Islamic law in Afghanistan and we are 10,000. Then, how we cannot enforce shariah.

USA Foreign Policy

US actual policy is letting him down in front of its own citizens who are against this hypocrite war of terrorism. They are not behind of intention to reduce poverty but to eliminate the poor people citizen of third world countries.

The proof is why they don't go to Haiti, Bangladesh and other poor countries to combat poverty? NEVER; we know why, because from the aforementioned countries has no richness or treasures from where they can filled up their empty barrels.

Lets talk about United Kingdom, The Great Britain, or England. The most oldest form of Darwinism. They do State Terrorist since they formed East India Company in India to run their illegimate business of Opium, Drug which now a days they consume more than any other nation.

Why they (UK and USA) don't stop immigration of third world countries citizen into the their territory . Never; because they play with the sentiments of poors. These countries yearly revenue through immigration services are higher than one year budget of any country like Pakistan.

In another word, their income depends upon to abuse poor people, and poor leaders, selling armaments, increasing crude prices without any reason and if there is any reason, this is certainly created by these big fishes. America and United Kingdom are big nations; they have progress a lot in terms of technology, armament, nuclear weapons and mode of public transport. But they are lacking of being nation to whom poor nation can trust to live in peace.

The advice for them is to take away their own interest from poor countries, let them produce their treasure (Black Gold) in our own way because Allah promised this treasure to the Muslim and by invading our Muslim countries, they will never be looked as a helpful nations but hypocrites.

Pakistan also need to revise the role of our leaders, Is our constitution is a piece of paper? That can be ripping off by any leader like the one Gen. Mohammad Zia-ul-haq said in Iran in the decades of seventies.The Pakistan cricket hero Imran Khan struggling to be the hero in his political life too and he can, because he has potential to bring some drastic change in the Politics life of Pakistan.

Whoever respects the human rights, the constitution, and enforces law and order, could be the winner and can bring up Pakistan as a super power economically.

BEGINNING OF TERRORISM

Before the war against terrorism can come to any definitive conclusion, its underlying philosophy must first be identified, along with the means to be employed. We must deal with terrorism's basic starting point, as well as the disasters to which it leads. Its starting point is the assumption that violence is a virtue in itself and a powerful means to solve social or political problems. While killing the innocents, damaging public order, and disrupting peace, any terrorist acts under the influence of ideas that have been imposed on him, coaxing him to believe that he's engaged in a justified struggle. Terrorism can be healed only when such people understand the mistaken illogic of any ideology that inspires terrorism and incites to violence—and when they realize that going along with it can never get them anywhere. Until those ideologies' errors and contradictions are revealed, all measures taken against terrorism can be short-term only. Soon terrorism will emerge again, in different places and under different circumstances, behind a different mask.

We can put an end to terrorism only by destroying its ideological infrastructure. In later chapters, you'll see that modern terrorism's ideological foundations in fact go back to Social Darwinism and the materialist tendencies derived from it. People exposed to this indoctrination believe that life is a field of struggle, and that only the strong survive. The weak are condemned to be eliminated. Man and, in fact, the entire universe, are both products of chance. Therefore, no one is responsible for his actions to anyone else. These and similar ideas inevitably coax people into leading an animalistic form of life, where ruthlessness, aggression and violence are regarded as acceptable or even virtuous.

Anyone who resorts to terrorism, maintaining that violence is the only way to achieve his aims, is actually under the influence of Social Darwinism and materialist thought, no matter what his religion or race, or what group he belongs to. Modern Islamic terrorist groups and other non-Muslim groups that claim to act in the name of religion are also under Darwinism's influence and materialism, even though they claim to carry out their terroristic acts in the name of religion. This is because for anyone who lives by the morality of religion revealed by God, it's impossible to approve of violence of any kind, much less achieve a "higher" aim by murdering others. Those who resort to such methods are therefore pursuing the exact opposite of the moral values upheld by religion, carrying out their actions under the influence of materialist ideologies.

Islam denounce Terrorism, it was made clear that Islam fiercely rejects all forms of terrorism, no matter whom it may be directed against. In the light of verses from the Qur'an, it was explained how religion's morality calls people to peace, tolerance, and convenience. Also stressed was the dishonesty of condemning only those acts of terrorism directed against one's own side: Such an attitude only weakens the fight against terrorism; and anyone living according to Islamic morality needs to fight terror in all its all forms. The foundation of that intellectual struggle is based on revealing the true morality of religion.

Today's politicians, political commentators and academics agree that by itself, military force isn't enough to root out terrorism. It can be eradicated: by means of peace, tolerance, and love. All the divinely-inspired religions that God sent down by means of His messengers are helpful guides. This book offers examples from the Qur'an as well as from the Bible (even though the latter has been partially distorted) to show how each of the three divine religions forbids the use of unjust violence. It also gives examples to show that the only way to fight terrorism is to heal the root causes through the love, affection, compassion, humility, forgiveness, tolerance and concepts of justice that religion's morality instill in people—whom, following the verse from the Qur'an (10:25): "God calls to the

Abode of Peace... "Such fortunate will do their utmost to build a world full of peace and love.

Terrorism is one of the gravest menaces facing our 21st-century world because it sees acts of violence as the only way to achieve political aims especially in Islamic Countries. The particular aim or problem depends on the terrorist's individual worldview. In a terrorist's eyes, political dilemmas and conflicts caused by ethnic and cultural differences can be resolved by violence alone. No group can get what it wants, except by "blood and iron".

The terrorist or group that created by Islamic or non Muslim seminaries believes that his objectives—enforcing his demands, spreading his organization's propaganda—can be attained only by damaging the fabric of society; when unease, fear, and conflict come to dominate daily life. Some groups aim to take advantage of the climate of chaos that their actions bring about. They think that it will be easier to achieve their aims where social stability has collapsed, individuals are wracked with fear and uncertainty. From the destruction, they claim, will rise what they call "righteousness and justice." But expecting that acts of terrorism can establish righteousness and justice, or that problems can be resolved by violence, is a terrible mistake. Violence is counter-productive: All they that live by the sword shall perish by the sword.

In the Qur'an (13:25), God describes such people as "those [who] cause corruption in the earth." So far, they have managed only to increase the number of deaths among the innocent—and among their own supporters as well. Every year, terrorist attacks cause thousands to live in fear and anxiety and suffer economic harm, not to mention those who are wounded or killed. Terrorism threatens all of mankind, its toll so very terrible that fighting has become urgently essential.

TERRORISM GROUPS

There are an estimated 500 terrorist groups in the world. These include international cartels controlling trade in drugs, arms and prostitution, as well as underground organizations, marginal movements, various radical ideological groups, and deviant cults that stage actions allegedly in the name of religion. Many terrorist organizations do operate within their own countries' borders, but a number target what they have decided as "enemy" countries, through attacks on prominent sites and individuals that, they calculate, will elicit a huge public reaction. From the reaction, they seek to achieve fame, in fact notoriety, which they hope that will add to their power. Though terrorism has existed since the earliest times, through esoteric organizations like the Sicarii or Assassins, and flourished in the modern times through revolutionary cadres like the sans-cullottes of the French Revolution or the Russian Nihilism of the 19th century, its threat really came to the fore in the 20th century, which saw an explosion in acts of terror and in the number of terrorists who committed them. Weapons of mass destruction and the rapid advance of technology made terrorist attacks much easier and vastly increased their destructiveness.

By the 1960s, people began to wonder seriously, what might happen, if a terrorist group managed to acquire some kind of nuclear weapon that could result in the deaths of tens of thousands. A biological or chemical attack could wipe entire populations off the map. No such attack happened, fortunately. But by the 1990s, the chances of such attacks increased. These concerns only heightened with the collapse of the Soviet Union and the weakening of control over its nuclear arsenal. The spread of the Internet and the facilitation of all forms of information increased worries still further.1 Fear of terrorism became the subject of hundreds of films and books. Reports were written about the possible consequences; research was carried out. Now, all too obviously, terrorists could go beyond familiar, limited actions like bombings, armed robberies, skyjackings and kidnappings, to attack entire communities. Such attacks could be carried out by remote control or computer, with no direct human intervention.

A number of recent fears in the US and UK involving biological weapons like of the anthrax bacteria revealed the scale of the threat posed by bio-terrorism and biological weapons. With the help of an experienced chemist in a simple laboratory, terrorists can now threaten the lives of thousands. One of the first examples of this occurred in 1984, when 750 people were poisoned in four restaurants in a small town in Oregon.2 Later, it was revealed that a Hindu-inspired New Age cult under the leadership of Baghwan Shree Rajneesh was responsible. Disciples had grown salmonella bacteria on their farms and placed them in salad bars in area restaurants. In 1995, the Aum Shinrikyo ("Higher Truth") cult released the poison gas sarin in the Tokyo underground subway system, leading to the deaths of 12 people and another 5,500 injured. Subsequent inquiries revealed that the cult had tried to construct biological weapons in its own laboratories—revealing just how large threat terrorism poses to the public.

In the 21st century, computer technology is expected to play an important role in terrorist attacks. Meanwhile, more "conventional" ways of terrorism, like bombings, arson attacks, skyjackings and kidnappings impeding writing books like this are still going on all over the world, from Europe to America, from Asia to Africa. Since 1962, for example, members of the ETA (Euskadi Ta Askatasuna) terrorist organization, fighting for the Basque region's independence, has carried out many terrorist attacks in Spain, resulting in the deaths of more than 800.4 For years, the Irish Republican Army has seized world headlines with its bloody attacks to gain independence for Northern Ireland. The central aim of the IRA is to end British control of Northern Ireland and to achieve the reunification of the island of Ireland. Generally it has operated in Northern Ireland and London, but has also been involved in bombings in various European countries such as Germany. Since 1969, the IRA's terrorist attacks, and Britain's methods of "counter-terrorism", have caused the deaths of more than 3,200 on both sides of the conflict.5 Millions of dollars' worth of damage has been caused by IRA bombings of airports and underground stations, again aimed at civilians. During a European Football Championship match on June 15, 1996, an IRA car bombing in a Manchester shopping center resulted in some 200 injuries.

Currently, no country can feel safe from this kind of threat. The few examples just cited show just how deeply terrorism has come to influence peoples' lives. No longer the problem of just a few specific nations, it's a threat that faces all mankind. Because no one can tell when, where or how terrorists will strike, the fight against them can no longer be considered the duty of a handful of countries or organizations. Terrorism, threatening the entire world, can be resolved only if well-intentioned people support each other in search of peace, friendship and brotherhood.

Terrorism is currently inflicting suffering and physical damage all over the world, not only in the United States, but in the African countries of Uganda, Angola and Nigeria; in the European nations of Great Britain, France and Spain; in Asian countries like Japan, and throughout the Middle East and Latin America. At any moment, civilians can find themselves facing a terrorist attack, whether sitting at home or at a movie theater, in a shopping center, riding a bus, or at their workplace. Naturally, terrorism's ability to enter peoples' homes has led to considerable anxiety and alarm. People are hesitant to enter crowded areas or use public transport; their daily lives are becoming intolerable. But that is exactly what terrorism wants to see: whole communities living in fear and alarm.

The evidence of terrible attacks throughout in the world certainly confirms that concern. In 1996, there were 296 incidents with 314 people killed and 2,912 injured. In 1997, terrorism's scope began to expand: Out of 439 attacks, 398 were aimed at workplaces or non-official premises, leading to the loss of 139 civilian lives, 39 of them civil servants or military personnel.

According to the U.S. State Department, the number of terrorist attacks in 2000 saw an eight percent rise over 1999, with 423 deaths and 791 injured. Between 1981 and 2000, the total number of dead resulting from terrorist attacks was 9,184. nor do these figures include all the people who died in all terrorist attacks across the globe. The report considered only attacks by international terrorist organizations, not those inflicted by local terrorist groups. In Turkey alone there were 21,866 terrorist attacks between August 15, 1984 and October 31, 2001, costing the lives of 5,605 security personnel and 4,646 civilians. A further 16,562 security forces and 5,091 civilians were injured.

Terrorist actions' physical damage and economic harm add yet another sobering dimension to the picture. The chaos and anarchy provoked by such incidents prevent investment in the affected regions. Attacks aimed at the economic infrastructure don't just hold back development. Existing resources are also destroyed, creating economic difficulties that impede social life across a wide spectrum of areas, particularly education. Military costs of the struggle against terrorism impose yet another burden. This diversion of resources that should be spent on raising standards of living affects not just the nation in question, but the entire global economy.

This summary reveals the grim picture that terrorism represents—bringing destruction all over the world and causing untold harm to human lives. If a sick person is to be treated properly, an accurate diagnosis is essential. Whatever treatment follows that diagnosis must be followed meticulously and decisively, until the sickness is finally expelled from the body. If not, the illness will inevitably recur. The same applies to one of the most serious ills affecting society.

One of the chief reasons why we can't find effective solutions to this century's social problems is that their causes aren't properly identified. When dealing with any social problem, the first thing to do is establish what causes give rise to it. Otherwise, whatever measures are taken can only be temporary.

The roots of terrorism are often sought in concrete matters; and thus the fight against it, aimed at these superficial targets, cannot provide lasting results. In order to free the world from terrorism, the principal factors behind it must be identified and eliminated.

It's not possible to defeat terrorism by security measures. By itself, military force is only likely to meet with increased violence, producing a vicious circle in which bloodshed continues to be answered with more bloodshed. When embarking on the fight against terrorists, we need to understand—and then combat—their way of thinking, the way they view life and other human beings, and how they justify their use of violence.

A terrorist believes that he can succeed only by using violence. He wants people around to fear him, and cloaks himself in pitilessness, ruthlessness and aggression to bring that fear about. Anyone opposing his ideas is an enemy, whom he regards as an object that needs to be eliminated. In his article, "Terrorists View us as Targets, not as Humans," psychotherapist and *Journal Sentinel* writer Philip Chard examines the terrorist mindset and how they justify violent attacks aimed at defenseless people:

"Researchers have glimpsed aspects of [the terrorists'] psyches. Most prominent among these is their capacity to view their victims as things, as objects, as statistics that, they hope, will show up on a casualty list.

"They don't want to experience their victims as human beings, as they would a friend or loved one. Rather, they strive to view them as pawns on a political chessboard. Consequently, from their own vantage point, terrorists don't perceive themselves as killing 'people.' In order to slaughter with ease and callous indifference, they mentally dehumanize us into 'targets' ...Their 'cause,' whatever it may be, is sufficiently sacred, noble or desperate that it justifies the carnage they instigate ... For most terrorists, their chief interest resides in effects, not persons ... They are after ... the impact of the massacre, not the experience of the massacre itself. Terrorists want to murder hope, or a way of life, or the spirit of a group of people or an entire nation. They destroy human beings because they believe doing so is the fastest and most direct route to that goal."

Philip Chard draws our attention to a most important matter: that terrorist feel not the slightest pang of remorse at the death of others. On the contrary, the more they can kill, the more successful they consider themselves to be, and rejoice in that fact. Such minds can quite happily shoot innocent people and bomb small children. For them, shedding blood becomes a source of pleasure. They cease to be human and turn into savage monsters. If one of them does evidence the slightest remorse, he is immediately branded a traitor by his more radical comrades. Being more radical and bloodier is considered to be more devout in the cause, so the zeal to kill increases constantly. Since any dispute can easily be defined as treacher, terrorists invariably use guns against each other, and carry out attacks on other splinter groups within their own ranks.

This passionate attachment to violence goes deeper beyond political ideologies and in fact stems from an underlying misconception about human nature. The terrorist mindset finds its inspiration from the materialist philosophy and Darwinist thought. Darwinism regards human beings as animals and maintains that living things evolve through a struggle for survival in nature. Eliminating the weak, so that the strong can emerge victorious, forms the essence of any terrorist's twisted thinking.

DARWINISM BUILT TERRORISM

According to Charles Darwin's theory of evolution, there is constant conflict in nature, and a ruthless competition for survival. The strong always defeat the weak, thus enabling progress. Out of that concept came the idea of the "struggle for survival" and such terms as "the favored races" (European whites) and "inferior" ones (Asian or African races). This racist logic laid the groundwork for hatred and conflicts all over the world. In turn, Darwin's idea of "the survival of the fittest" justified a great many movements that led mankind to hatred, enmity, conflict and war.

Darwinism still indoctrinates people with the deception that humans are no more than a highly developed animal species, the result of blind chance and have no Creator. This theory maintains that the world once consisted of nothing but inanimate rock, soil, and gasses. By sheer coincidence, life emerged as a result of the effect of natural forces like wind and rain and lightning on organic molecules. The theory goes on to explain all life on earth, including human beings, as a product of the blind forces of nature and mere chance. Yet this theory of evolution is a huge deception that violates the most basic laws of chemistry and biology and defies all reason and logic. However, the theory is imposed on modern society with an enormous propaganda and people indoctrinated with this idea believe themselves to be the products of chemical and biological accidents — free of all responsibility to the Creator and His moral code. Moreover, those under the spell of Darwinist logic—seeing life as a battlefield and therefore, justifying all kinds of wickedness in the struggle for survival—are brainwashed with the terrible idea that it's normal to treat other people like animals, even to exterminate them.

People educated with such ideas transformed the 20th century into one of savagery, supported conflict as part of Darwinism, and even regarded war as the most important means of furthering their aims. "Dialectical conflict" became the so-called justification for the massacres carried out by Communist ideologues. Over the course of the century, Communist terror cost the lives of some 120 million people. Darwin's nonsensical "struggle for survival between the races " and "natural selection" became the foundations for Nazism. Adolf Hitler claimed that only the superior races could—or should—survive. The Fascist terror he inspired unleashed a wave of slaughter across the entire world. Some 55 million people died in World War II, which began as a result of the Nazis' policies of war and occupation. Those in the 21st century, who still follow those ideas, regard violence as the only way and want this century to go down in history as one of terror.

Darwinism's theory that man is a warring animal, with which so many are subconsciously indoctrinated, has wreaked dreadful harm on humanity. Terrorist attacks are echoes of that. Darwinist slogans that maintain only the strongest can survive, praise violence, support conflict, and see war as a virtue need to be thrown, once, into the dustbin of history. Darwinism's overthrow can undermine all of those ideologies that support conflict and violence.

On the other hand, the definition of human nature by the monotheist faiths is much different Christianity, Judaism, and Islam—the three religions believed in by most people in the world—all oppose the Social Darwinist value called conflict. As we will see in detail in subsequent sections, each of these religions aims at bringing peace and security to the world, while opposing the oppression, torture, and killing of the innocent. Conflict and violence, they agree, are abnormal and unwanted concepts, violating the morality that God has set out for Man. Darwinism, on the other hand, regards violence and conflict as essential, and therefore justified. In short, the source of the world's terrorist nightmare lies in atheism and its contemporary equivalents: Darwinism and materialism.

Since schools in many countries teach Darwinism as clear scientific fact, new generations of terrorists are inevitable. From that point of view, it's urgent to prevent young people from being taught that they're the result of chance, descended from animals, totally unfettered with no duties towards God, and can survive only by emerging victorious in the struggle for survival. Anyone brought up to believe such concepts would inevitably be selfish, aggressive, ruthless, and prone to violence. Such young people are easily susceptible to anarchic and terrorist indoctrination. Following such ideologies, they can become cruel enough to kill children and murder their own brothers and sisters, without batting an eyelid. The communist, racist, and fascist terror groups that have plagued the world for the last hundred years are the products of just such an educational system.

That being so, we need to expose the true rottenness of terrorist logic. People need to be awakened to the fact, as effectively as possible, that all those who support and believe in Darwinism are mistaken. Man is not unfettered and irresponsible. We do have a Creator who watches us at all times, knows even our innermost thoughts and who, in the hereafter, will call us to account for all our deeds. Our Lord has created Man different from the animals, in that we possess a soul, reason, free will, judgment, and powers of discrimination. If a weak-willed person, easily angered, regards him self and others as mere animals, he can act in a very ruthless manner and easily do them harm. It makes no difference if those others are totally innocent children. Nevertheless, anyone who possesses reason and conscience and knows that he bears a soul, given him by God, holds his anger in check—no matter what the circumstances. His judgment and conscience will always prevail. Never will he do the slightest thing for which God might one day call him to account.

In the Qur'an (91: 7-10), God reveals that Man is inspired by both evil and the will to avoid it. Therefore, it's not some imaginary evolutionary process that underlies moral degeneration and the commission of crimes. Immorality and crime come from the evil side of human nature, which can only be defeated by personal devotion to the moral values that God has taught to humanity through religion. If people have no faith in God and don't believe they must ever account to Him for their actions, they have no reason to avoid committing evil in the forms of personal greed and dishonesty or social evils like wars, racist killings, gang wars or ruthless skinhead assaults. On a less dramatic level, it accounts for why people left to starve and for the rampant injustice and ruthlessness in the world today. There is no end to the cruelties of those who regard Man as only an animal species, believing that they, like animals, are engaged in a struggle for survival. Not believing in God and the hereafter, they induce others to forget about them too.

Every human being bears a soul breathed into him by God, and is responsible to the Creator Who created him out of nothing. In the Qur'an (75: 36-40), God reminds those who think of themselves as totally unfettered that they were created, and will be resurrected after death: "Does Man reckon he will be left Togo on unchecked? Was he not a drop of ejaculated sperm, then a blood clot that He created and shaped, making from it both sexes, male and female? Is He who does this, not able to bring the dead to life?"

So far, we have concentrated on how Social Darwinism, believing that violence is the solution to every problem, encourages violence, and is the foundation of terrorism. That is why demolishing the Darwinistic theory—which teaches that man is an animal, that only the physically powerful can survive, and that human life is a battleground—will also demolish one of terrorism's mainstays. The most effective means of protecting people from the nightmare of terrorism is spiritual education. Societies can achieve permanent peace only when their individuals learn to live by proper morality. Beyond that, other measures, rules, and precautions to regulate the life of society can go only so far, but can never eradicate the scourge of terrorism.

Worship can defeat Terrorism.In the Qur'an (32: 9) , God reveals that He has breathed His own soul into Man, His creation, and that Man is His representative on earth (Qur'an, 6: 165). One of the most important differences between Man and the animals is that Man was created with both earthly desires and with a conscience. Every person possesses desires that incite him to evil, along with a conscience that inspires him to avoid it. Alongside such pleasing attributes inspired by that conscience—love, sacrifice, compassion, humility, affection, honesty, loyalty and kindness—he also possesses destructive and undesirable tendencies, stemming from his earthly desires. Thanks to his conscience, however, the believer can distinguish between right and wrong and opt for what is morally right. Strong belief in and fear of God, faith in the hereafter, powerful fear of the endless torments of hell and a yearning for Paradise all keep the temptations of his earthly desires at bay. Therefore, he always behaves well towards people, is forgiving, responds to wickedness with good, assists that in need, and shows compassion, love, affection and tolerance. God commands justice and doing good and giving to relatives. And He forbids indecency and doing wrong and tyranny. He warns you so that hopefully you will pay heed. (Qur'an, 16:90)

Terrorists on the other hand, listen to their earthly desire for violence instead of their consciences, and can easily turn to all forms of wickedness. They become loveless, aggressive people who easily hurt others without the slightest pang of conscience. Having no fear of God, they do not know the morality of religion, nor do they practice it. Nothing can stop them from committing crimes.

In restraining its citizens, society's prevailing rules can go only so far. Thanks to its law enforcement units, the state may be able to partially protect streets and public spaces, and—thanks to a powerful system of justice—may be able to take necessary means to ensure public order and ensure that the crime rate drops. However, since it's impossible to keep watch on every individual, 24 hours a day, it's essential that peoples' consciences enter the equation at some stage. Someone who doesn't heed the voice of his conscience can easily turn to crime when on his own, or surrounded by people of like mind. The result is a society of individuals who gladly lie when they feel it necessary, have no compunction against enjoying unfair profits, and feel no qualms about oppressing and exploiting the weak. In a society that has lost all spiritual values and has no fear of God, purely physical measures are clearly not going to solve every problem. The morality of religion, on the other hand, commands a person to avoid evil deeds, even when on his own and when he knows that nobody in his community will ever punish him for his misdeeds. The person who knows that God will call him to account for his every deed, his every decision, and his every word—and will reward him for them accordingly in the hereafter—will always avoid evil.

Terrorist organizations can't possibly have any place in a society whose people avoid evil of their own free will. Where religion's morality prevails, problems that give rise to organizations supporting the use of violence will disappear naturally. If the whole society possesses superior virtues like honesty, sacrifice, love and justice, there can be no place for such things as poverty, unequal distribution of income, injustice, the oppression of the weak, or limitations on freedoms. On the contrary, a social order will emerge that meets the wants of the needy; where the wealthy protect the poor and the strong, the weak; where everyone can enjoy the very best health care, education, and transport systems. There, tolerance and understanding will dominate the relationships between different ethnic groups, religions and cultures.

For these reasons, proper morality is the key to solving so many social problems. The source of that key, in turn, is the Qur'an, which God has revealed as a guide for humankind.

TRUE ISLAM

For half a century after the first verse was revealed to the Prophet Muhammad (may God bless him and grant him peace), Islam underwent such an expansion as has seldom been seen. It spread from the Arabian Peninsula to the whole of the Middle East, North Africa and even Spain, drawing the attention of many in the West. In the words of the famous Islamic expert John L. Esposito, "What is most striking about the early expansion of Islam is its rapidity and success. Western scholars have marveled at it." Over the next centuries, Islam reached all corners of the world, from Indonesia to Latin America. Today, Islam is accepted as the fastest growing religion, and its roughly one billion followers represent about one-fifth of the world's population. Interest in Islam particularly increased after the terrorist attacks of September 11, 2001.

Looking at today's Islamic world today, we see a wide range of religious practices, depending on societies' different customs and traditions, their cultural heritage, and worldviews. This has led some individuals researching or trying to understand Islam to form mistaken impressions. Those differences may symbolize only the traditional values of the society under examination, but Islam itself. The only way of arriving at an accurate opinion of Islam is to put aside these differences and turn to the Qur'an, where the essence of Islamic morality is set out, and to the actions of our Prophet (may God bless him and grant him peace). Even if Muslims comprise neither the majority in a community, that does not mean that community's behavior, views and judgments will necessarily be Islamic, nor that need they be defended in the name of Islam. When evaluating an individual's—or community's—view of Islam that must always be borne in mind. Differences may stem from prevailing conditions. The only way to ascertain whether those views are correct is by turning to the Qur'an, the most accurate source of truth about Islam, and to the actions of our Prophet (may God bless him and grant him peace).

It is most unfair to pass judgment on Islam and Muslims without studying the Qur'an to learn whether a particular practice appears in it. Examining the lifestyle of a single community only can seriously mislead anyone who tries to understand Islam and form opinions about it. First, what needs to be done is to learn about Islam from its true source. Then, once the various models in different parts of the world are considered in the light of those criteria, many who only imagined they knew about Islam will actually come to do so for the first time; and can free themselves from the errors they have been laboring under so far.

ISLAM FORBIDS THE KILLING OF INNOCENTS

According to the Qur'an (5:32), it is a great sin to kill an innocent person, and anyone who does so will suffer great torment in the hereafter: ... If someone kills another person—unless it is in retaliation for someone else or for causing corruption in the earth—it is as if he had murdered all mankind. And if anyone gives life to another person, it is as if he had given life to all mankind. Our Messengers came to them with Clear Signs, but even after that, many of them committed outrages in the earth."

If one is looking for the cause of an act of terrorism, one must look for its source in anti-religious ideologies. Religion enjoins love, compassion, forgiveness, peace and living according to high moral standards. Terrorism, on the other hand, is on the side of cruelty and violence, causing pain, bloodshed and committing murder.

This verse equals the killing of one innocent to slaughtering all of humanity! Another verse (25:68) expresses the importance that the faithful attach to life:

Those who do not appeal to any other deity besides God [alone]; nor kill any soul whom God has forbidden [them to] except with the right to do so; nor fornicate. Anyone who does so will incur a penalty.

In yet another verse (6:151), God issues the following commandment:

Say: "Come, and I will recite to you what your Lord has forbidden for you": that you do not associate anything with Him;

that you are good to your parents; that you do not kill your children because of poverty—We will provide for you and them; that you do not approach indecency – outward or inward; that you do not kill any person God has made inviolate – except with the right to do so. That is what He instructs you to do, so that hopefully, you will use your intellect.

Any Muslim who believes in God with a sincere heart, who scrupulously abides by His holy verses and fears suffering in the hereafter, will avoid harming even one other person. He knows that the Lord of Infinite Justice will suitably reward him for all his deeds. In one of the hadiths, our Prophet (may God bless him and grant him peace) listed the kinds of people who are not pleasing to God:

"Those who act cruelly and justly in the sacred lands, those who yearn for the ways of the ignorant, and those who wrongly shed human blood."

Islamic morality commands believers to behave justly and morally in making a decision, speaking, or working—in short, in every area of their lives. God's commandments in the Qur'an and the sunnah of our Prophet (may God bless him and grant him peace) describe that understanding of justice in great detail. With their warnings, all the Messengers revealed to us in the Qur'an brought peace and justice to all the communities where they were sent. The prophets helped lift cruelty and despotism from the shoulders of the community of the faithful. As God has revealed in one verse (10:47):

Every nation has a Messenger, and when their Messenger comes, everything is decided between them justly. They are not wronged.

A most important feature of Islamic understanding of justice is that it commands justice at all times, even if one is dealing with a person who is near and dear. As God commands in another verse (4:135):

You who believe! Be upholders of justice, bearing witness for God alone, even against yourselves or your parents and relatives. Whether they are rich or poor, God is well able to look after them.

Do not follow your own desires and deviate from the truth. If you twist or turn away, God is aware of what you do.

That verse clearly states that to a believer, the wealth or social status of whomever one deals with is of no importance. What is important is fairness—no one should be treated unjustly—and to scrupulously implement the holy verses of God. In another verse (5:8), it is commanded:

You who believe! Show integrity for the sake of God, bearing witness with justice. Do not let hatred for a people incite you into not being just. Be just. That is closer to heedfulness. Heed God. God is aware of what you do.

In that verse, God orders the faithful to act justly always, even with their own enemies. No Muslim can make a spontaneous decision, based on the fact that the person he's dealing with has once harmed him or left him in a difficult situation. Even when he is a personal enemy, if the other side is genuinely in the wrong, any Muslim has the duty to respond with good will and to display the morality God has commanded. To believers, God has issued the following commandment (60:8): "God does not forbid you from being good to those who have not fought you in the religion or driven you from your homes, or from being just towards them. God loves those who are just." Here, He informs Muslims how their relationships with other people should be. These verses are the very foundation of a believer's attitude towards others, formed not by the nature of the people he is dealing with, but by God's revelations in the Qur'an. That is why Muslims with pure hearts always support what is right. Their determination on this matter is revealed in these terms (Qur'an, 7:181): "Among those We have created, there is a community who guide by the Truth and act justly according to it."

Other verses in the Qur'an on the subject of justice read:

God commands you to return to their owners the things you hold on trust and, when you judge between people, to judge with justice. How excellent is what God exhorts you to do! God is All-Hearing, All-Seeing. (4:58)

Say: "My Lord has commanded justice. Stand and face Him in every mosque and call on Him, making your religion sincerely His. As He originated you, so you will return." (7:29)

God commands justice and doing good and giving to relatives. And He forbids indecency and doing wrong and tyranny. He warns you so that hopefully, you will pay heed. (16:90)

All over the world, people are subjected to cruel treatment because of their race, language or skin color. Yet according to the view of justice as set out in the Qur'an, a person's ethnicity, race or gender are of no importance, because Islam maintains that all people are equal. However, Muslim nation don't follow Quran's words since for Rich nations, The power is Money, they can drive Islamic laws in the favor of people who have money power.

Our Prophet's (may God bless him and grant him peace) words, *"All of you belong to one ancestry of Adam, and Adam was created out of clay,"14* stress that there is no difference between people. Skin color, social status, and wealth confer no superiority on anyone.

According to the Qur'an, one reason why different tribes, peoples, and nations were created is so that they "might come to know one another." All are servants of God and must come to learn one another's different cultures, languages, customs and abilities. One intent behind the existence of different nations and races is cultural wealth, not war and conflict. All true believers know that only godliness —in other words, the fear of God and faith in Him— can impart superiority. As God has revealed in the Qur'an (49:13):

Mankind! We created you from a male and female, and made you into peoples and tribes so that you might come to know each other. The noblest among you in God's sight is that one of you who best performs his duty. God is All-Knowing, All-Aware. Elsewhere (30:22), He has revealed that: Among His Signs is the creation of the heavens and earth and the variety of your languages and colors. There are certainly Signs in that for every being.

History offers many examples of the faithful behaving with complete justice towards other peoples, helping Islam grow with unbelievable speed over a wide area, taking in North Africa, the whole Middle East and even the Iberian Peninsula. By means of these conquests, the civility and tolerance of Islamic morality was spread to many races, nations, communities and individuals, bringing together millions in a bond of mutual tolerance, the likes of which had never been seen before. The renowned researcher Joel Augustus Rogers has examined the various races and the relationship between the black race and other countries. In his book *Sex and Race,* he describes Islam's influence on the world in these terms:

One reason why Islam was able to survive so brightly for centuries is the almost complete absence in this religion of value-judgements based on race and class, the disregarding of the colour of an individual's skin or his social class and the fact that promotion to the highest levels of a community is based on ability alone... Islam established the greatest and at the same time the freest racial melting-pot in history, and the mixing of these races took place within the body of the most extensive empire the world has ever seen. At the height of its power, the Islamic Empire stretched from Spain and central France in the West to India, China, and the Pacific Ocean in the East, including Central Asia. The rulers of these extensive territories were of various colours. The colour of peoples' skins was even less important for Muslims than the colours of the flowers in a garden is to the flowers themselves.

Professor Hamilton Alexander Rossken Gibb is one of the world's foremost experts on Islam. In his book *Whither Islam?*, he describes the Islamic view of other races:

No other society has such a record of success uniting in an equality of status, of opportunity, and of endeavors so many and so various races of mankind... Islam has still the power to reconcile apparently irreconcilable elements of race and tradition. If ever the opposition of the great societies of East and West is to be replaced by cooperation, the mediation of Islam is an indispensable condition.

Islamic morality aims at a society built on brotherhood and peace, freedom and security. That is why all communities that come into contact with Islam have given up their oppressive, cruel and aggressive ways and have, instead, built peaceful and civilized societies. In their works, many Western historians have documented Islam's deep and positive affects on communities that came into contact with it. In *The Making of Humanity*, Professor Robert Briffault discusses the relationship between Western society and Islam:

The ideas that inspired the French Revolution and the Declaration of Rights, that guided the framing of the American Constitution and inflamed that struggle for independence in the Latin American countries [and elsewhere] were not inventions of the West. They find their ultimate inspiration and source in the Holy Quran. These extracts indicate how, down through the centuries, Islamic morality has taught people about peace, tolerance and justice. Nowadays, nearly everyone is seeking just such a model, and there is no reason why such a culture should not come about once again. All that is needed is people's desire to live by the morality of the Qur'an, starting with themselves and later, making efforts to convey it to others. When everyone, from the highest ranks to the very lowest, begins to implement the morality commanded in the Qur'an, they will become just, compassionate, tolerant, full of love, respectful and forgiving. That, in turn, will bring peace to all of society.

Every Muslim has the duty to call others to the morality of Islam, to inform them of the existence of God and the proofs of His creation. God Himself has revealed that responsibility in Verse 3: 104: "Let there be a community among you who call to the good, and enjoin the right, and forbid the wrong. They are the ones who have success." He also reveals how that invitation is to be made:

Call [them] to the way of your Lord with wisdom and fair admonition, and argue with them in the kindest way. Your Lord knows best who is misguided from His way, and He knows best who are guided. (16:125)

Correct and courteous words accompanied by forgiveness are better than charity followed by insulting words. God is Rich Beyond Need, All-Forbearing. (2:263)

True believers know the importance of this responsibility, described in Verse 3:114: "They believe in God and the Last Day, and enjoin the right and forbid the wrong, and compete in doing good. They are among the righteous." Therefore, they call on all those around them—friends, relatives, everyone they can reach—to believe in God, fear Him, and display a proper morality. This pleasing characteristic of Muslims is described in Verse 9:71:

The men and women of the believers are friends of one another. They command what is right and forbid what is wrong, and perform prayer and pay charity tax, and obey God and His Messenger. They are the people on whom God will have mercy. God is Almighty, All-Wise.

From this verse, it's clear that all believers, throughout the course of their lives, are charged with explaining that proper morality, living by it themselves, recommending good deeds to others and advising them to avoid evil. God commands believers to use soft words, "Say to My servants that they should only say the best..." (17:53)

God describes good words and bad in this analogy in the Qur'an (14:24-27):

Do you do not see how God makes a metaphor of a good word: a good tree whose roots are firm and whose branches are in heaven? It bears fruit regularly by its Lord's permission. God makes metaphors for people so that hopefully they will be reminded. The metaphor of a corrupt word is that of a rotten tree, uprooted on the surface of the earth. It has no staying-power. God makes those who believe firm with the Firm Word in the life of this world and the hereafter. But God misguides the wrongdoers. God does whatever He wills.

Anyone who wishes to lead a virtuous life should encourage others toward virtue. Anyone who wants to see good should make an effort to help spread it. Anyone who wants to see others behave according to their conscience should encourage them to do so, and anyone who opposes cruelty should warn those who engage in it.

In short, anyone who wants right to prevail should call on all others to abide by it. When issuing that call, however, it's most important to keep in mind that only God can inspire people to become Muslims, and cause words pleasing to them to have any effect. God has revealed that our Prophet (may God bless him and grant him peace), as a result of his noble character and superior morality, always treated people well—and has recommended him as a role model for all mankind.

In the Qur'an (5:2), God has issued this command.

... help each other to goodness and godliness. Do not help each other to wrongdoing and enmity. Have fear of God. God is severe in retribution.

As that verse makes clear, the faithful struggle only for what is good. They consider the words of God in Verse 4:127 of the Qur'an: "Whatever good you do, God knows it." They never forget that they will be recompensed for all they do in the sight of our Lord, but God reveals that pleasing mutual aid needs to be in a framework of "good and godliness." The meaning of goodness is also explained in Verse 2:177:

It is not devoutness to turn your faces to the East or to the West. Rather, those with true devoutness are those who believe in God and the Last Day, the Angels, the Book and the Prophets, and who, despite their love for it, give away their wealth to their relatives and to orphans and the very poor, and to travelers and beggars, and to set slaves free, and who perform prayer and pay charity tax; those who honor their contracts when they make them, and are steadfast in poverty and illness and in battle. Those are the people who act loyal. They are the people who guard against evil.

True goodness, therefore, is rather different from the way society in general perceives it. Those who do not live by the morality of the Qur'an view good deeds as favors they confer, whenever they happen to feel like it. Usually they restrict such good deeds to giving money to a beggar, or giving up their seat on the bus to an elderly person.

Yet as we have seen from the above verse, the Qur'an describes goodness as a concept encompassing the whole of a believer's life, as an obligation that must be fulfilled throughout the course of his life, not only when he feels like it or happens to remember it. As a servant, any Muslim possesses true sincerity and helps the poor and needy, even if he himself is in need, even giving up the things he loves (Qur'an, 76:8). In Verse 51:19, which reads, "And beggars and the destitute received a due share of their wealth," God has revealed that rendering assistance, helping others, and doing good are all incumbent upon Muslims. They give help unconditionally; and believers are ready to make any sacrifice to encourage others towards what is good. They expect nothing in return, apart from winning the pleasure of God. In Verse 76:9-10, God describes such behavior by believers:

We feed you only out of desire for the Face of God. We do not want any repayment from you nor any thanks. Truly We fear from our Lord a glowering, calamitous Day.

Muslims know that God is the Lord of infinite justice, and never forget that their good behavior will be suitably rewarded in the hereafter. Nor do they forget that life in this world is only temporary, and that their true home lies in the sight of God. In the Qur'an, He warns people of their inevitable end, and calls on them all to behave in a manner pleasing to Him:

We did not create the heavens and earth and everything between them, except with truth. The Hour is certainly coming, so turn away graciously. (15:85)

Worship God and do not associate anything with Him. Be good to your parents and relatives and to orphans and the very poor, and to neighbors who are related to you and neighbors who are not related to you, and to companions and travelers and your slaves. God does not love anyone vain or boastful. (4:36)

The recompense for those who exhibit pleasing behavior is of great good news for all of mankind, and is revealed in these verses, in these terms:

But as for those who believe and do right actions, We will not let the wage of good-doers go to waste. (50:30)

When those who have done their duty are asked, "What has your Lord sent down?" their reply is, "Good!" There is good in this world for those who do good, and the abode of the hereafter is even better. How wonderful is the abode of those who guard against evil: Gardens of Eden which they enter, with rivers flowing under them, where they have whatever they desire. That is how God repays those who guard against evil. (16:30-31)

Muslims spend their whole lives implementing their awareness of the good and evil, as described in the Qur'an. Yet they take another important responsibility onto their shoulders: inviting others to see the truth, to avoid evil, and live by the morality of the Qur'an. Believers spend their lives telling people about the difference between good and evil, because to the faithful, God has given the following command (3:104):

Let there be a community among you who call to the good, and enjoin the right, and forbid the wrong. They are the ones who have success.

In Verse 3:110, God stresses how those who abide by this commandment are much more auspicious than others:

You are the best nation ever to be produced before mankind. You enjoin the right, forbid the wrong and believe in God. If the People of the Book were to believe, it would be better for them. Some of them are believers, but most of them are deviators.

The faithful perform that Qur'anic duty not only in respect for those ignorant of the difference between right and wrong and with no knowledge of religion, but also in respect for the faithful themselves. People fall into error not only out of ignorance, but sometimes out of forgetfulness, by mistake, or when driven by earthly desires. That being so, the faithful encourage good and prevent evil by reminding one another of the Qur'an's commandments. They warn each other that in this world, those who fail to avoid evil will suffer the torments of hell; that only those who do good and devoutly carry out their religious obligations will be rewarded with Paradise. That delightful responsibility means that they never need feel wearied or discouraged while continuing to warn others compassionately and affectionately, no matter what mistakes they might have made. In many verses, God reveals that He loves those who have patience, and calls on the faithful to be patient when practicing the morality of the Qur'an:

You who believe! Seek help in steadfastness and prayer. God is with the steadfast. (2:153)

… Those who are steadfast and do right actions. They will receive forgiveness and a large reward. (11:11)

A good action and a bad action are not the same. Repel the bad with something better and, if there is enmity between you and someone else, he will be like a bosom friend. (41:34)

Ward off evil with what is better. We know very well what they express. (23:96)

In these verses, God promises the faithful that they can secure positive results, so long as they adopt a pleasant attitude in the face of wrongdoing. The Qur'an emphasizes that even when a believer is dealing with an enemy, still he can establish a warm friendship. Responding to evil with good is also an essential part of compassion. When any believer sees others adopting an attitude that will not be pleasing to God, he considers first of all how that will affect them in the hereafter. Then he approaches them with toleration and humility, refusing to let himself become puffed up with pride.

Over the course of their lives, believers may come across people of very different characters. Yet they will not change their view of morality according to the people they meet. Others may speak mockingly, use ugly words, become angry, or even behave in a hostile manner. Yet the true believer never ceases to be polite, modest, and compassionate. He will not respond to ugly words with more of the same. He will not laugh at those who mock him, nor answer anger with anger, but remains patient and tolerant. In the face of insulting behavior, he will respond with proper morality, and with such compassion that the other will feel ashamed. That is the morality our Prophet (may God bless him and grant him peace) recommends to us. In one of the hadiths, he says, "*You do not return evil for evil, but excuse and forgive.*"— 18 In another hadith, he calls on the faithful in these terms: '*None of you must be the kind of weak person who says, 'He who has no compassion will receive none.'* "

In the Qur'an (5:13), our Prophet (may God bless him and grant him peace) was told to be forgiving when betrayed by some of the children of Israel: ... They have forgotten a good portion of what they were reminded of. You will never cease to come upon some act of treachery on their part, except for a few of them. Yet pardon them, and overlook. God loves good-doers.

As this verse shows, poor morality displayed by someone else is no justification for displaying the same thing. Each individual is solely responsible to God for his actions. According to the Qur'an, acting with compassion, affection and proper morality in the face of someone else's bad behavior is a sign of superior morality that reveals the extent of a believer's devotion to God. One verse (10:26) reveals the reward that such a pleasing attitude will bring:

Those who do good will have the best, and more! Neither dust nor debasement will darken their faces. They are the Companions of the Garden, remaining in it timelessly, forever.

Islam Commands to be Forgiving, Always

One important sign of compassion is a person's ability to forgive. In Verse 7:199, God calls upon His servants to "make allowances for people, command what is right, and turn away from the ignorant."

Some may find this attitude difficult, but in the sight of God, it will be well rewarded. Those caught up in anger may well refuse to forgive mistakes. But to the faithful, God has revealed that it is better to forgive and, in Verse 26:40, has recommended this morality:

The repayment of a bad action is one equivalent to it. But if someone pardons and puts things right, his reward is with God...

In another verse (26:43), God reveals, "But if someone is steadfast and forgives, that is the most resolute course to follow." Verse 24:22 emphasizes that this is a very superior form of morality:

Those of you possessing affluence and ample wealth should not make oaths that they will not give to their relatives and the very poor and those who have emigrated in the way of God. They should rather pardon and overlook. Would you not love God to forgive you? God is Ever-Forgiving, Most Merciful."

In these words, He encourages the faithful to consider their own positions when it comes to forgiveness. Because everyone wants God to forgive him, to protect and show him mercy, so do we hope that all others will excuse and forgive our mistakes. Therefore, God has commanded the faithful to treat others in the same way they would like to be treated themselves. That important responsibility encourages the faithful to be forgiving towards one another. Our Prophet (may God bless him and grant him peace) encouraged them in these words: *"That person is nearest to God, who pardons, when he has someone in his power, one who would have injured him."*

Believers, knowing that at any moment they may make a mistake, behave tolerantly towards others. Those verses in the Qur'an dealing with repentance make it clear that never making mistakes isn't as important as the determination never to repeat them. One of these verses (4:17) reads: God accepts only the repentance of those who do evil in ignorance and then quickly repent after doing it. God turns towards such people. God is All-Knowing, All-Wise.

Under conditions that reveal an individual's sincerity, the faithful behave forgivingly and compassionately towards one another. If he who has committed error sincerely repents having done so, they cannot judge him for his past deeds. Even when the faithful are totally in the right and the other completely in the wrong, still they have no compunction about forgiveness, because God recommends such behavior as an example of proper morality (3:134):

Those who give in times of both ease and hardship, those who control their rage and pardon other people—God loves the good-doers. When it comes to forgiving, the faithful don't distinguish between great and small errors, nor do they tailor their view of forgiveness accordingly. Someone may have committed an error inflicting severe harm on others, great financial loss, even loss of life. Yet the faithful know everything happens by the permission of God, as part of His destiny. When it comes to such things, they therefore place themselves in the hands of God and feel no personal anger.

Alternatively, if someone transgresses this Qur'anic rule and exceeds the bounds set by God, only God can judge that person's behavior. It is never up to the faithful to judge—or refuse to forgive—anyone on any matter. The truly sorry and repentant person will have his reward only in the sight of God. In many verses, God has revealed that apart from "associating partners to Him," He will forgive the errors of the faithful who repent sincerely. Since one man cannot know another's repentance, the faithful simply forgive in the manner God revealed to them. If the Qur'an has anything to say on a particular subject, they treat the person who has committed error in that light.

God has infinite compassion, and is forgiving, protective and gentle toward believers. The Compassionate and Merciful has placed all the blessings in the universe at Man's disposal, supporting him with messengers to reveal the true path. He directs all men to be His sincere servants by means of His revelations, each of which is a guidepost to that path. Our Lord is the *Halim* (the Clement), *Adl* (Lord of Infinite Justice), *'Afuw* (the Pardoner), *Asim* (the Protector), *Barr* (the Source of All Goodness), *Ghafir* (the Forgiver), *Hafiz* (the Protector), *Karim* (the Generous One), *Latif* (the Subtle One), *Muhsin* (Lord of Infinite Kindness), *Ra'uf* (the Compassionate), *Salam* (the Author of Safety), *Tawwab* (the Accepter of Repentance) and *Wahhab* (the Bestower).

Believers know that they are under our Lord's protection and are aware of His infinite goodness and kindness. For that reason, they are eager to become the kind of servants that are pleasing to

Him, who merit His mercy, and Paradise. As we have seen, one characteristic distinguishing believers is they are full of love and compassion. A Muslim behaves very gently, always treating others kindly. God has offered our Prophet's (may God bless him and grant him peace) gentle nature as an example to all believers (3:159):

It is a mercy from God that you were gentle with them. If you had been rough or hard of heart, they would have scattered from around you. So pardon them and ask forgiveness for them, and consult with them about the matter. Then when you have reached a firm decision, put your trust in God. God loves those who put their trust in Him.

That verse describes how our Prophet's (may God bless him and grant him peace) gentle, moral nature exerted a positive influence on people, whereby they grew even more devoted to him. The Qur'an gives the gentle natures of other loving prophets as role models. One verse (11:87) recounts how, when the Prophet Shuayb (peace be upon him) was sent to the people of Midian, they told him, "... You are clearly the forbearing, the rightly-guided!" The superior morality of the Prophet Abraham (peace be upon him) is another example for everyone. The Qur'an tells us that he was sensitive, gentle and full of love. The verses in question read:

Abraham would not have asked forgiveness for his father, but for a promise he made to him, and when it became clear to him that he was an enemy of God, he renounced him. Abraham was tenderhearted and forbearing. (9:114)

Abraham was forbearing, compassionate, penitent. (11:75)

God has commanded his believers always to behave in a pleasant manner, to speak kindly, and to treat others well. His prophets behaved accordingly. For example, when the Prophet Musa (Moses) (peace be upon him) was about to go to Pharaoh, one of the most repressive and cruel rulers of all times, God called on Moses in these terms (20:42-44):

Go, you and your brother, with My Signs, and do not slacken in remembering Me. Go to Pharaoh; he has overstepped the bounds.

But speak to him with gentle words so that hopefully, he will be reminded or show some fear.

These verses are an important reminder that everyone has a duty to live by the morality that the Qur'an reveals, and to adopt the morality of the prophets. The Qur'an proposes the following ideals for mankind: Love to all creatures God created; being kind and gentle in the best possible ways; always favoring compromise and tolerance; never speaking harshly, even under the most trying circumstances; making sacrifices happily and willingly; always desiring and seeking the best for others; pushing one's own personal desires to the background; wishing for others exactly what one wishes for oneself; being always quick to offer assistance in cases of need; and rejecting all forms of cruelty. That, no doubt, is exactly the ethical model that mankind is searching for.

Freedom of Belief

In matters of belief, Islam offers people complete freedom, and in the very clearest language. That has been so ever since Islam was first revealed, and forms the basis of today's Islamic morality. The verses on the subject (2:256) are perfectly clear:

There is no compulsion where religion is concerned. Right guidance has become clearly distinct from error. Anyone who rejects false gods and believes in God has grasped the Firmest Handhold, which will never give way. God is All-Hearing, All-Knowing.

According to Islam, people are free to choose whatever beliefs they wish, and nobody can oblige anyone else. Yes, a Muslim has a duty to communicate Islam and explain the existence of God, to state that the Qur'an is the book of His revelation, that the Prophet Muhammad (may God bless him and grant him peace) was His messenger, to speak of the hereafter and the Day of Judgment and of the beauty of Islamic morality. Yet that duty is restricted to explaining the religion only. In one verse (16:125), God informs our Prophet (may God bless him and grant him peace) that he is only a messenger: Call to the way of your Lord with wisdom and fair admonition, and argue with them in the kindest way. Your Lord knows best who is misguided from His way. And He knows best who are guided.

Another verse (18:29) states, "... It is the truth from your Lord; so let whoever wishes believe and whoever wishes disbelieve..." In Verse 26:3, our Lord warns the Prophet (may God bless him and grant him peace), "Perhaps you will destroy yourself with grief because they will not become believers." He also issues His Prophet (may God bless him and grant him peace) this reminder (50:45):

We know best what they say. You are not a dictator over them. So remind, with the Qur'an, whoever fears My Threat.

People are free to choose correctly or wrongly. When Islam—the true path that God has revealed—is explained, they come to believe of their own free will, reaching this decision with no pressure being put on them. If they make wrong choices, they will face its consequences in the hereafter. On this subject, Verse 10: 99 of the Qur'an contains the clearest command and reminder: "If your Lord had willed, all the people on the earth would have believed. Do you think you can force people to be believers?"

When one of the faithful explains matters, one person might come to believe straightaway, whereas another might adopt a mocking and aggressive attitude. One who follows his conscience might decide to devote his life to pleasing God, even while another, doing as the deniers did, might respond to those same kind words with wickedness. Yet his denial won't lead whoever issued the invitation to suffer or despair. In Verses 12: 103-104, God has stated, "But most people, for all your eagerness, are not believers. You do not ask them for any wage for it. It is only a reminder to all beings."

What's important is that no matter what reaction he meets with, the person who abides by the Qur'an keeps on displaying the kind of morality that is pleasing to God, refuses to make any concessions on it, and leaves matters in God's hands. God has told us that His religion is to be explained in the most pleasing manner. In the words of the Qur'an (29:46):

Argue with the People of the Book only in the kindest way—except in the case of those of them who do wrong–saying, "We believe in what has been sent down to us and what was sent down to you. Our God and your God are one and we submit to Him."

We must not forget that every event, large or small, takes place according to a destiny created by God. He reveals the true path to anyone invited to believe in Him. For that reason, the faithful feel no distress at the behavior of those who reject Him. The Qur'an gives several examples. In Verse 18:6, God tells our Prophet (may God bless him and grant him peace) not to be distressed when those whom he calls on to believe refuse to do so: "Perhaps you may destroy yourself with grief, chasing after them, if they do not believe in these words." Another verse (28:56) reads, "You cannot guide those you would like to, but God guides those He wills. He has best knowledge of the guided."

That means that whatever invitations an individual issues, all his pleasant words, and every detail he goes into can make an effect only by the will of God.

A believer's only responsibility is to call people to the Qur'an. He cannot be blamed for atheists' refusal to amend their ways, nor with how they will earn the torments of hell for themselves. In Verse 2:119, our Lord told our Prophet (may God bless him and grant him peace), "We have sent you with the Truth, bringing good news and giving warning. Do not ask about the inhabitants of the Blazing Fire."

God has given mankind both reason and a conscience. His messengers and the divine books revealed to them have shown the true path, and people are responsible for their own choices. Islamic morality can be lived only by a sincere decision to do so—by surrendering oneself to God and listening to one's conscience, which always commands one to do what is right. It is a total violation of Islamic morality to force anyone to believe, because what matters is an individual's surrendering himself to God with all his heart and believing sincerely. If any system obliges people to have faith, then those "converts" will become religious only out of fear. The only acceptable way to live a religion is within an environment that leaves one's conscience completely free. This is what God revealed to our Prophet (may God bless him and grant him peace) (88:21-26):

So remind them! You are only a reminder. You are not in control of them. But as for anyone who turns away and disbelieves, God will punish him with the Greatest Punishment. Certainly it is to Us they will return Then their Reckoning is Our concern.

It's worth emphasizing that Islam leaves people free to make their own choices regarding religion and commands them to respect other religions. Even if someone believes in what the Qur'an describes as superstition, still he can live in peace and security in Muslim lands and freely perform his own religious obligations. In Verses 109:2-6, God commanded our Prophet (may God bless him and grant him peace) to tell those who denied Him:

"I do not worship what you worship, and you do not worship what I worship. Nor will I worship what you worship, nor will you worship what I worship. You have your religion, and I have my religion."

Under the morality of Islam, everyone is free to carry out the obligations in accord with his own particular belief. Nobody can prevent any others from performing their particular religious duties, nor can he oblige them to worship in the manner he desires. That violates the morality of Islam, and is unacceptable to God. In the Islamic model of society emerges in which everyone is free to worship and perform the obligations attendant upon his particular chosen beliefs. The Qur'an (22:40) describes monasteries, churches, synagogues, and the places of worship of the Peoples of the Book as all under God's protection:

... If God had not driven some people back by means of others, [then] monasteries, churches, synagogues and mosques, where God's name is mentioned much, would have been pulled down and destroyed. God will certainly help those who help Him—God is All-Strong, Almighty.

Our Prophet's (may God bless him and grant him peace) life is full of such examples. When Christians came to see him pray in his own mosque, he left it for them to use. 21That kind of tolerance was maintained during the times of the caliphs who succeeded the Prophet (may God bless him and grant him peace). After Damascus was captured, a church that had been turned into a mosque was divided into two, so that Christians might worship in one half and Muslims in the other.22

Muslims should never remain silent in the face of oppression that they witness, or even hear about secondhand. Their compassion, stemming from the morality of the Qur'an, directs them to oppose all tyranny, wickedness and oppression, to defend the oppressed, to wage a war of ideas on their behalf. Whether dealing with their closest friends or with strangers with whom they share no interests in common, they behave in a manner determined to prevent any such oppression. Rather, they seize on this opportunity to win the good pleasure of God and implement the morality of the Qur'an. Because a believer's conscience is so very sensitive, his compassion never lets him turn a blind eye to the slightest injustice or cruelty. He will take his place in the vanguard of that morality by avoiding any actions that might be unfair to or oppress anyone else. Whenever he sees anyone else behaving that way, his conscience gives him no peace until he's done everything possible to right matters. True compassion has no room for forgetting about oppression, ignoring it or underestimating it.

The ignorant seldom act until oppression stands at their very own doorstep. This stems from their forgetting or denying that in the hereafter, they will be brought face to face with all the good and bad deeds that they encountered in this world. But the faithful, well aware of this, will treat even total strangers he has never met with great compassion and seeks to rescue them from oppression. Even if no one else supports him, he will muster all his strength to forestall wickedness. Even though the majority may behave differently, their lack of conscience never rubs off on the true believer. In the hereafter, Muslims know, they will be called to account for what they did to prevent evil. They won't be able to get away with excuses like, "I didn't see it," or, "I didn't hear it," or "I never knew what was going on."

As is revealed in the Qur'an (19:80), "... he [man] will come to Us all alone," every human being will return to his Creator on his own. People will be brought into the presence of God, put to the trial, and called to account for their deeds in this world. Only those who followed the dictates of their conscience will come out of that questioning at all well. Those who have behaved well, opposed all forms of cruelty, fought evil, and remained on the path of God can expect a suitable reward. God mentions this matter in another verse (2:112):

All who submit themselves completely to God and are good-doers will find their reward with their Lord. They will feel no fear and will know no sorrow.

A CALL TO PEACE IN ANOTHER RELIGIONS: TOLERANCE IN THE OLD AND NEW TESTAMENTS

The preceding section considered the Qur'an's calls for people to live in love and security, emphasizing that Islam is a religion of peace. Like other divine religions, Islam proposes a model society of compassionate, mature, moderate, mild, gentle, kind, sympathetic, loyal, understanding, forgiving and tolerant people who avoid fighting and conflict. It also commands believers to strive to bring such a society about.

Divine books revealed before the Qur'an may have undergone a number of distortions, but they still contain sections that agree with it. These books are the Torah and the Gospels. Today, although mixed with human words and thus distorted, they make up the core of what is called the Bible. The Bible's two basic parts, the Old and the New Testaments, are based on the Torah and the Gospels relatively, including many other books and letters. Both the Old and New Testaments favor love, peace and tolerance, also prohibiting terror and oppression. In this section, we'll consider how Jews and

Christians from all over the world must take action in light of these commands to oppose terrorism.

The Old Testament consists of five books comprising the Torah given to the Prophet Moses (peace be upon him), the Book of Psalms, and other writings by Jewish prophets and accounts of their lives. Jews believe in the Old Testament. Christians also believe in the New Testament, an addition to the Old, which consists of the four gospels, the Acts of the Apostles following Jesus's death, and a number of letters. According to the Qur'an, however, the divine books of the Bible were distorted after being revealed to mankind. That means that both the Old and New Testaments are no longer the uncorrupted word of God. We should regard them as containing divine elements that agree with the Qur'an, but also various human errors. When making use of the Old and New Testaments, therefore, we need to consider whether their contents are in harmony with the Qur'an.

Seek good and not evil, that you may live; so the Lord God of hosts will be with you, as you have spoken. Hate evil, love good... (Amos 5, 14-15)

As emphasized earlier, the divine books sent down by God to guide His servants describe an ideal society full of love, peace, tolerance and justice. In the Qur'an, for example, God describes the Torah revealed to the Jews as a guide:

We sent down the Torah containing guidance and light, and the prophets who had submitted themselves gave judgment by it for the Jews—as did their scholars and their rabbis—by what they had been allowed to preserve of God's Book to which they were witnesses... (5:44)

Today, we can find part of the Torah's divine commandments in the Old Testament, directing people to avoid evil, tyranny, theft, corruption, falsehood and cruelty; and to display proper morality. In fact, God states in the Qur'an that:

He [God] said, "Moses, I have chosen you over all mankind for My Message and My Word. Take what I have given you and be among the thankful." We wrote about everything for him on the Tablets as an admonition and making all things clear. "Seize hold of it vigorously and command your people to adopt the best in it. I will show you the home of the deviators!" (7:144-145)

The Old Testament describes in considerable detail the fate awaiting those who commit evil and want to spread it, and warns people against going down that road. Flying into a rage and harming others, trying to turn them away from the true path, shedding blood and quarrelling are all described as forms of behavior displeasing to God, which He has forbidden. He condemns all those who go down the path of evil and oppression, revealing that such people will never be saved. Some Old Testament accounts emphasize this:

Simeon and Levi are brothers; instruments of cruelty are in their dwelling place. Let not my soul enter their council; let not my honor be united to their assembly; for in their anger they slew a man, and in their self-will they hamstrung an ox. Cursed be their anger, for it is fierce; and their wrath, for it is cruel! (Genesis 49, 5-7)

But the wicked are like the troubled sea, when it cannot rest, whose waters cast up mire and dirt. "There is no peace," says my God, "for the wicked." (Isaiah 57, 20-21)

You children of Israel... "There is no truth or mercy or knowledge of God in the land. By swearing and lying, killing and stealing and committing adultery, they break all restraint, with bloodshed upon bloodshed. Therefore, the land will mourn; and everyone who dwells there will waste away with the beasts of the field and the birds of the air; even the fish of the sea will be taken away. " Now let no man contend, or rebuke another; for your people are like those who contend with the priest. (Hosea 4, 1-4) Gilead is a city of evildoers and defiled with blood. As bands of robbers lie in wait for a man, so the company of priests murder on the way to Shechem; surely they commit lewdness. (Hosea 6, 8-9)

The merciful man does good for his own soul, but he who is cruel troubles his own flesh... But he who sows righteousness will have a sure reward. As righteousness leads to life, so he who pursues evil pursues it to his own death... The wicked will not go unpunished; but the posterity of the righteous will be delivered. (Proverbs 11, 17-21)

An ungodly man digs up evil, and it is on his lips like a burning fire. A perverse man sows strife, and a whisperer separates the best of friends. A violent man entices his neighbor, and leads him in a way that is not good... He who is slow to anger is better than the mighty. . . (Proverbs 16, 27-32)

The Lord is far from the wicked... (Proverbs 15, 29)

The Old Testament describes in considerable detail the deeds of people who did evil and acted tyrannically, making it clear that the wicked will receive their just deserts. But it also states that those who repent will be accepted as good, if they abide by God's religion:

Yet the house of Israel says, "The way of the Lord is not fair." O house of Israel, is it not My ways which are fair, and your ways which are not fair? When a righteous man turns away from his righteousness, commits iniquity, and dies in it, it is because of the iniquity which he has done that he dies. Again, when a wicked man turns away from the wickedness which he committed, and does what is lawful and right, he preserves himself alive. Because he considers and turns away from all the transgressions which he committed, he shall surely live; he shall not die. Yet the house of Israel says, "The way of the Lord is not fair." O house of Israel, is it not My ways which are fair, and your ways which are not fair? Therefore I will judge you, O house of Israel, every one according to his ways," says the Lord God. "Repent, and turn from all your transgressions, so that iniquity will not be your ruin. Cast away from you all the transgressions which you have committed, and get yourselves a new heart and a new spirit. For why should you die, O house of Israel? For I have no pleasure in the death of one who dies," says the Lord God. "Therefore turn and live!" (Ezekiel 18, 21-32)

... Thus says the Lord: "... I am fashioning a disaster and devising a plan against you. Return now every one from his evil way, and make your ways and your doings good." And they said, "That is hopeless! So we will walk according to our own plans, and we will every one obey the dictates of his evil heart." (Jeremiah 18, 11-12)

Do not be like your fathers, to whom the former prophets preached, saying, "Thus says the Lord of hosts: 'Turn now from your evil ways and your evil deeds.'" But they did not hear nor heed Me," says the Lord. (Zechariah 1, 4)

To Harm Others

Many Old Testament commandments prohibit doing harm to others, killing, ruling without justice, or behaving unfairly.

You shall not murder. You shall not commit adultery. You shall not steal. You shall not bear false witness against your neighbor. You shall not covet your neighbor's house... (Exodus 20, 13-17)

You shall do no injustice in judgment ... nor honor the person of the mighty. In righteousness you shall judge your neighbor. You shall not go about as a talebearer among your people; nor shall you take a stand against the life of your neighbor: I am the Lord... You shall not take vengeance, nor bear any grudge against the children of your people, but you shall love your neighbor as yourself: I am the Lord. (Leviticus 19, 15-18)

Lest innocent blood be shed in the midst of your land which the Lord your God is giving you as an inheritance, and thus guilt of bloodshed be upon you. (Deuteronomy 19, 10)

Deliver those who are drawn toward death, and hold back those stumbling to the slaughter. If you say, "Surely we did not know this," Does not He who weighs the hearts consider it? He who keeps your soul, does He not know it?.. (Proverbs 24, 11-12)

Be Good to Others

The Old Testament contains a number of statements commanding brotherhood and love, sacrifice and humility. Just like Muslims, the Jews and Christians have been ordered to treat others well, to do good deeds, never to deviate from the path of righteousness, and to be mild-mannered, tolerant and forgiving.

Some examples include: Sow for yourselves righteousness; reap in mercy... You have plowed wickedness; you have reaped iniquity. You have eaten the fruit of lies, because you trusted in your own way, in the multitude of your mighty men... (Hosea 10, 12-13)

Just like Muslims, Jews and Christians are commanded to avoid war and in particular, to establish peace. The book *Hristiyan Ahlaki* (Christian Morality) describes the kind of behavior a Christian should display, according to the Old and New Testaments, and sums this situation up in these terms: "The conflicts mentioned in the Holy Book are for the purposes of self-defense."23 It is forbidden to harm non-combatants, like children in the event of war.

Now it happened, as soon as the kingdom was established in his hand, that he executed his servants who had murdered his father the king. But the children of the murderers he did not execute, according to what is written in the Book of the Law of Moses, in which the Lord commanded, saying, "Fathers shall not be put to death for their children, nor shall children be put to death for their fathers..." ... (2 Kings 14, 5-6)

In the same way as Islam, Judaism and Christianity propose an exemplary model for society. With their strong faith, proper morality and the scrupulous adherence to His verses, the messengers whom God sent as guides to Man are the very finest examples. For this reason, it's most important for believers to try to adopt the prophets' morality of as their own, and to live similarly. If features of religion's proper morality can spread throughout all mankind, the resulting atmosphere will closely resemble heaven. In such a society, the nightmares of anarchy and terror will disappear. Scrupulous adhering to God's commands, those who fear and believe in Him will eagerly avoid all forms of wickedness and mischief. The world will come to be filled with peace and tolerance, moderate and understanding people. The Old Testament describes with a number of examples the life style, once the morality of religion prevails:

Then justice will dwell in the wilderness, and righteousness remain in the fruitful field. The work of righteousness will be peace, and the effect of righteousness, quietness and assurance forever. My people will dwell in a peaceful habitation, in secure dwellings, and in quiet resting places. (Isaiah 32, 16-18)

The wilderness and the wasteland shall be glad for them, and the desert shall rejoice and blossom as the rose; it shall blossom abundantly and rejoice, even with joy and singing… They shall see the glory of the Lord, the excellency of our God. Strengthen the weak hands, and make firm the feeble knees. Say to those who are fearful-hearted, "Be strong, do not fear!.. " Then the eyes of the blind shall be opened, and the ears of the deaf shall be unstopped. Then the lame shall leap like a deer, and the tongues of the dumb sing. For waters shall burst forth in the wilderness, and streams in the desert. (Isaiah 35, 1-6)

He who walks righteously and speaks uprightly, he who despises the gain of oppressions, who gestures with his hands, refusing bribes, who stops his ears from hearing of bloodshed, and shuts his eyes from seeing evil: He will dwell on high; his place of defense will be the fortress of rocks; bread will be given him, his water will be sure. (Isaiah 33, 15-16)

... To loose the bonds of wickedness, to undo the heavy burdens, to let the oppressed go free, and that you break every yoke? Is it not to share your bread with the hungry, and that you bring to your house the poor who are cast out; when you see the naked, that you cover him, and not hide yourself from your own flesh? Then your light shall break forth like the morning, your healing shall spring forth speedily, and your righteousness shall go before you; the glory of the Lord shall be your rear guard. Then you shall call, and the Lord will answer; you shall cry, and He will say, "Here I am." If you take away the yoke from your midst, the pointing of the finger, and speaking wickedness, if you extend your soul to the hungry and satisfy the afflicted soul, then your light shall dawn in the darkness, and your darkness shall be as the noonday. (Isaiah 58, 6-10)

"... You shall love the LORD your God with all your heart, with all your soul, and with all your mind." This is the first and great commandment.

And the second is like it: "You shall love your neighbor as yourself." (Matthew 22, 37-39)

The Christian New Testament also contains many sections forbidding evil and oppression. People are called on to be forgiving, peaceful, tolerant and compromising at all times. For these reasons, Christianity expects people to be understanding and joyful, and to refrain from conflict. Christians who abide by the injunctions revealed by the Prophet Jesus (peace be upon him) and who take his morality as their own are described in these terms in the Qur'an (57: 27): Then We sent Our Messengers following in their footsteps and sent 'Isa (Jesus) son of Maryam (Mary) after them, giving him the Gospel. We put compassion and mercy in the hearts of those who followed him . . .

In another verse (5:82), God states, "... You will find the people most affectionate to those who believe are those who say, 'We are Christians.' That is because some of them are priests and monks and because they are not arrogant," and praises Christians who turn to God with a sincere heart.

This positive morality of Christians is based on the commandments in the Bible. They are commanded to return good for evil, to love their fellow human beings unconditionally and to help the needy in the same manner. In fact, the New Testament uses a special word for the "unconditional love" that believers have for Our Lord and the faithful. One work dealing with Christianity describes the situation in these terms: The word agape is used 116 times in 105 verses of the New Testament. It is a very high form of love. Agape Enterprises simply means "Love Enterprises." Our ministry reaches out to those who need, and have nothing to repay. A number of extracts from the New Testament command people to avoid evil and bloodshed and encourage them to display proper morality.

Love and Compassion

"A new commandment I give to you, that you love one another; as I have loved you, that you also love one another." (John 13, 34)

Let love be without hypocrisy. Abhor what is evil. Cling to what is good. Be kindly affectionate to one another with brotherly love, in honor giving preference to one another; not lagging in diligence, fervent in spirit, serving the Lord; rejoicing in hope, patient in tribulation, continuing steadfastly in prayer; distributing to the needs of the saints, given to hospitality. Bless those who persecute you; bless and do not curse. (Romans 12, 9-14)

Owe no one anything except to love one another, for he who loves another has fulfilled the law. For the commandments, "You shall not commit adultery," "You shall not murder," "You shall not steal," "You shall not bear false witness," "You shall not covet," and if there is any other commandment, are all summed up in this saying, namely, "You shall love your neighbor as yourself." Love does no harm to a neighbor; therefore love is the fulfillment of the law. (Romans 13, 8-10)

And may the Lord make you increase and abound in love to one another and to all, just as we do to you. (1 Thessalonians 3, 12)

Then one of the scribes came... and asked him, "Which is the first commandment of all?" Jesus answered him, "The first of all the commandments is: 'Hear, O Israel, the Lord our God, the Lord is one. And you shall love the Lord your God with all your heart, with all your soul, with all your mind, and with all your strength.' ... And the second, like it, is this: 'You shall love your neighbor as yourself.' There is no other commandment greater than these."

So the scribe said to him, "Well said, Teacher. You have spoken the truth, for there is one God, and there is no other but He. And to love Him with all the heart, with all the understanding, with all the soul, and with all the strength, and to love one's neighbor as oneself, is more than all the whole burnt offerings and sacrifices." (Mark 12, 28-33)

Since you have purified your souls in obeying the truth through the Spirit in sincere love of the brethren, love one another fervently with a pure heart… (1 Peter 1, 22)

Finally, all of you be of one mind, having compassion for one another; love as brothers, be tender hearted, be courteous; not returning evil for evil or reviling for reviling, but on the contrary blessing, knowing that you were called to this, that you may inherit a blessing… (1 Peter 3, 8-10)

And above all things, have fervent love for one another, for "love will cover a multitude of sins." Be hospitable to one another without grumbling. As each one has received a gift, minister it to one another, as good stewards of the manifold grace of God. (1 Peter 4, 8-10)

Loving Your Enemy

"You have heard that it was said, 'You shall love your neighbor and hate your enemy.' But I say to you, love your enemies, bless those who curse you, do good to those who hate you, and pray for those who spitefully use you and persecute you. (Matthew 5, 43-44)

A Proper Morality

"Blessed are the merciful, for they shall obtain mercy. Blessed are the pure in heart, for they shall see God. Blessed are the peacemakers..." (Matthew 5, 7-9)

"Judge not, and you shall not be judged. Condemn not, and you shall not be condemned. Forgive, and you will be forgiven. Give, and it will be given to you: good measure, pressed down, shaken together, and running over will be put into your bosom. For with the same measure that you use, it will be measured back to you." (Luke 6, 37-38)

And why do you look at the speck [of sawdust] in your brother's eye, but do not perceive the plank in your own eye? Or how can you say to your brother, "'Brother, let me remove the speck that is in your eye,'" when you yourself do not see the plank that is in your own eye? Hypocrite! First remove the plank from your own eye, and then you will see clearly to remove the speck that is in your brother's eye. (Luke 6, 41-42)

Therefore, as the elect of God, holy and beloved, put on tender mercies, kindness, humility, meekness, longsuffering; bearing with one another, and forgiving one another, if anyone has a complaint against another… But above all these things put on love, which is the bond of perfection. (Colossians 3, 12-14)

Finally, brethren, whatever things are true, whatever things are noble, whatever things are just, whatever things are pure, whatever things are lovely, whatever things are of good report, if there is any virtue and if there is anything praiseworthy—meditate on these things. (Philippians 4, 8)

"... God resists the proud, but gives grace to the humble." Therefore submit to God. Resist the devil, and he will flee from you. Draw near to God, and He will draw near to you. Cleanse your hands, you sinners; and purify your hearts, you double-minded. Lament and mourn and weep! Let your laughter be turned to mourning and your joy to gloom. Humble yourselves in the sight of the Lord, and He will lift you up. Do not speak evil of one another, brethren. He who speaks evil of a brother and judges his brother, speaks evil of the law and judges the law. But if you judge the law, you are not a doer of the law but a judge. There is one Lawgiver, who is able to save and to destroy. Who are you to judge another? (James 4, 6-12)

Helping the Needy and Doing Good Deeds

"For a good tree does not bear bad fruit, nor does a bad tree bear good fruit. For every tree is known by its own fruit. For men do not gather figs from thorns, nor do they gather grapes from a bramble bush. A good man out of the good treasure of his heart brings forth good; and an evil man out of the evil treasure of his heart brings forth evil. For out of the abundance of the heart his mouth speaks." (Luke 6, 43-45)

But as for you, brethren, do not grow weary in doing good. And if anyone does not obey our word in this epistle, note that person and do not keep company with him, that he may be ashamed.

Yet do not count him as an enemy, but admonish him as a brother. (2 Thessalonians 3, 13-15)

So the people asked him, saying, "What shall we do then?" He answered and said to them, "He who has two tunics, let him give to him who has none; and he who has food, let him do likewise." Then tax collectors also came to be baptized, and said to him, "Teacher, what shall we do?" And he said to them, "Collect no more than what is appointed for you." Likewise the soldiers asked him, saying, "And what shall we do?" So he said to them, "Do not intimidate anyone or accuse falsely, and be content with your wages." (Luke 3, 10-14)

For this is the will of God, that by doing good you may put to silence the ignorance of foolish men - as free, yet not using liberty as a cloak for vice, but as bondservants of God. Honor all people. Love the brotherhood. Fear God… (1 Peter 2, 15-17)

Where do wars and fights come from among you? Do they not come from your desires for pleasure that war in your members? You lust and do not have. You murder, covet, and cannot obtain. You fight and war. Yet you do not have because you do not ask. You ask and do not receive, because you ask amiss, that you may spend it on your pleasures. Adulterers and adulteresses! Do you not know that friendship with the world is enmity with God? Whoever therefore wants to be a friend of the world makes himself an enemy of God. (James 4, 1-4)

Let all bitterness, wrath, anger, clamor, and evil speaking be put away from you, with all malice. And be kind to one another, tender hearted, forgiving one another, just as God forgave you. (Ephesians 4, 31-32) "Blessed are the peacemakers..." (Matthew 5, 9)

If it is possible, as much as depends on you, live peaceably with all men. Beloved, do not avenge yourselves... for it is written, "Vengeance is Mine, I will repay," says the Lord. Therefore "If your enemy is hungry, feed him; if he is thirsty, give him a drink; for in so doing you will heap coals of fire on his head." (Romans 12, 18-20) Take heed to yourselves. If your brother sins against you, rebuke him; and if he repents, forgive him. (Luke 17, 3)

Our Prophet (May God bless him and grant him peace) Mohammed's (pbuh) Noble Morality

Our earlier chapters concentrated on the physical and spiritual damage that terrorism inflicts, and cited how conveying the morality of religion on the level of ideas is the most important step in the cultural struggle against terrorism. Explaining the features of proper morality described in the Old and New Testaments and the Qur'an—love, compassion, tolerance and moderation—is the only way to do away with terrorism's endless bloodshed. In particular, the solution to terrorism in the name of religion in particular lies in religion being correctly explained—in other words in understanding the model of morality we discussed earlier especially of Islam. Whatever model people take for themselves must be a source they can regard as a guide. That source is the Qur'an; the model is the life of our Prophet (may God bless him and grant him peace). This chapter examines his life in the light of the Qur'an's verses and the *hadiths*—his teachings and sayings.

At every moment, our Prophet (may God bless him and grant him peace) displayed a morality that was pleasing to God and lived in the most perfect manner. Any society that model itself on the exemplary messengers of God will provide a most significant obstacle to social evils such as terrorism, which will be unable to survive in such an environment. Terrorists lack any concept of human love. Aggressive, uncompromising, intolerant, incapable of entering a dialogue with those who think differently, seeing no value in others' ideas, they try to resolve every argument through violence. In any social morality built on love and tolerance, they can never achieve their aims.

Mohammed (PBUH) Was a Man of Tolerance and Love

In the time of the Prophet Mohammed (May God bless him and grant him peace), Arabia was home to communities of different religions, cultures and ideas. Jews, Christians, Sabians, Zoroastrians and idol worshippers all lived side by side, together with many different tribes hostile to each other. Yet no matter what their tribe or beliefs, our Prophet (may God bless him and grant him peace) called people to religion with affection, patience, tolerance and love. The Qur'an (3:19) describes his pleasing attitude to those around him:

It is a mercy from God that you were gentle with them. If you had been rough or hard of heart, they would have scattered from around you. So pardon them and ask forgiveness for them...

As pointed out earlier, the Qur'an reveals that no one should be pressured to embrace Islam. Muslims are charged only with explaining the religion of God. No one can force anyone else to believe or worship. Only by the will of God can another find the true path and come to believe. Our Prophet (may God bless him and grant him peace) always scrupulously abided by that prohibition and stated frequently that a man could live by religion only when, in his heart, he really wanted to. God told our Prophet (may God bless him and grant him peace) in one holy verse (50:45) how he should behave towards those around him:

We know best what they say. You are not a dictator over them. So remind, with the Qur'an, whoever fears My Threat.

Our Prophet (may God bless him and grant him peace) once told the faithful, "I have been sent to show mercy." The key to his noble morality is also described in these terms:

Those who have mercy will receive the mercy of the Most Merciful.

A great many hadiths concern our Prophet's (may God bless him and grant him peace) compassion, affection and tolerance. For example, he once said, *"Those who show no mercy will be shown no mercy."* Other words of his include:

My Cherisher has ordered me nine things: To reverence Him, externally and internally; to speak true, and with propriety, in prosperity and adversity…

I swear by whom my soul is in his hand, you will not enter paradise until you believe, and you will not believe until you love each other. Do you want me to guide you to something which if you practice, you will love each other? Spread greeting with peace among of you.

In his collection of information from the world of the hadiths, the great Islamic scholar Imam Ghazali sums up our Prophet's (may God bless him and grant him peace) attitude to those around him in these terms:

... Everyone thought that the Prophet (may God bless him and grant him peace) honored him more. Whoever came to him could see his face.

... He used to call his companions by their surnames with honor and he used to give one surname who had no surname.

... He was very affectionate and kind in dealing with the people. ... Nobody could speak loudly in his assembly.

Our Prophet's (may God bless him and grant him peace) love of his fellow man, his consideration and affection, tied those around him and encouraged them to believe. His superior example of morality is one that all Muslims should dwell on. One verse (9: 128) describes the features of our Prophet (may God bless him and grant him peace) that set an example to all mankind:

A Messenger has come to you from among yourselves. Your suffering is distressing to him; he is deeply concerned for you; he is gentle and merciful to the believers.

Love and affection, tolerance and compassion are common traits of the messengers whom God has sent as leaders to the true path. The Qur'an states that the other prophets have been honored with "loving sensitivity" and gives the Prophet John (peace be upon him), to whom He gave wisdom, as an example in this regard to all mankind. Verse 19:13 describes that holy personage in these terms: ... and tenderness and purity from Us – he was conscientious.

Our Prophet's (may God bless him and grant him peace) Gentle Consideration

Our Prophet (may God bless him and grant him peace) was in constant contact with all sections of society and spoke to everyone, from those at the very pinnacle of power to prisoners of war, children and orphans. With people of all different social standings, lifestyles, natures and customs, he established positive dialogues, winning their affection and treating them all with kind patience and pleasant understanding.

As reported by those companions who were close to him, our Prophet (may God bless him and grant him peace) was "most kind, morally above reproach, graceful, amiable and considerate." His words, "*I have been sent to perfect good qualities of character*" are an expression of his high nature. Aisha, who knew him very well, described his pleasant morality in the following words: "The Prophet's (may God bless him and grant him peace) nature was the Qur'an."

Anas, who was brought up in the Prophet's (may God bless him and grant him peace) house and served him for years, describes his courtesy in these terms: God's Messenger *(may God bless him and grant him peace)*, when he shook hands with anyone, he did not withdraw his hands till the other man withdrew his. Similarly, he did not turn away his face from anyone till that man turned his face to the other side. And he was never seen to put forward his knees in front of one with whom he was sitting.

Whenever one spoke to him the other would keep quiet and listen till he would finish.

Anas bin Malik ("may Allah be pleased with him") says, 'I remained in the service of the Rasulullah (saas) for ten years. He never once spoke me a word of contempt. When I did something, he never asked me. "Why did you do so?" When I did not do a certain task, he never asked me why I did not do it.

Throughout his life, our Prophet (may God bless him and grant him peace) educated thousands. Through his influence, people who knew nothing about religion came to be considerate, willing to make sacrifices, have a pleasing attitude and possess a superior morality. Even now, centuries after his death, Our Prophet (may God bless him and grant him peace) remains the very best guide and teacher, whose words and morality continue to inspire billions.

Our Prophet (may God bless him and grant him peace) declared it was particularly important for the faithful to love one another with sincere affection, taking no account of personal interests, and never to harbor negative emotions like hatred, anger or jealousy.

In the Qur'an (42:23), God commands His Prophet (may God bless him and grant him peace) to say the following:

That is the good news which God gives to His servants who believe and do right actions. Say: "I do not ask you for any wage for this–except for you to love your near of kin. If anyone does a good action, We will increase the good of it for him. God is Ever-Forgiving, Ever-Thankful."

Some hadiths regarding the Prophet's (may God bless him and grant him peace) affection, friendship and brotherhood read:

A believer loves for others what he loves for himself.

God's Apostle (saas) used to accept gifts and used to give something in return.

He who is presented with a flower of sweet basil should not reject it, because it is light in weight and pleasant in odor.

Don't hate one another, don't envy one another don't sell over the sale to another, don't dispute with one another and don't back-bite one another. The servants of God are brethren to one another.

The habits of earlier generations have attacked you–envy and hatred. Hatred is shaving. You will not enter Paradise till you believe. You will not believe till you love one another. Shall I not inform you what thing will establish you on it? Spread peace among you.

The strong man is not the one who is strong in wrestling, but the one who controls himself in anger.

Beware of envy, for envy devours good [deeds] as fire devours firewood.

Muslims are brothers to one another. They should neither cheat, lie, nor humiliate each other.

With the rules he gave to the Muslims; with his just and tolerant attitude towards other religions, languages, races and tribes; and in his equal treatment of everybody, rich and poor, our Prophet Mohammed (may God bless him and grant him peace) is a great example to all of mankind. In one verse (5:42), God tells him "But if you do judge, judge between them justly. God loves the just." The Prophet (may God bless him and grant him peace) never made the slightest concession on that justice, not even under the most difficult conditions.

Many incidents from his life bear witness to the Prophet's (may God bless him and grant him peace) exemplary attitude. In the land where he lived, a variety of religions, races and tribes all lived together. These communities found it very difficult to live together in peace and security, much less restrain those who wanted to sow dissent. However, our Prophet's (may God bless him and grant him peace) justice was a source of peace and security, as much for these non-believers as it was for Muslims. During his lifetime, everyone on the Arabian Peninsula— Christian, Jew, or pagan—was treated justly, with no discrimination.

Our Prophet's (may God bless him and grant him peace) pleasing attitude, in conformity with the Qur'an, sets an example for those of different religions and shows how they should behave to one another. His justice brought about compromise between people of different races. In many of his addresses, even in his Farewell Sermon, he made it known that no one's race or class endowed him with any superiority. This lay only in godliness, as God has revealed in the Qur'an (49:13). Other hadiths on this subject say:

You are sons of Adam, and Adam came from dust. Let the people cease to boast about their ancestors. These genealogies of yours are not a reason to revile anyone. You are all children of Adam. No one has any superiority over another, except in religion and taqwa [godliness].

Our Prophet (may God bless him and grant him peace) Always Favored Peace

Our Prophet (may God bless him and grant him peace) never desired war but over the years, made great efforts to spread Islam by peaceful means. He was patient in the face of heavy assaults and pressure, except when dealing with such pressure became imperative, he did give permission for war, in the light of a revelation from God. He never declared war so long as there was still the slightest possibility of peace, and as long as an enemy's attacks and pressure represented no mortal danger.

During our Prophet's (may God bless him and grant him peace) lifetime, the Mu'tah Expedition was the bloodiest and most difficult waged by the Muslims. He appointed Zayd ibn Harithah to command the army, and admonished the troops:

> Wage war in the name of God, on the path of God, against those who deny God. Engage in no treachery. Do not cut off ears and noses and other parts of the body. Do not kill women and children, the elderly, and men of religion in their places of worship. Do not cut down date and other trees, and do not tear down buildings.

Based on the prophetic orders on war, the following principles, which may be called "The Islamic Principles of Combat", are outlined by Muslim scholars:

1. War is to be waged only with those who encourage and engage in it.
2. Priests in churches, children, women, and the elderly must never be harmed.
3. Sown fields must not be damaged.
4. Treaties and agreements must not be broken.
5. Animals must not be harmed.
6. There must be no cruelty and torture.
7. Towns must not be destroyed.

The Treaty of Medina, signed by our Prophet (may God bless him and grant him peace) and the Jewish and polytheist communities in the city, was also an important example of justice and mutual respect between different communities. The treaty, drawn up to establish a kind of constitution between communities of different beliefs and allowing each one to observe its own principles, brought peace to those who for years had been hostile to one another. One of its most striking features was how it enshrined freedom of belief. The article on that subject reads:

The Jews of Banu 'Awf are one nation with the Muslims; the Jews have their religion, and the Muslims have theirs…

Article 16 of the Treaty of Medina reads, "*The Jew who follows us is surely entitled to our support and the same equal rights as any one of us. He shall not be wronged nor his enemy be assisted.*" The Prophet's (may God bless him and grant him peace) successors stayed loyal to that rule he agreed to, extending it even to Berbers, Buddhists, Hindu Brahmans and those of other beliefs.

One reason why the time of the Prophet (may God bless him and grant him peace) was blessed with peace and security was his position of justice, so in line with the morality of the Qur'an. Foreign writers, too, have been impressed by his superior character and praise our Prophet's (may God bless him and grant him peace) morality in their works. In *The Genuine Islam*, George Bernard Shaw described these superior traits:

I have always held the religion of Mohammed in high estimation because of its wonderful vitality. It is the only religion which appears to me to possess that assimilating capacity to the changing phase of existence which can make itself appeal to every age.

I have studied him ... he must be called the Savior of Humanity. I believe that if a man like him were to assume the dictatorship of the modern world, he would succeed in solving its problems in a way that would bring it the much needed peace and happiness...

In our own time as well, abiding by the Qur'an's morality is the only answer to all the conflicts, fighting, and instability of the world.

Like our Prophet (may God bless him and grant him peace), never we should depart from the path of justice, and should always respect the rights of different communities and indivdiuals, whatever their beliefs and identities may be.

Solutions to Terror And Anarchy, From Beduizzaman Said Nursi

Throughout history, there have been periods when the scourges of terror and anarchy have intensified, posing a threat to entire populations. Numerous solutions have been proposed. One of those who stressed the importance of an all-out struggle against terror and anarchy was the great Turkish Islamic scholar, Bediuzzaman Said Nursi (1877-1960). He said that the first thing people must do is spread the morality of the Qur'an; to that end, he made a number of recommendations.

At the time Bediuzzaman lived, the world was going through radical changes. The First World War had a particularly impact on his life. During the War, he had led the Ottoman militia forces on the Caucasian Front against the invading Russians for which he was later awarded a War Medal. He was taken prisoner in March 1916 and was held in Russia for two years. In early 1918, he escaped from prison and made his way back to Istanbul via Warsaw, Berlin and Vienna.

Thus he had a front-row seat to witness the collapse of the Ottoman Empire and the establishment of the Turkish Republic. He also saw the Russian Revolution bring Communism to power, the conflict between the great European powers, and the difficulties that both World Wars inflicted on the Turkish Republic. As can be seen in his writings, he made a detailed analysis of all these events, evaluating all political developments in the light of the verses of the Qur'an. Always he emphasized how any society that turns its back on religion will suffer great damage; and that only if Muslims joined forces, could they enjoy great success against atheist ideologies.

Bediuzzaman knew that terror and anarchy would emerge in his own time, and afterwards. He therefore tried to alert people to a number of possible solutions for these terrible problems. In his words, "... Religion fiercely condemns strife and anarchy. Anarchy recognizes no rights. It turns human morality and the works of civilization into the morality of animals," This was the best possible expression of Islam's views on terror and violence, which Bediuzzaman spent his life expounding. As he once said, "Patience and endurance to put a stop to anarchy and maintain public order are necessary, with all sincerity in the service of the faith. I am therefore perfectly content to sacrifice my repute to that end." He stated that in the fight against anarchy and terror—a fight that required patience and endurance—believers bore a great responsibility.

His experience and guiding words are of great value today. We should carefully consider every statement made by this worthy individual, who spent his life trying to build a world of love and wisdom, based on the morality of the Qur'an.

Only by Love, Bediuzzaman Always Said, Could Terrorism be Overcome

The most noteworthy aspect of his statements is the importance he attaches to human love and life, inspired by the morality of the Qur'an. As he once said,

The true lesson from the Qur'an is this: If there are ten monsters and one innocent person in a house... is it permissible to burn that house... even though the morality of the Qur'an forbids such a thing... [to] ruin ten innocent people for the sake of one monster? Would not burning that house down be the greatest possible cruelty and betrayal? ... the morality of the Qur'an forbids the endangering of the lives or the harming of the 90 percent of innocent people for the sake of the ten percent of monsters who threaten security. We must be aware that we are bound by religion to preserve security and abide by that lesson from the Qur'an...

In these words, Bediuzzaman revealed the great importance of human life, that every possible sacrifice should be made to save the life of just one individual, that doing the opposite means committing great cruelty. Muslims should work to establish peace and security. Because that responsibility is a command from God, believers use all means at their disposal to help spread the morality of religion. Where terror and anarchy become terrible scourges, an environment in which Islamic morality is lived resembles heaven. Bediuzzaman said as much in a number of statements:

If a Muslim departs from the Muslim community, he turns from the religion and becomes an anarchist and has a poisonous effect on society. Because anarchy recognizes no rights, and turns the proper nature of mankind into the morality of savage animals.

A true Muslim, a sincere believer, never supports anarchy and wickedness... the religion fiercely condemns strife and anarchy. Because anarchy recognizes no rights, and turns the proper nature of mankind and the works of civilization into the morality of savage animals.

He made it clear that conveying the morality of religion would open up a great dialogue, even in the hearts of the intolerant, the uncompromising and aggressive. The love of God would keep people from all forms of tyranny. He stressed that every Muslim's duty is to relate the beauties of religion and the truths of the Qur'an, so as to bring that love into peoples' hearts. Bediuzzaman once stressed that his *Risale-i Nur* ("Letters of Light", a collection of all his writings) fulfilled that function:

Yes, the *Risale-i Nur* and faith based on truth and proof and the truths of the Qur'an, explains and elucidates matters in a manner appropriate to the times and in such a way that the community can accept them, has led to millions of people examining faith and belief, awoken Islamic love and dialogue in their souls, and built a spiritual wall against atheism and immorality, the signs of anarchy. Yes, the union of the sacred ideal and purpose form an invincible force, an impassable wall, a spiritual power in peoples' souls, hearts and minds.

At every opportunity, Bediuzzaman reminded people that in the fight against terror and anarchy, the most important weapon was the spread of religious morality. As he commented,

Towns are also households for their inhabitants. If belief in the hereafter does not govern the members of that large family, vices like malice, self-interest, false pretences, selfishness, artificiality, hypocrisy, bribery, and deception will dominate—displacing sincerity, cordiality, virtue, zeal, self-sacrifice, seeking God's pleasure and the reward of the hereafter, which are the bases of good conduct and morality. Anarchy and savagery will govern under the superficial order and humanity, poisoning the life of the town. Children will become troublemakers, the youth will take to drink, the strong will embark on oppression, and the elderly start to weep.

In societies that turn their back on religion, deceit, oppression, anarchy, violence and terror emerge. Virtues like cooperation, sacrifice and honesty go by the board. People think only of their own self-interests, desiring only their own comforts and working only for themselves. Yet when a society lives by religion, then cooperation, friendship and brotherhood prevail. Later in this same statement, Bediuzzaman gives examples of the advantages that religious morality can bring to family and social life:

By analogy, the country is also a household, and the fatherland, the home of the national family. If belief in the hereafter rules, then true respect, earnest compassion, disinterested love, mutual assistance, honest service and social relations, unhypocritical charity, virtue, modest greatness, and excellence will all start to develop. It says to the children, "Give up messing around; there is Paradise to be won!" and teaches them self-control through instruction in the Qur'an. It says to the youth, "There is Hell-fire; give up your drunkenness!" and brings them to their senses.

To the oppressor, it says, "There is severe torment; you will receive a blow!" and makes them bow to justice. To the elderly it says, "Awaiting you in the hereafter is everlasting happiness, far greater than all the happiness you have lost here, and immortal youth; try to win them!" It turns their tears into laughter. It shows its favorable effects in every group, particular and universal, and illuminates them. Sociologists and moralists, who are concerned with the social life of mankind, should take special note. If the rest of the thousands of benefits and advantages of belief in the hereafter are compared with the five or six we have alluded to, it will be understood that only belief is the means of happiness in this world and the next, and in the lives of both.

As these examples suggest, once people live by religious morality, it's easy to advise them, forbid them to commit evil, and turn them to the true path. Bediuzzaman often said that terror and anarchy could be destroyed only if people live by the morality of the Qur'an—commanding love, tolerance, peace, forgiveness, affection and compassion; standing against all forms of evil and wickedness. These words of his call on Muslims to embrace the truths of the Qur'an, again emphasizing that only prevailing religion can end anarchy in the world:

The only solution to the ruin and destruction caused by anarchy, which menaces and has wreaked terrible calamities on mankind, is the eternal and timeless truths of a sacred and divine religion.

Bediuzzaman frequently stressed that the morality of the Qur'an, and its interpretation in the *Risale-i Nur* made a great contribution in eliminating terror and anarchy, and would continue to do so in future. Every effort to explain Qur'anic morality and invite people to the path of true Islam helps fulfill that duty and plays an important role in the struggle against terrorism. Bediuzzaman drew attention to the importance of that: "The *Risale-i Nur* definitely has no connection with politics. But since it has smashed absolute disbelief, it destroys and repulses anarchy, which underlies absolute disbelief, and absolute despotism, which overlies it."

In another statement, he sets out some essentials to get rid of anarchy: "Respect, compassion, refraining from sin, security, the giving up of lawlessness and being obedient to authority." Later in the same statement, he describes how the *Risale-i Nur* fulfills the duties they have taken on:

When the Risale-i Nur looks to the life of society, it establishes and strengthens these five principles in a powerful and sacred fashion and preserves the cornerstone of public order... Over the last twenty years, the "Risale-i Nur" has made one hundred thousand people into harmless, beneficial members of this nation and country.

In his works, Bediuzzaman Said Nursi offers a detailed description of the form that struggle against terror, atheism, anarchy and the problems of the Islamic World should take: "Our enemies are ignorance, poverty and inner conflict. We shall fight these three foes with the weapons of wisdom, skill and unanimity of purpose." These vital words draw attention to three grave dangers: ignorance, poverty and conflict.

It's essential to warn the public against the first of these, ignorance. In today's Islamic world, the great majority has some a knowledge of religion and belief in God. Yet seldom does that same majority deeply examine religion and spiritual values. Because their knowledge is generally superficial and picked up secondhand, it's impossible for them to translate religion's proper morality to be, in its true sense, into life. It's essential, therefore, to do away with that lack of knowledge.

The poverty of the Muslim world is the second danger Bediuzzaman cites. The poverty prevents people from having a proper education and thus feeds ignorance. It also makes Muslims feel weak and thus feeds both frustration and radicalization. The third danger is the inner conflict over so many issues in the Muslim world. When parties can reach no agreement on basic values, their debate over ideas usually degenerates into hostilities, conflicts and even civil wars. Tolerance and mutual respect are not only inter-civilizational but also intra-civilizational necessities.

But the truth is, a constructive attitude can resolve these problems and conflicts. The paths of reason and conscience are one and the same. For that reason, truth needs to be stated openly, in the face of the chaos and strife that conflict brings with it. Against these three dangers, Bediuzzaman also stressed the measures to be taken.

The first of these, art, occupies an important place and means several things: First, that people should be taught to understand beauty and aesthetics. These blessings from God will turn human souls away from brute force. Knowing that art is a blessing from God, and giving thanks for it, increases peoples' spiritual depth. For that reason, it's most important to show the full beauty of the God's art all around us. Artists should act in that knowledge, and the devout need to turn to art with that same awareness. Every explanation of the morality of religion must bear artistic values in mind. It's highly important to demonstrate the devout's superior artistic understanding in all written works, with colored pictures, simple and clear language, and high-quality printing.

Wisdom embodied in the written word is equally a form of art. The words employed, the examples used, and the striking, effective means of expression all make a very important impressions on the reader. When it comes to explaining the beauties of religion, simple means of expression—as opposed to unclear, confusing and abstruse methods—make it much easier to grasp the truth and understand it.

The "wisdom" Bediuzzaman refers to means the possession of knowledge. Muslims need to be the masters of knowledge in the age in which they live. That, of cource includes science and social sciences. Because a Muslim is an earthly representative of the religion that God has chosen for Man, he needs to be well versed in the sciences, cultures, thought and technology of his time, as well as being able to employ that knowledge efficiently.

The final method Bediuzzaman recommends, unanimity of purpose, needs to be brought about by every Muslim who wants to achieve security and well being and to see the Islamic world flourish again. History shows that unification and harmony in the Islamic world have always brought success. The golden age of the Prophet (may god bless him and grant him peace) and the first caliphs, the Abbasid Empire, the empire of Saladin, or the Ottoman Empire; all these examples indicate that unification among the Muslims themselves created powerful and victorious, yet fair and tolerant states. In times of turmoil, both Muslims and non-Muslims suffered.

Thus, a revival of the Islamic world is due to the unification of Muslims all around the globe, transcending ethnic, sectarian or social disputes. Once this is achieved, the formation of a political unity — in terms of an Islamic Union — will also be at hand. Such a Union will resolve the disputes both among the Muslims themselves and among the Muslims and non-Muslims; heal the radical elements in the Islamic world by means of education and persuasion; and establish good relations between the Islamic civilization and other civilizations.

THE EVOLUTION MISCONCEPTION

Every detail in this universe points to a superior creation. By contrast, materialism, which seeks to deny the fact of creation in the universe, is nothing but an unscientific fallacy.

Once materialism is invalidated, all other theories based on this philosophy are rendered baseless. Foremost of them is Darwinism, that is, the theory of evolution. This theory, which argues that life originated from inanimate matter through coincidences, has been demolished with the recognition that Allah created the universe. American astrophysicist Hugh Ross explains this as follows:

Atheism, Darwinism, and virtually all the "isms" emanating from the eighteenth to the twentieth century philosophies are built upon the assumption, the incorrect assumption, that the universe is infinite. The singularity has brought us face to face with the cause – or causer – beyond/behind/before the universe and all that it contains, including life itself.64

It is Allah Who created the universe and who designed it down to its smallest detail. Therefore, it is impossible for the theory of evolution, which holds that living things are but products of chance, to be true.

Unsurprisingly, when we look at the theory of evolution, we see that this theory is denounced by scientific findings. The design in life is extremely complex and striking. In the inanimate world, for instance, we can explore how sensitive are the balances which atoms rest upon, and further, in the animate world, we can observe in what complex designs these atoms were brought together, and how extraordinary are the mechanisms and structures such as proteins, enzymes, and cells, which are manufactured with them. This extraordinary design in life invalidated Darwinism at the end of the 20th century.

We have dealt with this subject in great detail in some of our other studies, and shall continue to do so. However, we think that, considering its importance, it will be helpful to make a short summary here as well.

Darwin's theory was not based on any concrete scientific finding; as he also accepted, it was just an "assumption." Moreover, as Darwin confessed in the long chapter of his book titled "Difficulties of the Theory," the theory was failing in the face of many critical questions.

Darwin invested all his hopes in new scientific discoveries, which he expected to solve the "Difficulties of the Theory." However, contrary to his expectations, scientific findings expanded the dimensions of these difficulties.

The defeat of Darwinism against science can be reviewed under three basic topics:

(1) The theory can by no means explain how life originated on the earth.

(2) There is no scientific finding showing that the "evolutionary mechanisms" proposed by the theory have any power to evolve at all.

(3) The fossil record proves completely the contrary of the suggestions of the theory of evolution.

In this section, we will examine these three basic points in general outlines:

The Origin of Life

The theory of evolution posits that all living species evolved from a single living cell that emerged on the primitive earth 3.8 billion years ago. How a single cell could generate millions of complex living species and, if such an evolution really occurred, why traces of it cannot be observed in the fossil record are some of the questions the theory cannot answer. However, first and foremost, of the first step of the alleged evolutionary process it has to be inquired: How did this "first cell" originate?

Since the theory of evolution denies creation and does not accept any kind of supernatural intervention, it maintains that the "first cell" originated coincidentally within the laws of nature, without any design, plan, or arrangement. According to the theory, inanimate matter must have produced a living cell as a result of coincidences. This, however, is a claim inconsistent with even the most unassailable rules of biology.

"Life Comes from Life"

In his book, Darwin never referred to the origin of life. The primitive understanding of science in his time rested on the assumption that living beings had a very simple structure. Since medieval times, spontaneous generation, the theory asserting that non-living materials came together to form living organisms, had been widely accepted. It was commonly believed that insects came into being from food leftovers, and mice from wheat. Interesting experiments were conducted to prove this theory. Some wheat was placed on a dirty piece of cloth, and it was believed that mice would originate from it after a while.

Similarly, worms' developing in meat was assumed to be evidence of spontaneous generation. However, only some time later was it understood that worms did not appear on meat spontaneously, but were carried there by flies in the form of larvae, invisible to the naked eye.

Even in the period when Darwin wrote *The Origin of Species*, the belief that bacteria could come into existence from non-living matter was widely accepted in the world of science.

However, five years after the publication of Darwin's book, Louis Pasteur announced his results after long studies and experiments, which disproved spontaneous generation, a cornerstone of Darwin's theory. In his triumphal lecture at the Sorbonne in 1864,

Pasteur said, *"Never will the doctrine of spontaneous generation recover from the mortal blow struck by this simple experiment."*

Advocates of the theory of evolution resisted the findings of Pasteur for a long time. However, as the development of science unraveled the complex structure of the cell of a living being, the idea that life could come into being coincidentally faced an even greater impasse.

Inconclusive Efforts in the Twentieth Century

The first evolutionist who took up the subject of the origin of life in the twentieth century was the renowned Russian biologist Alexander Oparin. With various theses he advanced in the 1930's, he tried to prove that the cell of a living being could originate by coincidence. These studies, however, were doomed to failure, and Oparin had to make the following confession: "Unfortunately, however, the problem of the origin of the cell is perhaps the most obscure point in the whole study of the evolution of organisms."

Evolutionist followers of Oparin tried to carry out experiments to solve the problem of the origin of life. The best known of these experiments was carried out by American chemist Stanley Miller in 1953. Combining the gases he alleged to have existed in the primordial earth's atmosphere in an experiment set-up, and adding energy to the mixture, Miller synthesized several organic molecules (amino acids) present in the structure of proteins.

Barely a few years had passed before it was revealed that this experiment, which was then presented as an important step in the name of evolution, was invalid, the atmosphere used in the experiment having been very different from real earth conditions.

After a long silence, Miller confessed that the atmosphere medium he used was unrealistic.

All the evolutionist efforts put forth throughout the twentieth century to explain the origin of life ended with failure. The geochemist Jeffrey Bada from San Diego Scripps Institute accepts this fact in an article published in *Earth* Magazine in 1998:

Today as we leave the twentieth century, we still face the biggest unsolved problem that we had when we entered the twentieth century: How did life originate on Earth?

The Complex Structure of Life

The primary reason why the theory of evolution ended up in such a big impasse about the origin of life is that even the living organisms deemed the simplest have incredibly complex structures. The cell of a living being is more complex than all of the technological products produced by man. Today, even in the most developed laboratories of the world, a living cell cannot be produced by bringing organic chemicals together.

The conditions required for the formation of a cell are too great in quantity to be explained away by coincidences. The probability of proteins, the building blocks of cell, being synthesized coincidentally, is 1 in 10950 for an average protein made up of 500 amino acids. In mathematics, a probability smaller than 1 over 1050 is practically considered to be impossible.

The DNA molecule, which is located in the nucleus of the cell and which stores genetic information, is an incredible databank. It is calculated that if the information coded in DNA were written down, this would make a giant library consisting of 900 volumes of encyclopaedias of 500 pages each.

A very interesting dilemma emerges at this point: the DNA can only replicate with the help of some specialized proteins (enzymes). However, the synthesis of these enzymes can only be realized by the information coded in DNA. As they both depend on each other, they have to exist at the same time for replication. This brings the scenario that life originated by itself to a deadlock. Prof. Leslie Orgel, an evolutionist of repute from the University of San Diego, California, confesses this fact in the September 1994 issue of the *Scientific American* magazine:

It is extremely improbable that proteins and nucleic acids, both of which are structurally complex, arose spontaneously in the same place at the same time. Yet it also seems impossible to have one without the other. And so, at first glance, one might have to conclude that life could never, in fact, have originated by chemical means.

No doubt, if it is impossible for life to have originated from natural causes, then it has to be accepted that life was "created" in a supernatural way. This fact explicitly invalidates the theory of evolution, whose main purpose is to deny creation.

The Tale of Human Evolution

The subject most often brought up by the advocates of the theory of evolution is the subject of the origin of man. The Darwinist claim holds that the modern men of today evolved from some kind of ape-like creatures. During this alleged evolutionary process, which is supposed to have started 4-5 million years ago, it is claimed that there existed some "transitional forms" between modern man and his ancestors. According to this completely imaginary scenario, four basic "categories" are listed:

1. Australopithecus
2. Homo habilis
3. Homo erectus
4. Homo sapiens

Evolutionists call the so-called first ape-like ancestors of men *"Australopithecus"* which means "South African ape." These living beings are actually nothing but an old ape species that has become extinct. Extensive research done on various Australopithecus specimens by two world famous anatomists from England and the USA, namely, Lord Solly Zuckerman and Prof. Charles Oxnard, has shown that these belonged to an ordinary ape species that became extinct and bore no resemblance to humans.

Evolutionists classify the next stage of human evolution as "homo," that is "man." According to the evolutionist claim, the living beings in the Homo series are more developed than Australopithecus. Evolutionists devise a fanciful evolution scheme by arranging different fossils of these creatures in a particular order.

This scheme is imaginary because it has never been proved that there is an evolutionary relation between these different classes. Ernst Mayr, one of the most important proponents of the theory of evolution in the twentieth century, contends in his book *One Long Argument that "particularly historical [puzzles] such as the origin of life or of Homo sapiens, are extremely difficult and may even resist a final, satisfying explanation."*

By outlining the link chain as "*Australopithecus* > *Homo habilis* > *Homo erectus* > *Homo sapiens*," evolutionists imply that each of these species is one another's ancestor. However, recent findings of paleoanthropologists have revealed that Australopithecus, Homo habilis and Homo erectus lived at different parts of the world at the same time.

Moreover, a certain segment of humans classified as Homo erectus have lived up until very modern times. *Homo sapiens neandarthalensis and Homo sapiens sapiens* (modern man) co-existed in the same region.

This situation apparently indicates the invalidity of the claim that they are ancestors of one another. A paleontologist from Harvard University, Stephen Jay Gould, explains this deadlock of the theory of evolution although he is an evolutionist himself:

What has become of our ladder if there are three coexisting lineages of hominids (A. africanus, the robust australopithecines, and H. habilis), none clearly derived from another? Moreover, none of the three display any evolutionary trends during their tenure on earth.

Put briefly, the scenario of human evolution, which is sought to be upheld with the help of various drawings of some "half ape, half human" creatures appearing in the media and course books, that is, frankly, by means of propaganda, is nothing but a tale with no scientific ground.

Lord Solly Zuckerman, one of the most famous and respected scientists in the U.K., who carried out research on this subject for years, and particularly studied Australopithecus fossils for 15 years, finally concluded, despite being an evolutionist himself, that there is, in fact, no such family tree branching out from ape-like creatures to man.

Zuckerman also made an interesting "spectrum of science." He formed a spectrum of sciences ranging from those he considered scientific to those he considered unscientific. According to Zuckerman's spectrum, the most "scientific" – that is, depending on concrete data – fields of science are chemistry and physics. After them come the biological sciences and then the social sciences. At the far end of the spectrum, which is the part considered to be most "unscientific," are "extra-sensory perception" – concepts such as telepathy and sixth sense–and finally "human evolution." Zuckerman explains his reasoning:

> We then move right off the register of objective truth into those fields of presumed biological science, like extrasensory perception or the interpretation of man's fossil history, where to the faithful [evolutionist] anything is possible - and where the ardent believer [in evolution] is sometimes able to believe several contradictory things at the same time.

The tale of human evolution boils down to nothing but the prejudiced interpretations of some fossils unearthed by certain people, who blindly adhere to their theory.

Those who believe in the theory of evolution think that a few atoms and molecules thrown into a huge vat could produce thinking, reasoning professors, university students, scientists such as Einstein and Galileo, artists such as Humphrey Bogart, Frank Sinatra and Pavarotti, as well as antelopes, lemon trees and carnations. Moreover, the scientists and professors who believe in this nonsense are educated people. That is why it is quite justifiable to speak of the theory of evolution as "the most potent spell in history." Never before has any other belief or idea so taken away peoples' powers of reason, refused to allow them to think intelligently and logically and hidden the truth from them as if they had been blindfolded. This is an even worse and unbelievable blindness than the Egyptians worshipping the Sun God Ra, totem worship in some parts of Africa, the people of Saba worshipping the Sun, the tribe of the Prophet Abraham worshipping idols they had made with their own hands or the people of the Prophet Moses worshipping the Golden Calf.

In fact, this situation is a lack of reason Allah pointed to in the Qur'an. He reveals in many verses that some peoples' minds will be closed and that they will be powerless to see the truth. Some of these verses are as follows:

As for those who disbelieve, it makes no difference to them whether you warn them or do not warn them, they will not believe. God has sealed up their hearts and hearing and over their eyes is a blindfold. They will have a terrible punishment. (Qur'an, 2: 6-7)

... They have hearts they do not understand with. They have eyes they do not see with. They have ears they do not hear with. Such people are like cattle. No, they are even further astray! They are the unaware. (Qur'an, 7: 179)

Even if We opened up to them a door into heaven, and they spent the day ascending through it, they would only say, "Our eyesight is befuddled! Or rather we have been put under a spell!" (Qur'an, 15: 14-15)

Words cannot express just how astonishing it is that this spell should hold such a wide community in thrall, keep people from the truth, and not be broken for 150 years. It is understandable that one or a few people might believe in impossible scenarios and claims full of stupidity and illogicality. However, "magic" is the only possible explanation for people from all over the world believing that unconscious and lifeless atoms suddenly decided to come together and form a universe that functions with a flawless system of organization, discipline, reason and consciousness, the planet Earth with all its features so perfectly suited to life, and living things full of countless complex systems.

In fact, Allah reveals in the Qur'an in the incident of the Prophet Moses and Pharaoh that some people who support atheistic philosophies actually influence others by magic. When Pharaoh was told about the true religion, he told the Prophet Moses to meet with his own magicians. When the Prophet Moses did so, he told them to demonstrate their abilities first. The verses continue:

He said, "You throw." And when they threw, they cast a spell on the people's eyes and caused them to feel great fear of them. They produced an extremely powerful magic. (Qur'an, 7: 116)

As we have seen, Pharaoh's magicians were able to deceive everyone, apart from the Prophet Moses and those who believed in him. However, the evidence put forward by the Prophet Moses broke that spell, or "swallowed up what they had forged" as the verse puts it. We revealed to Moses, "Throw down your staff." And it immediately swallowed up what they had forged. So the Truth took place and what they did was shown to be false. (Qur'an, 7: 117-119)

As we can see from that verse, when it was realized that what these people who had first cast a spell over others had done was just an illusion, they lost all credibility. In the present day too, unless those who under the influence of a similar spell believe in these ridiculous claims under their scientific disguise and spend their lives defending them abandon them, they too will be humiliated when the full truth emerges and the spell is broken. In fact, Malcolm Muggeridge, an atheist philosopher and supporter of evolution admitted he was worried by just that prospect:

I myself am convinced that the theory of evolution, especially the extent to which it's been applied, will be one of the great jokes in the history books in the future. Posterity will marvel that so very flimsy and dubious an hypothesis could be accepted with the incredible credulity that it has.

That future is not far off: On the contrary, people will soon see that "chance" is not a god, and will look back on the theory of evolution as the worst deceit and the most terrible spell in the world. That spell is already rapidly beginning to be lifted from the shoulders of people all over the world. Many people who see the true face of the theory of evolution are wondering with amazement how it was that they were ever taken in by it.

CONCLUSION

Unless necessary measures are taken, unless deep-rooted solutions are brought in, the 21st century will continue to be a time of terror and violence, just as the 20th was before it. The ideological fight against terrorism, therefore, must begin started with great and urgency, to include very great numbers of people. This fight will be fought on the level of ideas—between people who believe in the true religious morality, who are loving, forgiving, compassionate and in full possession of their conscience; and those who draw their strength from ignorance, arrogance and violence.

In one holy verse (Surah Hud: 116), our Lord asks, "Would there had been more people with a vestige of good among the generations of those who came before you, who forbade corruption in the earth…" Believers should possess the virtue that God describes in that verse. While terrorists hope to achieve their aims by violence, believers should know that true success can be achieved only by clinging tightly to the religion of God, and acting accordingly. If Jews, Christians, and Muslims join together in that struggle, in a spirit of respect for all beliefs and ideas and, by the will of God, they will enjoy definitive success.

A terrorist may learn by heart all the fundamental sources behind his beliefs. Yet such a person is still unaware of the one evident truth that will bring him happiness and inspiration, both in this world and the next. That's because all his life, he's been educated in radical ideologies, in the context of the idea that life is a battleground in which only the strong survive, where violence and oppression are the only means of survival. Anyone resorting to terrorism, no matter what his religion, race, or nation, must understand that he's acting under the influence of a misleading philosophy, that in the final analysis stems from materialist and Darwinist thinking, though it sometimes poses as a religious idea.

Those who resort to secular terrorism are unaware that God and the hereafter really do exist; that this world is merely a place of trial; and that only those who believe and carry out their religious obligations devoutly will be saved. Those who resort to allegedly "religious" terrorism, are far from understanding God's commandments against mischief and the value of human life, such as that "... If someone kills another person—unless it is in retaliation for someone else or for causing corruption in the earth—it is as if he had murdered all mankind. And if anyone gives life to another person, it is as if he had given life to all mankind." (Qur'an, 5: 32)

At this point, a great responsibility falls on all true believers, no matter what their religion. Jews must not ignore Old Testament statements calling mankind to peace and tolerance, and they must call on all other Jews to oppose terrorism — including the state terrorism employed by Israel in the occupied territories. So should Christians call on all other Christians, taking as their guide the morality most pleasing to God. They should also stress that "the war on terror" should not turn into violent revenge, and a peaceful "counter-terrorism" should be preferred, since the Christian faith proclaims that "blessed are the peacemakers". (Matthew, 5: 9) One should not forget that terrorism stems from wrong ideas and the basic struggle against terrorism should be on the level of ideas. Believers must explain that these ideas are wrong both in terms of their theory and practice. No idea can prevail by means of violence, oppression and cruelty; and despotism can never triumph.

Terrorist ideology is built on sand. Its foundations can easily be swept away by mobilizing a proper education campaign. Sincere believers in all parts of the world can help end the ignorance that breeds terrorism by searching for solutions, writing books and articles, promoting educational activities and disseminating their own cultural heritage.

8

Capitalism and Terrorism

Capital, as Karl Marx observed, came into the world "dripping from head to toe, from every pore, with blood and dirt" (Capital, Volume 1, Chapter 31). Yet Marxists recognize that the overthrow of feudalism represented an enormous leap forward for humanity: capitalism vastly accelerated the development of science and technology, increased labor productivity exponentially and opened up vast new possibilities for the expression of human individuality. That these contributions were limited and deformed by the straitjacket of private property should not blind us to capitalism's immensely progressive character in relation to all previous class societies.

The French Revolution of 1789, the decisive event that established the ascendancy of the bourgeoisie over the feudal aristocracy, pitted a dynamic new form of social organization against a decrepit old one. In place of feudal absolutism, the rising capitalist class established what Marx termed the "dictatorship of the bourgeoisie." The new social order was consolidated through the infamous Reign of Terror associated with Maximilien Robespierre. Contemporary bourgeois academics, who tend to view the Jacobin "Terror" as an unfortunate excess, generally prefer to ignore the role that violence played in establishing capitalist supremacy. For them, the development of human civilization is a gradual, evolutionary process that would be entirely peaceful if not for the activities of subversives, fanatics and other "evil-doers." But the Terror of the French Revolution, like all important events, must be seen in its historical context, as Mark Twain observed in A Connecticut Yankee in King Arthur's Court:

"There were two 'Reigns of Terror,' if we would but remember it and consider it; the one wrought murder in hot passion, the other in heartless cold blood; the one lasted mere months, the other had lasted a thousand years; the one inflicted death upon ten thousand persons, the other upon a hundred millions; but our shudders are all for the 'horrors' of the minor Terror, the momentary Terror, so to speak; whereas, what is the horror of swift death by the ax compared with lifelong death from hunger, cold, insult, cruelty, and heartbreak?"

The cumulative violence of the old order was infinitely greater than that of Robespierre and his associates. The Jacobin Terror was historically justified because it helped secure a new, progressive social order. Likewise, for ordinary Russians the violence of the "Red Terror" employed by the Bolsheviks to defend the October Revolution against the Whites and their imperialist backers, was nothing compared to the horrors of life under the Czarist autocracy. Leon Trotsky, who, after Lenin, was the central leader of the Bolshevik Revolution, wrote at the time:

"The State terror of a revolutionary class can be condemned 'morally' only by a man who, as a principle, rejects (in words) every form of violence whatsoever—consequently, every war and every rising. For this one has to be merely and simply a hypocritical Quaker." — Terrorism & Communism

Revolutionaries judge everything, including the use of "violence," not on the basis of abstract moral categories, but rather by its consequences for social development. By this criterion, the terrorist attacks that destroyed the World Trade Center in New York on 11 September 2001 were not progressive; they were profoundly reactionary acts. Most of those killed were ordinary working people. We shed no tears for the military cadres in the Pentagon who died that day, but the mass murder of three thousand innocent civilians in the twin towers and aboard the four commercial airliners was a heinous, anti-working class crime. Nine days after the attacks, in an address to a joint session of Congress, George W. Bush took advantage of Americans' fear and sense of vulnerability to launch his cynical "war on terror." The Commander-in-Chief of the military apparatus that deliberately exterminated hundreds of thousands of civilians in Hiroshima and Nagasaki to "shock and awe" the Japanese into submission and intimidate the Soviets, proposed to launch a war—on behalf of the entire "civilized world"—against "terrorism." It was reminiscent of Ariel Sharon—the butcher of Sabra and Shatila—talking about eradicating "terrorist nests" in Palestinian communities in Gaza.

The U.S. "war on terror" is intended to terrorize other countries, in the first instance the so-called rogue states, into submitting to the dictates of American imperialism. Peter Ustinov once aptly observed that "terrorists" are people who have bombs but no air force to deliver them. Those officially designated "terrorists" tend to be the retailers—the wholesalers are the U.S. and other major imperialist powers (supported, in their own duplicitous, "peace-loving" ways, by weaker imperialists like Denmark and Canada).

Origins of Al Qaeda

The connection between wholesalers and retailers in the terror business is perfectly illustrated by Al Qaeda. We should not forget how Osama bin Laden and other leading cadres of Al Qaeda got their start—they were trained and equipped by the CIA to fight a jihad against the Soviets in Afghanistan in the 1980s. (This is the same period in which the United States and Britain were providing Saddam Hussein with his infamous "weapons of mass destruction" to use during his war with Iran).

In 1978, when the pro-Soviet People's Democratic Party of Afghanistan (PDPA) took power in Kabul, it immediately began distributing land to the peasants, reduced debt payments for the poor, and lowered the bride price. The PDPA also encouraged girls to go to school. The semi-feudal landowners, moneylenders and reactionary Muslim clerics considered this a threat to their traditional way of life and, aided by the CIA, began to organize an insurgency. In December 1979 the Soviet Union countered by sending its army into Afghanistan to back the left-nationalist government.

Zbigniew Brzezinski, Jimmy Carter's national security adviser at the time, later admitted that the U.S. had been actively supporting resistance by the clerics and landholders for months before the Soviets' intervention:

"[I]t was July 3, 1979 that President Carter signed the first directive for secret aid to the opponents of the pro-Soviet regime in Kabul. And that very day, I wrote a note to the president in which I explained to him that in my opinion this aid was going to induce a Soviet military intervention....

"That secret operation was an excellent idea. It had the effect of drawing the Russians into the Afghan trap…" — Le Nouvel Observateur, Paris, 15-21 January 1998

The U.S. spent billions of dollars training and equipping 100,000 radical Islamic mujahedin whose leaders were among those who, in the 1970s, had been throwing acid in the faces of unveiled women at Kabul University. Ronald Reagan praised the Afghan reactionaries as "freedom fighters" and called them the "moral equivalent" of America's founding fathers.

Marxists had a side in Afghanistan. We called for the military victory of the Soviet Army and the PDPA over the mujahedin, and would have welcomed the extension of the Soviet collectivized property system to Afghanistan. But in 1989, in a prelude to the August 1991 destruction of the Soviet degenerated workers' state, the Kremlin bureaucracy gave up and pulled out of Afghanistan.

After the Soviet retreat, the U.S. lost interest and a bloody war erupted among competing mujahedin factions that was eventually won by the Pakistani-backed Taliban in 1996. The United States welcomed the victory of the Taliban as a stabilizing factor in a region that, after the collapse of the Soviet Union, had assumed renewed importance due to the discovery of huge oil and natural gas deposits in the lands bordering the Caspian Sea. (The U.S. was particularly interested in the possibility of building a pipeline from Turkmenistan, through Afghanistan to Pakistan. This route would bypass both Iran, a country designated by the U.S. as part of the "axis of evil," and Russia, which opposes American expansion in the region.) The fact that the Taliban was a brutally repressive, misogynist theocracy was a matter of complete indifference to the apostles of liberty and freedom—Washington's only problem with the new Afghan government was that it was not sufficiently pliable. So plans were being laid long before 9/11 for installing a friendlier regime in Kabul. The destruction of the World Trade Center in New York in September 2001 provided a perfect pretext for removing the Taliban and establishing a string of military bases across formerly Soviet Central Asia—all in the name of fighting "terror." The real reason was to undercut Russian and Chinese influence and insert the American military into the region.

The Russians have been waging a reactionary war for more than a decade to crush the attempt by the Chechen people to win their independence. The U.S. has been happy to see the Russian military bogged down in a protracted guerrilla conflict in Chechnya and has been reluctant to include the Chechens as targets in the global "war on terror." Even after the horrific massacre of Russian school children in Beslan on 1 September [2004], the corporate media in the U.S. refused to endorse the Kremlin's brutal campaign against the Chechen resistance. The New York Times wrote that "despair and anger at Russians" drove Chechens to suicide attacks and observed:

"Mr. Putin is also responsible for Russia's stubborn refusal to deal with the political dimensions of Chechen separatism, as if punishing military offensives, puppet governments and fraudulent elections could somehow make the problem go away." — New York Times, 14 September 2004

Yet, like the rest of the American media, the Times "stubbornly refuses" to take a similarly broadminded approach to the question of why so many Iraqis are prepared to sacrifice their lives to deliver blows to American forces occupying their land. The transparently stupid assertions by President Bush that "the terrorists" hate America because of its freedom and democracy explain nothing. A retired U.S. Air Force lieutenant-colonel, Robert Bowman, offered a far more plausible explanation when he noted that the United States is:

"...the target of terrorists because, in much of the world, our government stands for dictatorship, bondage and human exploitation. We are the target of terrorists because we are hated. And we are hated because our government has done hateful things." — National Catholic Reporter, 2 October 1998

'Hateful Things'

The United States and every other imperialist power does violent and "hateful things" to the oppressed masses of the world because a social system that condemns half the world's population to life on less than $2 a day for the benefit of a tiny handful of billionaires can only be maintained by constant, massive brutality.

Within two months of the U.S.-led invasion of Afghanistan in 2001, more civilians were killed than perished in New York on 11 September. Tens of thousands of Iraqis have been killed by the "coalition of the willing" since March 2003 when the U.S. blitzkrieg was launched with an aerial bombardment designed to "shock and awe," i.e., terrorize, the population. Some 200,000 Iraqis were killed by the imperialists in the 1991 Gulf War. And more than a million Iraqis, many of them children, died during the 1990s as a result of the sanctions imposed by the United Nations on behalf of the U.S.-led imperialist coalition.

Last spring when four American mercenaries were killed in Falluja, the U.S. responded by attacking the city and killing 600 civilians. During the past few weeks U.S. aircraft have been relentlessly bombing residential neighborhoods in Falluja, as a prelude to the long-awaited assault. There is barely a pretense of winning hearts and minds—the clear intent is to terrify the population into submission. But it is not working. As one young Iraqi told the New

York Times (14 September 2004): "When the Americans fire back, they don't hit the people who are attacking them, only the civilians. This is why Iraqis hate the Americans so much. This is why we love the mujahedeen." The horrors of imperialist terrorism have been highlighted by recent reports of torture, rape and murder of prisoners in Baghdad's Abu Ghraib prison and other facilities. In waging its "war on terror" the Bush administration decided to suspend the Geneva Convention for any prisoners it chose to designate as "unlawful combatants," including those held at Guantanamo Bay, Cuba, so that they could be routinely subjected to what the New York Times decorously refers to as "brutal interrogation techniques," i.e., torture. At a U.S. Senate hearing last month General Paul Kern revealed that as many as 100 people detained by the American military in Iraq have not been officially recorded, to avoid the risk of embarrassing investigations into their torture or execution (Washington Post, 10 September 2004).

Imperialist rule has always been characterized by brutal repression. The French and American imperialists butchered two million Vietnamese workers and peasants in a long, losing counterrevolutionary war. At least half a million people were slaughtered in 1965 in a CIA-supported coup in Indonesia. Tens of thousands were killed in Chile under Augusto Pinochet, whose military dictatorship was backed by the U.S. During the 1980s, the CIA's "contra" terrorists in Nicaragua murdered thousands of people, many of them schoolteachers and healthcare workers, in an attempt to undermine the left-nationalist Sandinista regime. Of course, none of this qualifies as "terrorism" in the capitalist media.

A few months ago the Bush administration ordered three anti-communist Cubans with long-standing ties to the CIA to be admitted to the U.S. They had been convicted in Panama of planning to detonate 33 pounds of explosives to kill Fidel Castro, along with dozens of university students, when he visited in 2000. These terrorists are welcome in the United States.

In fact the U.S. "war on terror" provides employment for many terrorists. A good example is Ayad Allawi, the long-time CIA asset appointed by the U.S. as Iraqi "prime minister" last June, who Bush has praised as a "strong leader" in the fight against international terrorism. In the 1970s, Allawi ran a Mukhabarat death squad for Saddam Hussein. During the 1990s, while on the CIA payroll, he helped organize several bombings in Iraq, including one that killed several schoolchildren.

Bush's chief ally in the "war on terror" is British Prime Minister Tony Blair. In the 1920s, in an attempt to put down a popular uprising in Iraq, British airplanes dropped poisonous mustard gas in civilian areas. Eighty-odd years later, Blair sought to rationalize the invasion of Iraq by feigning outrage that Saddam Hussein had used chemical weapons "against his own people." Blair also neglected to mention that Britain and the U.S. had supplied the weapons in the first place.

Canada officially sat out the Iraq war, though Canadian military planners and 31 soldiers participated alongside British and American troops. Three Canadian warships with 1,300 sailors were in the Persian Gulf helping to protect American aircraft carriers. Canada's most important contribution was sending 3,000 soldiers to Afghanistan to free up American troops for Iraq. U.S. Ambassador Paul Cellucci, commenting on the Liberal government's refusal to officially endorse the assault, pointed out: "Ironically, the Canadians indirectly provide more support for us in Iraq than most of those 46 countries that are fully supporting us" (Globe and Mail, 31 March 2003). Canada is what we call a "jackal" imperialist—it tags along behind the big predators and picks up the scraps they leave behind.

'To Impose the Will of the United States'

The pretext for the attack on Afghanistan was that it was harboring terrorists. In a desperate attempt to ward off an imminent American assault, the Taliban offered to expel bin Laden and his cronies, but the U.S. wasn't interested. Al Qaeda was never the issue. The war on Afghanistan was part of a larger strategic military plan for control of Central Asia and the Middle East. In its September 2001 Quadrennial Defense Review Report, the U.S. Department of

Defense referred to the importance of "access to key markets and strategic resources," and noted:

"U.S. forces must maintain the capability at the direction of the President to impose the will of the United States and its coalition partners on any adversaries including states or non-state entities. Such a decisive defeat could include changing the regime of an adversary state or occupation of foreign territory until U.S. strategic objectives are met."

It's no coincidence that most of the countries targeted in the supposed "war on terror" are either sitting on important oil deposits or are strategically located in relation to them. Iraq, which possesses the world's second-largest oil reserves, is right next door to Saudi Arabia which has the largest. Iran, on Iraq's other flank, also possesses important oil and gas deposits. In a speech delivered on the first anniversary of the criminal assault on Iraq, Bush claimed that the "ultimate ambition" of "the terrorists" was "to control the peoples of the Middle East" and "blackmail the rest of the world with weapons of mass terror." That's U.S. foreign policy in a nutshell.

Under the Bush Doctrine, the United States claims the right to preemptively attack any country which might possess "weapons of mass destruction" which could fall into the hands of terrorists at some point in the future. That of course was the excuse for invading Iraq. Meanwhile, the U.S. is planning nuclear first strikes on "rogue states." In 2002, according to a leaked Pentagon document, there were seven countries on that list: China, Russia, Iran, Iraq, North Korea, Syria and Libya (Daily Mirror [London], 11 March 2002). Cuba, too, is in grave danger. The only reason it is not on the to-be-nuked list is because of its proximity to Florida. The imperialists are anxious to uproot the system of collectivized property and restore capitalism in China, Cuba and North Korea. While revolutionaries advocate the overthrow of the ruling Stalinist bureaucracies through workers' political revolution, we also stand for the unconditional defense of these states against both internal counterrevolution and imperialist aggression—and we defend their right to possess nuclear arms.

The War at Home

The "war on terror" is fought on two fronts. In addition to extending U.S. military power globally, it also serves as a tool for strengthening the position of the American ruling class at home by hobbling domestic political resistance, particularly from the left and labor movement. The social basis of capitalist profit is the exploitation of living labor in the process of material production. Without the socially necessary, productive activity of the working class, capitalist society would not function. Any imperialist power that seeks to dominate the planet must first ensure the subservience of its own proletariat.

The color-coded "war on terror" uses a time-honored mechanism for getting the oppressed to identify with their oppressors: fear of an external danger. Today in North America, particularly in the U.S., there is a concerted campaign to promote a level of fear, bordering on paranoia, that has resulted in widespread acquiescence to a whole range of repressive measures that many Americans would not normally tolerate. The elaborate security checks, fink lines, data mining of credit cards, library and health records, the "orange" and "red" alerts, are all accepted because of the supposed danger of terrorist attacks.

Do you know how many people were killed by terrorist attacks in the United States in 2002? In 2003? This year? No one. And yet the avalanche of anti-democratic legislation continues, all under the guise of protecting American "freedom." Marxists have no illusions in the capitalists' commitment to democracy, and we remember that the right to free speech, freedom of assembly, the right of habeas corpus and all other democratic rights were won through hard social struggle. They must be jealously guarded against infringement by the ruling class.

At a Senate hearing in December 2001, U.S. Attorney General John Ashcroft openly attacked those who dared to complain about the assault on civil liberties: "Your tactics only aid terrorists for they erode our national unity and diminish our resolve. They give ammunition to America's enemies and pause to America's friends" (CNN.com, 7 December 2001).

The supposed "war on terror" has meant attacks on organized labor, immigrants and minorities (especially Muslims, South Asians and Arabs). Since September 2001, more than 5,000 foreign nationals have been arbitrarily detained by the U.S. Justice Department as "suspected terrorists." Of those 5,000 only one has been convicted by a jury of anything related to terrorism. And last month, a federal judge in Detroit threw out that conviction citing a lack of evidence and gross prosecutorial misconduct.

The U.S. government has drawn up secret, arbitrary "no-fly" lists of Muslims, leftists, peace activists and other suspected "dissidents" who are not allowed aboard airplanes in the U.S. This is pure political harassment. The workers' movement has a vital interest in fighting all such attacks on democratic rights because an attack on any minority is an attack on all the oppressed and exploited. That is clear if you look at the scope of the Patriot Act, which defines "domestic terrorism" as acts that "appear to be intended" to "influence the policy of a government by intimidation or coercion" or "to intimidate or coerce a civilian population." The law was deliberately formulated so that it could be interpreted as applicable to picket lines, strikes or demonstrations. Proposals are floating around the U.S. Congress to ban unions for anyone deemed essential to "homeland security" (Washington Post, 27 September 2004), a category the government would like to expand to include longshore and other unionized workers. This is a proposal for government-organized union busting, under the guise of a "war on terror." The increasingly authoritarian climate in the U.S. was evident during the Democratic and Republican national conventions this summer, both of which featured massive cop intimidation, police pens, preventative arrests and other preemptive measures to suppress dissent. The FBI recently seized internet servers which host various Indymedia websites on the grounds that in the course of exposing police brutality by undercover cops in Europe, "personal information" had been revealed. In Italy, Indymedia is currently being investigated for supposed links to "terrorism." And here in Toronto people remember [police chief] Julian Fantino's denunciation of OCAP [Ontario Coalition Against Poverty] as a "terrorist" group after the police riot at Queen's Park in June 2000.

In the aftermath of 9/11, the Canadian government passed its own draconian "Anti-Terrorism Act" (Bill C-36) which defines terrorism as an act (or omission) "compelling a person, a government or a domestic or an international organization to do or refrain from doing any act." Like the U.S. Patriot Act, this law defines terrorism broadly enough to include almost anything. It is an enabling act for police repression.

Only Socialist Revolution Can End Capitalist Terror!

Marxists adamantly oppose attacks on innocent civilians—whether office workers in New York, pizzeria patrons in Jerusalem or schoolchildren in Russia. We are opposed to violence directed against the working class and the oppressed, and to all acts that undermine the struggle for a better future. But Marxists are not pacifists. We do not oppose the use of force in principle. Pacifism is the ideology the oppressors recommend for their victims. It is, in Trotsky's phrase, a "debilitating narcotic" for the proletariat.

The capitalist media and politicians sometimes refer to the blows struck against the imperialist occupation by the Iraqi resistance as "terrorist attacks." There is no question that, as in Afghanistan, most of those actively resisting the imperialist occupation embrace extremely reactionary and virulently anti-working class ideologies. But that does not change the fact that the peoples of Iraq have a right to determine their own future free of coercion by foreign invaders and their puppets. In Iraq today the issue is not one of democracy versus dictatorship. It is a question of whether or not the U.S./British imperialist "coalition" will be able to re-impose colonial rule.

The "war on terror" is essentially a marketing device designed by the American ruling class to promote its campaign for global supremacy. It is used both to justify military adventures abroad and vicious repression at home. Under capitalist rule things are rarely called by their right names: exploitation is fair exchange, war is peace and occupation is liberation. The so-called war on terror is no exception. It is, in reality, a war of terror.

The only way to put an end to this system of chronic violence and brutality—which condemns some 40,000 children to starve to death every day—is through proletarian socialist revolution. The capitalists and their ideologues insist that "there is no alternative" to the tyranny of the market, but that is a lie. For the vast majority of humanity, capitalism is terrorism.

The Bolshevik Revolution of 1917 proved that with revolutionary leadership ordinary working people have the capacity to rise up and smash capitalism. The working class was victorious in October 1917 because of the existence of a revolutionary socialist organization – the Bolshevik Party of Lenin and Trotsky. Our job as socialists is to lay the political foundation for a mass-based, revolutionary workers' party capable of leading a successful struggle to expropriate the expropriators and open the road to a new world order in which human need, and not corporate profit, is the highest priority.

TERRORISM AND CONTAINER TRADE

When Malcolm Maclean, the founder of Sea-Land Service Inc., introduced container to the world in 1956 he would not have imagined that 50 years down the line the box would give a monumental head ache to his own country. For, in the wake of the 9/11 attack the Americans firmly believe that if there were to be future terrorist strikes on their country they will most probably come from the sea, in marine containers. They see bomb in every box.

Their presumption and fear is well-founded. Although the container is the most efficient, economical and reliable means of transporting international goods it is also vulnerable to intrusion, subversion, and misuse. The very characteristics of the container and the mechanics of the container system that allow large volumes of cargo to flow quickly and fluently can be leveraged by terrorist organizations to conceal and smuggle with same ease and effortlessness explosives and weapons to cause wholesale destruction of people and property.

The central principle of containerization is door to door service, meaning goods will be put inside the container at the exporter's place and taken out at the other end at importer's premises. In between no one will open the container, see or inspect or examine the contents of the container. One has to only believe what the shipper has shown on the document, such as shipping bill, Bill of Lading, he has packed into the container. This same anonymity and unobtrusiveness, which are the hall marks of containerization, can give an unfair advantage to terrorist outfits to pass out deadly weapons and materials. They have to only stuff a weapon of mass destruction (WMD) or materials for building such a weapon into a container in an exporter's shed, seal the container, show it as some legitimate cargo in the shipping documents, move it to the shipside, get it loaded routinely and thus bring it to the targeted destination to annihilate people and property.

Another weak link is the multiplicity of players involved in the transport chain. Consignor, freight broker, clearing agent, shipping company, container line, railways, transport operator, port, customs, importer, et al. Each one looking after only his interest and no single agency or authority responsible for the security of the container over its entire chain.

Coming to the container itself. It is just what the doctor has ordered for a healthy and safe passage of a weapon of mass destruction (WMD).The container is large, roomy and has a hefty pay load. Measuring up to 40 ft length, 9ft 6inch height and 8 ft width it has a volumetric capacity up to 67.5 cu.mtr and a load bearing capacity up to 35 tons. Made of solid, sturdy cladding material it is almost impregnable.

Marry these physical features of the container with the concept of door to door operation with no checking or inspection en route, and no single authority responsible for the entire transportation chain, you have a first-rate method for sending stealthily across the seas any respectable size weapon of mass destruction.

To carry out this brazen operation, terrorist organizations may adopt one of the following modus operandi:

(i) intercept a container stuffed with bona fide cargo and substitute it partially or fully with the mass destruction weapon or material. This substitution can be effected at any of the places en route to the port or terminal. The container may be opened to introduce the illicit cargo while it is sitting in railway yard waiting to be loaded on the train, or at a CFS before its haulage to the terminal for loading on the ship. A most likely interception point however would be the highway while the container is transported to the port. The transporter may be taken into confidence or he may be a willing accomplice to the nefarious deal or the driver may be intimidated or bribed to take the container to a lonely spot or to a remote warehouse where the substitution will be done.

(ii) set up a legitimate trading business and send illegitimate goods such as explosives, weaponry, etc under the cover of genuine shipment. The advantage is the initial stuffing operation will take place in the terrorist's premises itself and there will be no need to take the risk of waylaying the container or involving a third party like a transporter or his driver.

Up to the turn of the last century the primary concern of the trade with respect to container security was cargo theft and its aftermath. More appropriately how to deflect liability when there was loss of cargo due to pilferage, robbery, etc. So the security measures were focused more on documenting at every inter change point the condition of the container, the number of the seal and its condition. So that the liability could be fixed on the party responsible for the leg prior to noticing of the infarction, if any.

But the last thing on any body's mind was safeguarding the container from terrorist infiltration. Even though our terrorism woes began in the 80s, with the bombing of Air India flight 182 over Irish coast in which 329 people perished, and got intensified from the 90s no one connected extremism to freight system or maritime transport, although a direct association could have been drawn after the 1993 serial blasts in Mumbai for which RDX and other explosives were brought from abroad by sea and landed at water fronts in Ratnagiri and Raigad districts in Maharashtra.

But we had chosen to remain impervious to the possibility of terrorists using the container to convey and deliver deadly weapons and materials till Americans alerted the world to such a likelihood. But that warning came much later. Initially it appeared that Americans were inured from terrorism when many countries right, left and centre, especially India, were suffering horrendous and repeated attacks. Americans would have perhaps thought that terrorism too was predominantly a third world problem like poverty and infectious diseases. But all that started changing from 1993.There were three serious incidents before hell broke loose on Sep 11, 2001. These were:

The first one happened on the same World Trade Centre buildings that got flattened 8 years later. On the morning of 26 Feb 1993 bombs exploded on the basement of WTC that killed 6 and injured scores of others.

Five years later, on Aug 7, 1998, U S embassies in Kenya and Tanzania were bombed almost simultaneously in which a total of 213 people died.

The third incident was an audacious one. On October 12, 2000 when the American naval vessel, USS Cole was berthed in the port of Aden at Yemen a small craft with explosives fastened to its hull rammed the port side of the naval vessel killing 17 sailors as they were queuing for lunch.

Of course, there is no need to go into what happened 11 months later in New York, for even a child in womb, like Abhimanyu, would know the details backwards. But those temeritous and spectacular attacks of the World Trade Centre and other targets including Pentagon on that fateful day inevitably shook the Americans into taking some concrete preemptive action towards visualizing where the future attacks could come from, what will be the likely methods and strategies of the terrorists, and to formulate strategies to nip them at the bud. The result is setting up of a separate agency called Department of Homeland Security(DHS) whose job inter alia is to formulate policies, plans and programmes for preventing and deterring terrorist incidents, taking counter terrorism measures and generally to protect American people and property from future terrorist attacks.

One of the areas identified by DHS as having ominous potential for exploitation by terrorists is the containerized system. There were two incidents that point to such a correlation:

A) On Oct 26, 2001, just one and a half month after the Sep 11 attacks, Italian officials intercepted one Mr. Rizik amid Farid, a high-ranking Al Queda member, in a container bound for Canada. Farid was in possession of airport security passes and an aircraft mechanic certificate that allowed him free access to sensitive areas in several U S airports including New York's JFK, Newark International, Los Angeles International, and Chicago O'Hare.

B) In 2004, Abdul Qadeer Khan, the father of Pakistan's atom bomb, admitted to smuggling nuclear equipment and technology to Libya, Iran and North Korea. Khan purportedly shipped all of his nuclear materials in containers.

The Department of Homeland Security anticipates that terrorist outfits will take advantage of the weak points in the system to sneak weapons and high explosives into a target country and cause calamitous damage to economic infrastructure and decimate huge populations to cause maximum impact and effect.

Terrorists will try to achieve these evil intents in three ways :

1. Manage to smuggle large quantity of explosives or a ready-to-strike WMD in a container, and when the container is on

ship in a targeted country's port detonate the charge when the ship passes through vital areas such as main channel or lock gates . Or, when the container is on trailer on the quay or the yard set off the bomb under container cranes. Either of this will substantially cripple shipping and cargo handling in that port and if that port happens to be the gateway port of the country handling majority of the cargo the import-export trade of the country will suffer a long- time blow, pushing back the country's growth and prosperity.

2. In the second scenario the container with the weapon may be sneaked out of the port and exploded at a critical infrastructure like a power plant or oil installations or stock exchange.
3. To cause maximum damage to people and property the passed out weapon in container may be triggered at a busy place where large number of people are usually present, such as malls, railway stations, and popular shrines.

The above is not an exercise in exaggeration or scare mongering but indication of real, plausible scenarios. We have already been victims of countless attacks of the above kinds, to a moderate degree, if one could call 300 people dying in one incident as moderate. But if the terrorists could lay hands on larger quantities of the same materials or on more deadly substances and weapons, the employment of the same methods could escalate the destruction and death to gargantuan proportions.

So far the terrorists have been using conventional explosive materials such as arms and ammunitions, RDX, gelatin sticks, TNT, nitroglycerine, etc. The fear and worry is that far more powerful and deadly materials exist, and it may be a matter of time before they gain access to them. In particular are the chemical, biological, radiological or nuclear (CBRN) materials that the terrorists could use for making weapons and then move them internally or by sea to a foreign target .Virtually any back-yard assembled nuclear weapon could be put in a container along with a dense shielding material like lead to make detection difficult. So also are isotopes or other nuclear materials for a radiological device, or the so called dirty bomb. Chemicals such as chlorine, sarin gas and other such lethal substances can be carried for fitting into a WMD, or an already assembled WMD with a chemical war head could be moved in the container. Biological agents such as viruses (ebola, small pox) or bacteria(plague, anthrax) or toxins(botulinum, ricin) can be carried in ready-to use delivery systems or in small parcels to be used in a weapon later on.

The CBRN group of materials or weapons is extremely dangerous and devastating. Just one incident involving a nuclear device or a biological war head in a major port or in its immediate environment could have immense and dramatic consequences far beyond the target area. Human loss can run to lakhs and economic damage to billions of dollars. Two recent instances can put the scale of such devastation in perspective. The loss due to the attack on the World Trade Centre is estimated to be $ 83 billion. A labour dispute in 2002 that caused the shut down of U S west coast ports for 10 days resulted in a loss of $5 billion.

World trade is estimated to be $12 trillion per year (2007 figure) or approximately $ 30 billion per day. Global trade to a large extent is dependent on transportation of cargo in containers and in the year 2007 the container traffic was about 450 million TEUs. Out of this lot even if one container was used for a CBRN attack in a transshipment hub or a gateway port it would have had economic consequences far beyond the port or even the country, and brought the world trade itself to its knees.

Fortunately, at present the chances that terrorists will use container to send across CBRN materials or weapons to a foreign target are slender. Not because it is difficult for them to hood wink the various parties involved in the container logistics or to beat the security systems operating in the transportation chain. It's primarily because it's not easy for them to muster enough materials or to acquire the technology and other paraphernalia for making the CBRN, at the moment.

Nevertheless, weapons of mass destruction in wrong hands is a real threat, and determined terrorists will pursue doggedly to procure them, what ever time and effort it takes. There is intelligence that indicates that Al Qaeda is showing serious interest in CBRN weapons, and there are a few rogue nations who will oblige them with such materials. In the light of these disturbing possibilities it is urgent and imperative that the security of the container across its entire transportation chain is upgraded vastly from the present level of theft prevention to protection against terrorist misuse. In this regard the philosophy should be, like charity security too has to begin at home. It means no container will get out of the shores of the exporting country unless it has been completely screened and sanitized. Only then we can expect and demand that import boxes coming to our country are similarly sanitized. The next principle should be that the port or the terminal should be the last line of defence and not the first. So all the security measures applied on the container, at every stage of the intermodal chain, should be before it enters the terminal or the port. To meet these prerequisites a number of security measures are available ranging from simple devices to sophisticated technologies to common sense as well as heightened procedures. They include the following:

(1) manual container seals

(2) tracking devices and electronic seals

(3) sensors

(4) scanners

(5) smart container

(6) access control

(7) security protocols

(8) security procedures

Container Seals: Manual

Manual seals have been in use in the industry almost from the beginning. They are of two types, both for detecting tampering or intrusion.

(a) indicative seals : they are made of plastic, wire, or a combination of both with a unique serial number imprinted on each.

(b) barrier seals : they are made of tough, strong material which make them difficult to break. Examples of barrier seal are bullet seal, bottle seal. Special tools or bolt cutters are required to break them whereas indicative seals could be cut with wire cutters or ordinary knives.

Both indicative and barrier seals do not prevent intrusion or entry into the container. The condition of the seal is indicative of whether or not a container is violated. One has to only presume that if the seal is intact no intrusion has occurred, and if the seal is compromised the contents of the container also is compromised.

The problem with manual seals is that they do not offer precise information as to where, when and under what circumstances the seal was tampered and the container was broken into. Another draw back is that they can be easily counterfeited.

Tracking Devices and Electronic Seals

Several electronically operated systems are available for tracking of containers out of which two are significant to container security as they can be integrated with mechanical seals. Called e-seals they are a more efficient and effective tool for deterring, detecting and signalling tampering and intrusion incidents. These e-seal systems are:

(a) Radio Frequency Identification (RFID)

(b) Global Positioning System (GPS)

Radio Frequency Identification: RFID is an exploding and amazing technology that has potential use in almost every industry and business where large number of items is required to be identified and tracked continuously and constantly, such as the container trade. Its applications are wide and diverse including asset management, inventory control, automatic toll collection, guidance of physically challenged people, detection of counterfeit currency, and numerous others. It is essentially a technology that uses radio waves for identifying and tracking an object or item. The system consists of a label called RFID tag which is attached to an object or subject with desired information written into it in electronic form. As the item, say, a container moves from one area to another an antenna picks up the signal from the tag, which in turn triggers a reader or transreceiver. The reader interprets the information written on the tag and passes it to the main system through a server for processing and storing.

As the system thus captures information automatically on occurrence of every activity or event it makes the tracking more reliable and accurate. Another capability of RFID tag is that it can record as many details of the incident as required including time and location, how it occurred, by whom and so on. These capabilities of RFID to capture all the requisite information instantaneously without any human input has far-reaching value to container security. By integrating an RFID tag to a high quality mechanical seal and dovetailing it with a sensor the system can detect any violation of the seal or infiltration to the container immediately ,log all the details of the incident and can even send distress signal.

There are mainly two types of RFID tag: passive and active. A passive tag does not have power of its own; it gets activated only when it comes into contact with the antenna. Passive tags are cheap and disposable costing about 30 cents a piece. They have a short range of about 3 ft. The draw back of passive seals is since they have no inherent power they cannot detect and record any tampering of seal as and when it occurs. They can report the intactness or otherwise of the seal only when it is interrogated by the reader next time.

Active tag on the other hand has a longer range of 300ft and has its own power source. It is alive and alert all the time. So if a tampering or intrusion occurs it will immediately detect it and maintain a time log of the event including all the associated details. If the tag is integrated or interfaced with a GPS device it can log the exact location of the incident and some may even send 'may day" tampering reports. A significant disadvantage of active tag is its cost which can be up to $ 20 per tag but the reuse could reduce the cost per container substantially.

Because of low cost and operational simplicity passive seals were the preferred option prior to Sep 11 as the predominant concern at that time was theft prevention. But as post Sep 11 scenario has escalated the threat to terrorism misuse, it will be increasingly necessary to equip the containers with active RFID seal. In the long run and at macro level active tag will be a prudent option because global loss per year due to theft of containerized cargo is $ 20 billion whereas a study by the Brookings Institution, a non-profit public policy organization based in Washington, estimates that a single incident involving detonation of a WMD in a container at a major port will entail a cost of $ 1 trillion (1000billion).

Global Positioning System (GPS): Global positioning system is an appropriate technology for the tracking and monitoring of security while the container is on vessel. The software for its implementation is relatively inexpensive and the system provides instant information on the vessel's location through the use of satellites.

As mentioned earlier GPS can be a valuable adjunct to RFID as the combination of an active tag and GPS can detect, record and alert any intrusion or tampering even when the container is on the ship in high seas.

There are at present some drawbacks in the systems such as limited coverage in remote areas, battery dependence, human intervention and high maintenance. But GPS is a fast developing system and these deficiencies are bound to be overcome with considerable benefit to container tracking and container security.

Sensors

Despite using powerful active RFID, breaches to the container could occur as the seal could be evaded, or tricked into not detecting a violation. Ingenious thieves and terrorists can come around the electronic "eye" by operating away from the line of sight of the tag. For example, they can cut open the roof or any side of the container that does not fall on the line of sight, introduce the weapon or lethal substance, and weld back the cut portion to the container. Container doors can be detached and fixed back without breaking the seal or without making the seal getting wind of it. Another way of circumventing the e-seal is to load the explosive or other dangerous materials before the seal is fixed on the container.

In order therefore to further insure the container from infiltration another devise known as sensor is required to be integrated with the electronic seal. Sensors come in two types: one detects general infiltration and the second identifies the presence of a specific substance or material, say an explosive or a hazardous chemical.

General intrusion sensors use changes in ambient or physical conditions such as light, temperature, humidity, motion, vibration, etc to detect the intrusion.

Specific sensors identify the presence of a particular item from its emanation, such as vapor, gas, smell, heat. For example, a sensor designed for detecting a flammable substance will detect it by the vapor generated by it or from the charged atmosphere it has caused. Other examples are nitrous oxide sensor which can detect a nitrogen tetroxide rocket propellant. A carbon di oxide sensor can detect the presence of a human being inside the container from his exhalation. An ammonia sensor can uncover ammonium nitrate bomb made from fertilizer. This seems to be the favorite of terrorists as it is cheap and freely available. It is the material that was used in the 1995 Oaklahoma bombing, 2002 Bali bombings and the 2008 serial blasts in Bangalore and Ahmedabad.

Sensor cannot be a stand alone tool to give complete protection to the container, so also the other two security devises, namely, mechanical seal and active RFID tag. They have to be put together to form a formidable barrier against theft, intrusion and other violations.

Scanners

Scanner is the last line of defence against terrorism misuse before a container leaves the home port. It's a final tool to check and confirm that contents of the container are the same as shown in the shipping documents, and to make sure that no illegitimate materials have been sneaked into the container during its journey to the port from the shipper's premises or railway depot or CFS.

The scanners that are currently in use fall into two categories: X-ray machines and gamma ray detectors. They are basically imaging equipments, useful more for gross verification that no objectionable or no-conforming materials are carried in the container. Such a checking is done manually by the customs or security official by interpreting the images thrown by the x-ray or gamma ray scanner. Therefore, unless the people operating these equipments have been sufficiently trained, and are skilled and experienced misjudgements could occur, leading to ugly or disastrous consequences. An innocent cargo may be detained while a deadly chemical may be whisked away. A WMD in knocked down condition may be interpreted as automobile parts or vice versa. Therefore, for identification of deadly cargo such as WMD or high explosives or nuclear materials scanners that can pinpoint and self-detect will be imperative. Such specific and sophisticated machines are currently not available, but are under development.

One of them is thermal imaging equipment which tracks the natural heat generated by radioactive substances to nail them. Another scanner under development by Livermore National Laboratory, USA, is the neutron scatter, specifically for detecting nuclear materials and nuclear weapons. Development of this machine has become a top priority for the current sensors or scanners cannot easily detect nuclear weapons or nuclear fission materials carried in containers. For instance, if highly enriched uranium (HEU),whic: can be more easily turned into a bomb than plutonium or any other nuclear substance, is kept in a container shielded by a dense material like a led plate it may escape attention if a regular gamma ray detector or an x-ray machine is used to screen the container.

Therefore, the current machines should be more appropriately called screening equipment and not scanners as scanning may connote detailed scrutiny and self detection. Screening and scanning of containers, while complementary, they are not the same. Whereas 100% screening of containers is possible, if authorities decide to do so, 100% scanning is impractical with the technologies presently available.

Even 100% screening of all containers is an implausibility given the sheer volume of boxes handled at a terminal every day. Even the most efficient gamma ray scanner will take at least three minutes to screen a container. So a typical container terminal handling 5000 laden export boxes a day will have a 9-day back log if one scanner is used for screening all of them. Alternatively, at least 10 scanners will be required which very few terminals will be able to afford in terms of cost, space, manpower and logistics. Costing Rs 20 crores, each scanner will require 1 hectare space, at least about 20 to 25 technicians, many number of tractor-trailers. Besides it will inevitably lead to increased dwell time of the container. It's estimated that every extra day stay of the container raises the landed value of the cargo by 1%.

That precisely is the reason why a storm is brewing over a law enacted by US Government in August 2007. As per this rule, beginning 1st July 2012 all containers bound for American ports should be screened at the host port prior to loading. This has set a fierce opposition in many quarters including European Union and India.

However, given the sensitivities of the Americans after the 9/11 attacks a balanced and practical approach suggested by many is to screen the containers by judicious selection. That is, to choose the containers for screening based on risk assessment, by random selection, prior intelligence, cargo of suspicious or fly-by-night exporter, goods which can be used to mask or shield destructive materials, and any other criteria mutually agreed between the exporting-importing countries. If the screening reveals any thing suspicious that container may be put through a rigorous examination including unstuffing, physical inspection, etc.

Smart Box

The tracking-cum-security devises described above can give almost total protection to container against terrorist exploitation if they are put together as a composite unit in a container. But the question is who will take the responsibility for such an integration, who will bear the initial cost, who will operate the system and who will monitor and confirm that all the components are in place and working.

While the shipper may use tamper-resistant mechanical seals, he may not come forward to use it in tandem with RFID tag due to cost and other considerations. Same will be the case with GPS and sensors. The shipper may expect the container line to put up and operate these fixtures. Another problem is lack of standardization of these devises and systems.

A solution to the above could be to make the above security features a part and parcel of all containers so that these issues get settled automatically and naturally. The U S government is working towards such a move for which it has set up a technology research programme called Advanced Container Security Device.

The objective of this project is to develop a concept called Smart Box which will have all the security and tracking devises built into the container itself, including a super strong barrier seal, an active RFID tag, a GPS unit, a sensor and a software package. Such an "intelligent container" will monitor the integrity of the container on all the six sides; keep track of every movement and activity of the container and keep an eye on the contents of the container at all times. The container will also have the capability to store all relevant shipping data that could be fed to customs and other regulatory authorities. The software will identify if the container had an intrusion and set off an alarm both locally and remotely –to the shipper and customs.

American Customs intends that all future containers to be manufactured on this prototype and the existing containers to be retro fitted with these smart features. When cargo is transported in these next generation containers they can be expected to be whisked away in receiving ports without screening or inspection regardless of whether they have been prescreened or not in the host ports.

The cost of the integrated security devise will be around $ 60 per unit. It is considered not much compared to the cost of a 20 ft container at around $ 5000 and a 40 ft container $ 9000. It is negligible if one takes into account the $ 20 billion lost every year due to theft, and it is certainly nothing considering the billions of dollars and hundreds of thousands of human lives it would save by averting transportation of WMDs and other dreadful materials by terrorists in containers.

Access Control

Even though various security devises or their integration in futuristic smart box will detect tampering of seal or container, or any intrusion it is better to take measures to prevent any non-bona fide or un authorized access to container or container operation and container movement areas. It is therefore necessary to deploy technologies and systems that will be fool-proof in identifying authorized, genuine persons and rejecting bogus and illegitimate characters.

Biometric identification systems thus far are the most advanced and infallible tool for access control. There are several technologies presently available, each one using a different feature of human anatomy. These systems use one or more of the following unique characteristics of each person for recognition:

(a) fingerprint

(b) hand recognition

(c) eye-retinal

(d) eye-iris

(e) whole face

(f) voice

(g) dynamic signature

These systems are not elaborate, easy to install and operate, and are relatively inexpensive. Each can be used as stand-alone system, or in concert with others to provide added security.

Security Protocols

Terrorism has become as ubiquitous as the container with no part of the world escaping its deadly reach except perhaps the dictatorial regimes like Burma, North Korea. Even China which seemed to have been unaffected by terrorism started experiencing it from August 2008 as the Olympics was nearing. In the first fortnight of that month, just before and during Olympics there were 3 attacks in Xinjiang, in the north western region of the country. The attacks occurred on 1st, 10th and 12th in which a total of 27 people died including 19 policemen.

A side effect, a dangerous side effect, of globalization of commerce and trade could be cross border terrorism. As the trade and cargo flows quickly and seamlessly across countries terrorism may take advantage of the borderless movement to hitch a piggy back ride on the systems that make this transfer effortless and easy.

So if container terrorism has to be effectively and resolutely thwarted it has also to be done at world level and not at piece meal individual port or country level. Countries and international agencies and organizations have already banded together to take concerted action to block terrorists from hijacking the maritime trade, especially the container supply chain, to their evil ends.

United States, European Union and G8 as well as international organizations that regulate the maritime industry including International Maritime Organization (IMO), International Labour Organization (ILO), and World Customs Organization (WCO)- have all taken measures to prevent penetration of terrorism through ship and container. There are many initiatives, plans and protocols that drive these measures, out of which two need special mention as they will have a universal and significant impact on the way business is done in ports and shipping, and the manner in which container is moved from end to end. They are:

(1) International Shipping and Port Security Protocol or ISPS

(2) Container Security Initiative or CSI

International Shipping and Port Security Protocol: International Maritime Organization which is primarily an agency for enhancing and monitoring safety in maritime transport has taken the additional responsibility to improve security in ports and shipping. Accordingly IMO has, under Safety of Life at Sea (SOLAS) convention, developed a code called ISPS. The code lays down a set of security requirements that are obligatory for the governments, ports, terminals and shipping companies to implement.

Under the ISPS regime each port must conduct threat and vulnerability assessments and prepare a comprehensive security plan. The plan should spell out measures to counter these threats at varying levels including normal, medium and high. On the shipping side all sea going vessels are similarly required to carry out a vulnerability assessment and based on that develop and implement a security plan which should include an Automatic Identification System (AIS) that can be interrogated.

Thought he ISPS code, which came into effect from 1st July 2006, has been adopted by most of the major ports, its implementation needs further tightening. Some ports are still using for access control the conventional methods like manual entry system, physical verification of hard copy pass, etc. They need to adopt the automatic and more fool proof controls like biometrics, CCTVs, and other electronic devices to reduce human intervention to the minimum.

Another aspect is that ISPS does not extend to container operations sites outside the terminal or port. As the container is like the hatch of the ship and once the cargo is stuffed into it no further checking or inspection is carried on it, it is very necessary that the same measures taken under ISPS to sanitize the port and the vessel are applied on these container operation areas as well. The most vulnerable points for container intrusion are the sites where the stuffing takes place and where the container awaits further movement. These areas are the CFS and ICD. Hence it is paramount that the

ISPS code is made mandatory to these locations as well. A compromised container will compromise two places at one stroke—port and ship. Container Security Initiative: In the wake of the 9/11 attacks Department of Homeland Security of the United States considers that maritime supply chain, especially container, could be a potential source for transportation and delivery of materials and weapons of mass destruction by terrorists. Its customs wing, now called Customs and Border Protection (CBP), has initiated several measures to thwart terrorists from using containers to disrupt global trade or to cause loss of life and property in target countries.

A key and critical programme developed by CBP is the Container Security Initiative to ensure that only clean containers leave the port of origin. Launched in Jan 2002 the CSI has at its heart the following four elements:

(1) To identify high-risk containers by means of automated targeting system that use advance information and strategic intelligence

(2) To pre-screen and evaluate containers before they are shipped

(3) To use latest technology such as gamma ray scanner for pre-screening with a view to assessing the contents reliably and quickly

(4) To develop the concept of smart box which will have the requisite security features such as RFID tag, GPS, sensor and other devises built into the container itself to ensure the integrity of the container and its contents.

To support CSI in identifying high-risk containers at the load port the CBP has from Dec 2002 implemented a rule known as 24 hour rule requiring ocean carriers to provide manifest 24 hours prior to loading of containers. The US Customs screen the shipments contained in the manifest using their own information and intelligence system called Automated Target System. On that basis they determine which containers require further review or inspection. The suspect containers are then identified to the host port for thorough screening before they are loaded on the ship.

Container Security Initiative is a multi national programme in which customs officers of participating ports are stationed at each other's port. The U S Customs and Border Protection (CBP) have initially chosen the top 20 mega ports for implementation of CSI which was subsequently extended to other container ports. As of Jan 2008 a total of 58 ports, which account for 85 % of the containers exported to U S, are operational under CSI.

In CBP's view the Container Security Initiative will benefit a participating port in 3 ways: (a) Because of reciprocal arrangement the containers coming to that port would get prescreened in the exporting port, thereby reducing the chances of terrorist attack in the receiving port and country (b) It will provide a better security to the entire global container trade with less disruptions, delays and damages (c) The participating port's(country's) exports will not suffer delay at the other side since they would have been precleared by the receiving port or prescreened at the host port.

Standard Security Procedure

Container Security is a shared responsibility among all actors involved in the supply chain. Any breach in one link compromises the security of the entire chain. Nearly 75 % of the activities on a loaded container take place outside the restricted and controlled environment of a port or terminal. Hence the likelihood of the container getting violated is more in these 'free' areas including shipper's premises, road, railway yard and CFS.

Like standard operating practices (SOP) it is therefore necessary to establish standard security procedures for all actions and activities performed on the container outside the terminal. Similarly an institutional mechanism has to be put in place to ensure all players including shipper or forwarding agent, transporter, ICD manager and CFS operator follow these procedures strictly.

Following is a standard security procedure (SSP) suggested for activities outside terminal. This is only indicative, and a terminal or port or even a country may adopt all or some of these elements, and may add their own, to suit local conditions, practices and laws, but without diluting the security focus.

(1) Only reputed exporters, manufacturers, trading houses and other well-known and high-volume shippers should be allowed to stuff container in their premises.

(2) The stuffing area should be clearly defined, marked out and dedicated.

(3) All the people engaged in the activity including laborers, clerical staff, equipment operators, et al should have been screened, their antecedents checked, and cleared by police. Except them no body should be used under any circumstances.

(4) Other not so well known or low to medium volume shippers may be permitted on trial basis to carry out stuffing in their place provided their own back ground has been checked and vetted. If permitted, they should follow the steps indicated at 1 to 3 above.

(5) Customs may be the authority to decide who should be allowed to stuff in their premises. Customs may carry out surprise checks to ensure that all shippers are following the laid down safety procedures religiously.

(6) All others should stuff their cargo in the CFSs or ICDs only.

(7) CFSs and ICDs should be completely sanitized by employing or engaging persons whose back ground has been checked, and cleared. Similarly, the people connected with cargo, container and transport interests also should be authenticated or authorized after screening.

(8) Entry to the CFS and ICD should be regulated by automated access control systems including biometrics, smart card and CCTV.

(9) Every lorry load of loose cargo that enters the CFS or ICD should be screened by X-ray or any other imaging equipment.

(10) Stuffing operation should be diligently supervised by security personnel deployed at the CFS or ICD.

(11) On completion of stuffing a high quality barrier seal or e-seal, as standardized by the concerned authority, should be fixed.

(12) If the technology available, a GPS gadget and a sensor may be integrated with the seal to bolster security.

(13) Only prescreened and authorized transporters should be engaged for moving the container to the terminal. Their drivers too should have been cleared by police on verification of their back ground.

(14) The travel route to the terminal should be clearly defined and briefed to the driver, with a map, if necessary. Alternative roads also should be marked to cover emergencies like prolonged traffic hold-up, breaches due to rain or other adverse weather condition.

(15) One person should always be present on the vehicle-either the driver or cleaner. Only one person at a time should go for meals, bath room, etc.

(16) They should be especially careful while waiting at the parking lot, railway crossing where the miscreants could attack the container.

(17) Despite all the vigilance if any intrusion or tampering takes place they should immediately contact the nearest police station, and the shipper. The trailer should not proceed unless it is checked and cleared.

There may be high-tech container security devises, systems, and well meaning and lofty initiatives and protocols. But if people at the shipper's place or ICD or CFS, or the transporter and his men are slack or negligent intrusions can take place any where on the way to the terminal. Given that all containers cannot be screened at the terminal and only 5 to 7% of the boxes can be opened and contents examined, a casual and apathetic attitude may lead to disastrous consequences. In order therefore not to leave any thing to chance the parties involved in the activities may have to be mandated to follow such a security regimen at every stage of the container's journey from the factory or CFS or ICD up to the gate of the terminal.

The procedures and technologies, outlined above, to enhance the security of container may appear elaborate, and even counter productive. Containerization after all is one of the greatest innovations in the maritime industry that has accelerated the flow of cargo just as computerization has accelerated the flow of information. The apprehension is therefore well placed that any security overkill may retard the momentum, roll back containerization's benefits and take us back to the dark ages of snail-paced movement of general cargo.

At the same time we cannot be in denial about the vulnerability of container to intrusion and misuse by terrorists. We have seen too many carnages and destruction all over the world caused by ruthless terrorists who will spare no means to kill and devastate. If container trade is not to become a tool to the terrorist industry it is hugely important that every possible precaution and preventive action is taken to secure the container in the strongest manner possible. In that effort if some of the measures are abundant and even redundant, so be it. As the old wisdom goes it is better to be safe than sorry.

Speed and time saving are the crux of air travel. But are not people now reporting 2 hours before at the airport for a flight that takes only 1 hour? That is because too many planes had been hijacked and too many had been blown up. That is the price terrorism is extracting and people have no alternative but to pay it. Container traffic is no different.

Fortunately, however, it is possible to achieve a balance between quick commerce and secure commerce in container trade. The very same security devises and procedures that appear elaborate in fact will hasten the movement of containers. These automatic equipment and devises including RFID, GPS and sensor will monitor on their own the integrity of the container and its contents throughout the journey without the need for human intervention at every interchange point which will be otherwise necessary for verification of number and condition of seal, state of the container, and for recording details of each activity. Secondly, the security regime requires every place and every person involved in the handling and movement of container to be screened and sanitized. As this will greatly reduce the chances of a container incursion, hold-up of the container for examination, investigation and other procedures also will diminish.

Further, even elaborate systems will get stabilized and streamlined in no time as enforcers as well as users get familiar with it. Take once again the airport security. About 25 years ago a passenger could just walk into the plane after checking in his baggage at the airline counter. Now how many checks he has to go through. First his ID is verified at the entrance, his check-in baggage is then screened and sealed, he is then frisked, his hand luggage is then x-rayed, he has to then identify his checked in baggage which has already been screened. Only then he is allowed to board the plane. Is he not putting up with all this multiple checks for the sake of safety and security? In spite of the repeated screening is not the system working fairly quickly and effectively?

Anyway, whether the procedures are elaborate or simple, long or short, costly or cheap there cannot be two ways about implementing them as the magnitude of the threat is enormous and the stakes are humongous.

Terrorism cannot be wished away. It has to be only willed away. Collective will and commitment of all the players involved in the container supply chain alone can prevent terrorism from taking a new root and route in container. If on the other hand, despite the looming threat and the availability of the latest technologies and systems, if they take an ostrich-like attitude and continue with the old-fashioned procedures and methods of securing the container they will become accessory to terrorism by default.

9

The Faces of Terrorism: Social and Psychological Dimensions

THE PARADOXES OF TERRORISM

TERRORISM as a contemporary phenomenon teems with paradoxes. For at least three decades, many who have studied it have regarded it as the "conflict for our time" (Clutterbuck, 1977, p. 13). Yet the same author who advertised it in those words also regarded it as "rooted in history" (ibid., p. 22), to be found in military, political, and religious annals since classical times. Despite this duality of vision, it is true that terrorism has irregularly emerged as the world's most salient and worrisome form of combat during the past several decades, and to many it promises to remain so indefinitely into the twenty-first century.

It is also paradoxical that, despite being so conspicuous on the current scene, terrorism has never been defined properly by either scholars or political officials. Nor, with the exception of some political scientists and policy analysts, have behavioral and social scientists studied this critical phenomenon very much or very well. This situation is all the more curious because only a little observation or reflection is needed to conclude that the human sides—the psychological, social, political, economic, and cultural—are universally present dimensions in terrorism and the responses to it.

A third paradox is that observers frequently describe post–cold war or post-9/11 terrorism as something new—the end of war as we knew it, a facet of globalization, an aspect of postmodernity—yet close inspection of the actual goals, ideologies, strategies, and tactics reveals how few of these ingredients are novel. In light of this circumstance, in this book I treat terrorism not as a special thing or creature but as a kind of human behavior that has some distinctive characteristics but that also lends itself to explanation by mobilizing existing theoretical and empirical knowledge in the behavioral and social sciences.

In a single volume added to the increasing cascade of books, articles, and media discussion, I cannot hope to resolve these paradoxes fully, though one of my aims is to cast light on understanding them. I will do so in part by self-consciously shunning cosmic and dramatic depictions—some of which, I argue, are reactions to our ignorance and anxiety about terrorism. Instead, I treat contemporary terrorism as a peculiar combination of ingredients culminating in a specific form of violent behavior.

Although behavioral and social scientists have fallen short in studying and understanding terrorism, some knowledge has accumulated. In addition, we know much about phenomena that are parts of the terrorism package. This knowledge can be brought to bear on understanding it. Among the relevant areas of knowledge are the structural bases— economic, political, social, and cultural—of deprivation, dispossession, and protest; the nature and role of ideologies that accompany extremist behavior; the dynamics of recruitment to social movements, behavior in them, and political reactions to them; the dynamics of small groups and networks; public reactions to uncertain threats and actual disasters; deterrence; and the politics of fear. I will mobilize selected knowledge on these and other topics in the book.

A few words on my credentials—whether they are strengths or liabilities—are in order. I am a sociologist by profession, but prior to my retirement in 2001, I, like almost all my colleagues, was not a student of terrorism. Within sociology I have studied collective behavior, social movements, cultural traumas, organizational responses to uncertainty, and comparative social structure and social change. For better or for worse, my work has almost always been interdisciplinary, and at different times I have had one foot in history, economics, anthropology, and political science. I also mention research that has reached into psychology. As part of this effort, I have undertaken full psychoanalytical training, including some practice. For the study of terrorism I regard interdisciplinarity as a strength, because the topic itself knows no disciplinary boundaries and spreads into all of them.

My direct introduction to terrorism occurred almost immediately after my retirement on September 1, 2001. Shortly after the September 11 attacks in New York City and Washington, D.C., the presidents of the National Academies wrote a letter to President George W. Bush pledging the support and cooperation of scientists in dealing with the national crisis created by those events. The first tangible manifestation of this support was the creation of the Committee on Science and Technology for Countering Terrorism, which, within less than a year, issued a major report on scientific understanding and applications to defending the nation against most types of potential terrorist attack (Committee on Science and Technology for Countering Terrorism, 2002). I was one of two social scientists on that committee, and I drafted the chapter on terrorism and human populations. In addition, I chaired two National Research Council committees, one dealing with the social and psychological dimensions of terrorism generally (Smelser and Mitchell, 2002a) and one on the possibilities and limitations of deterrence theory in dealing with contemporary international terrorism (Smelser and Mitchell, 2002b). Subsequently I have been involved in a diversity of the National Academies' activities relating to research and policies on terrorism. Engaged in these experiences, I was more or less forced to become a scholar of the subject. The experiences with the National Academies, moreover, provided the background for my decision to write a general book on the subject.

This book is mainly academic in emphasis in that it synthesizes behavioral and social science research and seeks general understandings and explanations. To deflect any message of grandiosity that may be inferred from this statement of purpose, I hasten to add that no effort is made to cover all relevant social science materials; rather, I use materials selectively according to my own judgments of relevance and priority. Nor do I pretend that I am simply, automatically, and impersonally applying objective knowledge with no intrusion on my part. Some interpretations are my own, consistent, it is hoped, with our general knowledge of psychological and social processes. Nor, finally, can I avoid topics that are controversial. Terrorism in all its international and domestic ramifications is by now thoroughly politicized, and even statements intended to be objective about it excite partisan reactions. To take only one example, to "objectify" the ideological bases of terrorism and counterterrorism and to attempt to understand them as natural phenomena is to adopt a political distance from these ideologies that is offensive to those who believe in them. And as the shrillness of the American presidential campaign of 2004 amply demonstrated, almost no facet of our nation's policies toward terrorism escapes partisan tint. All one scholar can do is to strive (but never succeed fully) to overcome partisan implications by bringing the best knowledge available to bear on any issue.

I have supplemented my general analysis in two particular ways. First, in working through all the issues involved in the subject of terrorism, I came to locate a number of snarls in our thinking about it and practical predicaments in our dealing with it. I call these entrapments. Many of them arise because terrorism has foisted them on democratic societies. They are points of confusion and controversy—many touching the fundamentals of our political system—that result in repeated and seemingly irresolvable debates and conflicts. Furthermore, the entrapments do not yield solutions, because discourse seldom moves outside or rises above their own internal dynamics. Examples of entrapments are conflicts over defining terrorism, diagnosing the role of the media, and understanding the tension between security and civil liberties in responding to terrorism. I identify a number of points of entrapment as the work proceeds. Second, I have taken the occasion to add an autobiographical dimension in the form of boxed material in many of the chapters. These entries are illustrative personal experiences and observations arising from my work on terrorism, including work with other social scientists. They are designed to provide vivid and concrete illustrations of general issues and topics discussed in the text.

I have arranged the chapters in a mainly analytical way. One could argue that issues of definition should come first. However, this item is so nettlesome and so demanding of conceptual throat clearing that I decided to begin straightaway with substance, and discuss definitions in the appendix. Chapter 2 takes up the causes and conditions of terrorism, focusing on its insurgent and international forms but not on state terrorism—historically an equally important and certainly a more lethal form than the first two but the product of a quite different set of determining conditions. This chapter is a complex one, corresponding to the complexity involved in sorting out the multiple causes, their significance at different levels, and their permutations and combinations. Chapter 3 singles out the ideologies that inspire terrorism. Concentrating on them helps elicit their crucial importance in unraveling and explaining terrorist behavior. In chapter 4 I turn to a combination of topics: the motivation of individual terrorists, their recruitment, the significance of the groups they form, their decline, their audiences, and the roles of the media in terrorism. These topics are often treated separately in the literature. For reasons that will become clear, however, I will argue that all of them—and ideology, too, for that matter—are inseparable parts of the driving motivational complex for terrorists and the commission of terrorist acts.

Chapter 5 turns to the study of target societies and deals with the social psychology of anticipating. experiencing, and coping with the threat of rare but potentially catastrophic events; the social and psychological aspects of educating, preparing, and warning the population about terrorism; and the diversity of responses to terrorist threats and attacks. In chapter 6 I deal with the complexities involved in living with the possibility of terrorist attacks, including defending democratic societies against them. Chapter 7 takes up even more general historical issues involved in dealing with international terrorism and is concerned directly with the contemporary world situation, especially the United States' place in it, as well as domestic and foreign public policies. Chapters 6 and 7 are more reflective and evaluative than the others and include many judgments of my own that seem plausible in light of what we know, but they are in no sense disciplined "applications" of sure knowledge.

I envision that the book will have three audiences—other scholars, public officials concerned with terrorism and responsible for confronting it, and interested general readers. Communicating with the first and third of these audiences is relatively nonproblematical, but I am fully aware of the limitations of academic material for policy makers and policy executors. There are inherent reasons why knowledge produced by academics does not interest—and may even irritate—those in policy arenas. At the most general level, academics and policy makers (and most military officers and journalists) have different and noncomparable priorities. The former are typically interested in general explanations arrived at by objective examination of available evidence (Wieviorka, 1995, p. 605). Many of the explanatory factors they identify, moreover, lie beyond the possibility of political or public intervention. The latter are interested in applied, timely decisions and implementations intended to have desired effects. In consequence, people on both sides of the academy–policy divide often cannot hear one another, and become impatient as a result.

Terrorism policy reflects this disconnect in an extreme way. By its very nature, terrorism demands focus and urgency, because it is uncertain and because it carries threats of death and destruction. Most policy makers cannot afford to appreciate the nicety, conditionality, and qualifications of academic analysis (Ezekiel and Post, 1991, pp. 118–19). This tension is superimposed on a traditional residue of mutual stereotyping and distrust between "academic" people of thought and "policy" people of action (Merari, 1991, p.

88). Despite these general limitations, some parts of this book may be directly relevant to policy. For example, my analysis produces a critique of the reliance on "gadgets, game theory, and goodness"—that is, the combination of technological solutions, instrumentalism, and moralism—that appears to have dominated our nation's response to terrorism since September 11, 2001. In addition, the discussions of counterproductive effects of overreacting to terrorist threats, underpreparing and overpreparing populations for danger, and the vulnerabilities of first-responding agencies are surely relevant to planning and policy. Many other points on the political, economic, social, and cultural aspects of terrorism and terrorist groups should be relevant for longer-term policy. One must acknowledge, however, that in democracies facing danger and among politicians sensitive to the media and public opinion and ultimately accountable in the electoral process, short-term reactions and accommodations typically trump longer-term polices and general reflection.

Fighting International Terrorism with Social Science Knowledge

Social scientists, including numerous sociologists, will unite in defense of national security. The University of Maryland-College Park was named in January as the home for a major Department of Homeland Security (DHS) social and behavioral research center dedicated to reducing terrorism worldwide. The center's three main working groups will focus on the origins of terrorist groups, the dynamics of terrorist groups, and a group examining societal issues associated with terrorism in the United States.

Secretary of Homeland Security Tom Ridge and Charles McQueary, his undersecretary for science and technology, announced the $12-million, three-year grant to the University of Maryland and its academic partners to establish the Center of Excellence for Behavioral and Social Research on Terrorism and Counter-terrorism. It is the fourth university-based center of excellence funded by DHS. "A critical aspect of fighting terrorism is understanding terrorism, understanding how terrorist groups form and operate, how they grow and sustain themselves, and the social and psychological impacts of terrorist attacks," said Ridge at the center's dedication.

The center's team of scholars will be led by University of Maryland criminologist Gary LaFree. "This may be the social science equivalent of the Manhattan Project," said LaFree, an ASA member. "Too often, policymakers have had to counter terrorists on the basis of assumptions and guesstimates. Our job will be to give them more solid information to work with."

Team Approach

Teams of social scientists from many fields comprise the Center of Excellence. In the first year, one working group will study how terrorist organizations form and recruit, focusing on specific organizations that pose a clear and present danger. One line of research, for example, will ask whether terror groups inspired by religious zeal are more likely to use weapons of mass destruction than their secular counterparts. Another will look at the way terror groups have exploited the September 11, 2001, terrorist attacks to expand their base of popular support.

In all these studies, researchers will look for ways to intervene and disrupt the process. "We'll be a kind of academic rapid-response team," LaFree says. "Part of our job will involve getting timely advice to homeland and national security professionals in government."

"This new center award is a very important one and a real accomplishment for sociologists!" said Kathleen Tierney, University of Colorado-Boulder sociology professor and director of the Natural Hazards Research and Applications Information Center. Tierney will head the working group on the societal impacts of terrorism. In addition to the University of Maryland, the University of Colorado is one of the center's six academic partners, which include the University of California-Los Angeles, the University of Pennsylvania, the University of South Carolina, and the Monterey Institute of International Studies.

"We will be working to better understand the public perception of the terrorism threat, ways of communicating that threat to the public and to public officials, and preparedness issues in schools and communities," said Tierney.

Global Databases & Network Analysis

The researchers will rely on a variety of tools already in use by social scientists. These tools include major global databases of ethnic struggles over the past 60 years and the most comprehensive open data set on terror incidents. As part of his prior research, LaFree has been assembling the terror database and will begin to mine it for clues about the roots of terror and effective counter-measures. The researchers will look for patterns among terrorist events and study terrorist groups in the same fashion social scientists have long studied gangs, hate crimes, and social networks in general. In fact, social network analysis was employed to root out Saddam Hussein just prior to his capture in Iraq last year.

"We know a lot more about violence, group psychology, and international conflict than has been brought to bear on this problem," said LaFree. "Our teams will be more inclusive so we can tap this expertise." The center will also have a strong educational component, helping to train a new generation of researchers, graduates and undergraduates, in the field of terror-related social science. There will also be a certificate program associated with the program for graduate and undergraduate students, signifying that a student has concentrated in terrorism study within a traditional academic major.

The road leading to the inclusion of social science in criminal justice has been a long one. Sociologists and other social scientists have long collected and analyzed data on the social impacts of natural disasters and extreme events, but receiving recognition and federal government support took much lobbying by social scientists within the government. ASA's Executive Director Sally Hillsman, while Deputy Director of the National Institute of Justice, was among those social scientists serving on the Office of Science and Technology Policy (OSTP) cross-agency committee that helped the administration "understand the potential role of social science and sell the value of the social sciences in fighting terrorism and its causes," explained Hillsman.

Disasters Have Common Impact

"In terms of physical impacts and the ways in which people and organizations respond, such attacks have a great deal in common with natural disasters such as great earthquakes and hurricanes," Tierney said. "One of the goals of the center is to ensure that lessons learned from more than five decades of research on natural disasters and other extreme events are applied to the management of emerging terrorism-related threats."

In addition to LaFree and Tierney, the other team leaders include social psychologist Arie Kruglanski, University of Maryland; Clark McCauley, psychology professor at Bryn Mawr College and co-director of the Solomon Asch Center for Study of Ethnopolitical Conflict at the University of Pennsylvania; and Jonathan Wilkenfeld, professor of political science and director of the Center for International Development and Conflict Management, University of Maryland. Also, Gary Ackerman, senior research associate at the Center for Nonproliferation Studies, Monterey Institute of International Studies; Susan Cutter, professor of geography and director of the Hazards Research Lab, University of South Carolina; and Linda Bourque, department of community health sciences professor and associate director of the Center for Public Health and Disasters, University of California-Los Angeles.

After the January 10 announcement at the University of Maryland-College Park campus, the university and the federal government will engage in a 90-day negotiation of the final terms of the contract. After that the center will open.

Perspectives on Terrorism

Several years ago, while I was working operationally overseas, a team of analysts visited our office from headquarters in Washington, DC. These officers were on a tour of the region, and one of them offered to give a briefing to our local personnel regarding a terrorist group active in the country to which I was assigned and on which a lengthy piece of finished analysis had just been completed. The briefer, who had written the analysis, had reached a number of very interesting conclusions concerning the evolution of the group and believed that he was able to make a number of very detailed predictions regarding the direction this group would take in the future. Among other things, he was convinced that the group was losing support, was unable to maintain its previous level of activity and was likely to decline precipitously in significance in the months and years ahead. It was, in his opinion, no longer a serious threat to American interests. The briefing was well done, tight, focused, and, unlike so many such presentations, captivating.

It was also absolutely wrong.

I had run many of the sources which had produced the intelligence on which this analysis was based. I knew that the only thing that had changed regarding this group was our access. Where once we had significant detail on the internal workings of the terrorist organization in question, and a clear understanding of the complexity of its operations and the breadth of its capabilities, we were now slowly going blind. The group had not evolved. It was not losing support. We were simply unable to maintain access. The danger from this group was not declining. It was increasing.

It was a stark reminder of an obvious but frequently forgotten truth. You cannot analyze information you do not have, and your analysis is only as good as the intelligence on which it is based. You can listen to rumors, draw inferences from tiny snippets of information, and extrapolate from other known cases all you want. In the end, if you do not have hard facts, you are guessing, and, as events over the last many years show, in the business of terrorism you are often guessing wrong.

Seven years ago an al-Qaeda terrorist attack on U.S. soil killed roughly three-thousand Americans. Any number of American agencies and departments failed miserably in the discharge of their responsibilities on that occasion. First and foremost, 9/11 was a failure on the part of the Central Intelligence Agency (CIA). Put simply, we did not have the sources inside al-Qaeda we needed to warn us of the coming attack. Just as it had been on so many prior occasions, the U.S. was caught flat-footed and dealt a staggering blow. This time, however, the impact was that much greater in that the attack occurred on U.S. soil and the death toll was enormous.

In the wake of these attacks and the subsequent intelligence errors concerning WMD in Iraq, the United States Government instituted a whole raft of "reforms" within the American Intelligence Community (IC). The most notable of these was the creation of an office of Director of National Intelligence, the DNI, who was charged with the task of coordinating the activities and budgets of the numerous separate intelligence agencies, which make up the IC. Whether or not he has the power to do this task remains to be seen. It should be remembered that prior to 9/11 there already was an individual, the Director of the CIA, whose job it was to run the IC. That he failed completely to direct and coordinate the activities of this sprawling community, which is overwhelmingly under the direction of the Pentagon, was directly attributable to the fact that he had no substantial authority to back up what was in reality a largely symbolic position.

In like fashion, all sorts of other changes and "reforms" were rolled out across the IC. Additional layers of bureaucracy were added in many organizations. New procedures were implemented with the goal of ensuring wider distribution of sensitive information both within the IC and to local law enforcement. Some of these made sense and were long overdue. Many of them had nothing to do with the problems at hand and were a reflection of the fact that bureaucracies and bureaucrats, left to their own devices, will always do what they do best. They will create rules, procedures and regulations.

Nothing in any of this addressed the most significant issue: the failure of the CIA to collect the human intelligence required to have provided advance warning of the pending attacks. The fact remained that the CIA, the United States' premier intelligence organization, for a variety of reasons which I will delineate, remained incapable of performing its primary mission and safeguarding the nation it served.

The CIA is crippled by a whole host of ailments. Some of the wounds are self-inflicted. Many of them are not. None of them are curable by the addition of more bureaucracy and yet more layers of supervision, coordination and oversight. Meetings, PowerPoint presentations and long term strategic plans penned by individuals who have never met a terrorist and would not know one if they tripped over him do not produce intelligence reports.

The CIA, which began life once long ago in the mists of time as a band of bold, aggressive, highly creative individuals called the Office of Strategic Services (OSS), has become a stiff, rigid, overly bureaucratic structure dominated not by risk takers and rule breakers but by cautious, ladder-climbing bureaucrats. It has, in short, lost what made it special and capable of doing the impossible and transformed into just another plodding federal agency. In this context, therefore, all changes and "reforms" which add yet more bureaucracy and more "drag" take us not toward a solution but in exactly the wrong direction.

What exists as the CIA today is largely a product of the Cold War. It is a structure designed to collect information within the context of a long, largely static strategic struggle. It uses as its primary collection mechanism officially covered officers assigned abroad and targets mostly foreign officials. In the context of a worldwide confrontation with the Soviet Union, which lasted for decades, this structure generally made sense. It allowed the United States to place large numbers of personnel abroad, relatively quickly and cheaply, and it positioned those officers to work against their adversaries, Soviet intelligence and their allies.

Such a structure makes no sense whatsoever given the primary targets against which the organization is required to work today. If

I am serving under official cover in a Third World country today, I am likely in a good position to make contact with local officials, with prominent members of the business and academic communities and to focus on other officials from nations hostile to American interests. My status as an American official, however, will be of no value whatsoever in gaining me access to members of terrorist groups, individuals involved in the smuggling of radiological material or drug cartels. At best, my status in the country will be of no help at all. To the extent I am required to live and work in true name and attract attention to myself via my official duties, my cover may, in fact, be a great hindrance.

Just as important as the structure of the organization, however, is its culture and its philosophical approach to risk and the conduct of operations. An agency built to collect long-term strategic intelligence via officially covered officers placed abroad develops a certain approach to risk taking. The emphasis is placed on the avoidance of a "flap", a diplomatic incident. Operations which have the potential to turn ugly or to go wrong are avoided and the risk versus gain analysis is heavily weighted toward eliminating risk. If it comes to a choice between running an operation (op) or making sure that nothing goes wrong, the op is likely not to be run. There will always be time later to come back and make another attempt at collection. Threats are thought of as distant and slow in evolution.

Over time this approach becomes embedded in the culture of the organization. Officers are not routinely subjected to physical risk. They understand that, if caught, they may be questioned briefly, but the worst that will happen is that they will be sent home prematurely. They come to accept this as a way of life, and, gradually, they come to regard any level of risk beyond this to be unacceptable. An operation which has the potential to lead to the capture or death of a staff officer is simply considered "too risky".

This focus on risk avoidance has been intensified by the political pressures on the CIA. Again and again, the President of the United States has called upon the CIA to conduct activities which were not supported by the Congress. In some cases, such as the Iran-Contra affair, these activities were, in fact, conducted contrary to explicit legislative prohibitions. When uncovered, these activities have provoked vicious Congressional responses, and significant numbers of CIA officers have either been forced into early retirement or prosecuted as a result.

Congress for its part, while entrusted with oversight authority, has chosen to focus more on making political hay out of CIA mistakes than it has on constructive engagement. Agency officers routinely find themselves being used as pawns in a power struggle between the Executive and Legislative branches of the United States Government. The result is predictable. Career officers, with spouses, children, mortgages and college expenses to think about keep their heads down, choose the safe route and avoid pushing the envelope.

During the Cold War the consequences of these problem were often less apparent. When you are trying to collect information on Soviet missile forces within the broader framework of a worldwide generational conflict, taking the long, patient, safe approach is, after all, usually wise. Unfortunately, it makes much less sense within the context of a fast moving, global war against a vicious enemy determined to strike, not a decade from now, but next week.

For this kind of conflict a very different approach is needed, one which emphasizes creativity, daring and imagination over deliberation and caution. In essence, what is needed is an approach much like that which the original OSS utilized. While the OSS had a nominally military structure, it was a civilian organization and it employed a wide, eclectic mix of individuals ranging from paratroopers and Army officers to actors, professors and professional sports players. It also drew from the full cross-section of American society including in its ranks members of some of the oldest and most prominent families in the nation as well as recent immigrants still fluent in the tongues of their native lands.

The result was a free-wheeling organization staffed by what its leader William Donovan referred to as his "glorious amateurs" and characterized by what he described as "discipline daring". Nothing was too novel or risky to be considered. The only thing that was absolutely unacceptable was a lack of movement. Donovan could accept failure. He could not accept inactivity. In his words, "If you fall, fall forward."

The OSS understood precisely the level of risk which would have to be accepted in order to acquire the intelligence the nation needed. It posted officers abroad under a host of covers. Sometimes they operated as singletons, sometimes as armed teams working with local partisans. They were driven always, however, by the same dynamic: to do whatever was required to collect the needed intelligence. In many cases, this meant sending staff officers into occupied territory where they lived and worked undercover for months or years at a time stealing German, Italian and Japanese secrets. A significant number of these officers were caught, and many died a horrible death, but the OSS continued to do whatever it took to complete the mission. It did not relish the death of officers in the line of duty, but it understood that it was the inevitable cost of success.

This attitude and approach were not necessarily unique to the OSS. The British Special Operations Executive (SOE), for example, on which much of the OSS was patterned, shared a similar approach. Regulations and procedures were not regarded with much favor. Results were.

In the case of the OSS, those results were staggering. An organization which was created in 1942 was by war's end in 1945 operating worldwide and running sources under the most extreme circumstances imaginable from the heart of the Third Reich to the jungles of Burma. The conditions under which the organization operated were often brutal, but, despite this, the organization forged ahead, and the United States acquired the intelligence it needed to win the Second World War.

Just as the OSS's approach to intelligence collection was not necessarily unique, so too are the problems the United States faces in the collection of human intelligence not unique either. The United States has been struck by terrorists without warning over a period of many years, beginning in Lebanon in the 1980s and culminating on September 11, 2001. Other nations have endured and continue to endure their own intelligence failures: the Madrid train bombings, the London underground bombings, the Beslan school massacre and a long list of attacks in India perpetrated by Pakistani militants and their supporters. It has, in fact, become commonplace that terrorists strike without warning and that civilized nations are left to focus on managing the after effects of the event and deliberating regarding retaliation.

We have come to think of this as inevitable. It is not. The fact that intelligence agencies using current methodologies are not collecting the information that we need does not mean that it is impossible to collect this information. It does mean, however, that we are going to have to change our methodologies in order to achieve success. Approaches evolved to gain access to information on the strategic plans of hostile governments are not likely to prove useful in helping us get inside of small, highly compartmented organizations composed of brutal fanatics. For that task, we are going to have to go back to an approach which accepts as a given a level of risk much higher than that we have been tolerating and which employs techniques more in tune with those used to penetrate organized crime syndicates and drug cartels than those of the classic Cold War espionage cases.

Officers may still be placed abroad under official cover when this makes sense. More frequently, however, we are going to have to move to a system of placing officers overseas without the benefit of any official status. They will need to live and work in the milieus they are expected to penetrate. Their lives, when posted abroad, may be more analogous to those of Bureau of Alcohol, Tobacco, and Firearms (and Explosives) agents penetrating motorcycle gangs in the United States than they will to those of current officially covered intelligence officers. This will afford them much greater natural access to targets of current interest, but it will also mean that they will be subjected to much greater risk and that we will have to accept that level of risk to operate.

As noted earlier, if I am an intelligence officer serving abroad under official cover, and I get caught in the act of violating local laws, I am likely to be held for a short period of time, declared persona non grata and then sent home. It may not be the best day I ever had, and it may mean a great deal of disruption for my family, but I will survive.

Once we step across the line and begin to place significant numbers of officers abroad without the benefits of official cover and ask them to penetrate violent terrorist groups and organized crime cartels, we are entering an entirely different world. Now if I am caught, it is likely that I will die. That death may well be slow, painful and horrifying. The first notice that my home office has of a problem may be that my body is found by the side of the road downtown.

This is not glamorous. It is not pretty. It is not easy. It will require not only an acceptance of this kind of risk on the part of the organization, but also on the part of the individual officers called upon. It will also, frankly, call for a cadre of tough, well-trained and very disciplined operatives, who have been brought up from the point of their induction into the organization to cope with these demands.

That said, I would submit that we have no choice but to move in this direction. The failure of the United States Government and other allied nations to focus on the necessity for reform in the collection of human intelligence has had massive negative consequences to date. Continued inaction may well prove to be infinitely more damaging.

The world around us is evolving at a phenomenal pace. In many parts of the world the artificial "order" imposed by nation states that are largely the creation of former colonial powers is disintegrating. Lawless areas which hold the potential to serve as safe havens for terrorist groups appear with ever increasing frequency.

We may or may not succeed in keeping Afghanistan from reverting to its role as a base for terrorist operations. Meanwhile, much of the Northwest Frontier Province is already serving as the de facto headquarters for al-Qaeda and Somalia is spiraling yet again into total chaos. Absent a miracle, the bulk of that war-ravaged nation will once be under the control of Islamic extremists within months.

Given the pressures of over-population, energy and water shortages, unemployment and religious fanaticism there is no reason to think this situation will improve anytime soon. We are living in a world which for the foreseeable future will include large, ungoverned areas wracked by tribalism, violence and extremism. These will be the base camps for terrorism for a long time to come, and if we are going to prevent future attacks we are going to have to field intelligence services which are capable of grappling with the organizations bred in such areas.

Nor is the nature of the attacks we face likely to remain static. While significant portions of the globe seem to be unraveling, the pace of technological advancement continues to quicken. Pakistan may be on the brink of implosion, but it's still possible for a scientist in Peshawar operating with limited resources to do a credible job of creating both biological and chemical weapons for use by an extremist group. Particularly when it comes to biological agents, this threat will only become worse in coming years. We may soon, in fact, be faced not only with threats from known, naturally occurring pathogens but from genetically engineered ones as well.

In short, while the impact of terrorism to date has been horrific it is likely that this impact will increase dramatically in the future and that we will be feeling it for many years to come. We do not have the luxury of continuing to treat this issue as something that can be resolved by the application of standard bureaucratic measures. New lines on wiring diagrams and ever larger staffs will not win this conflict. Small numbers of highly trained, disciplined and creative individuals empowered to take risks and push the envelope will.

None of this is code for an acceptance of some of the more questionable practices of the Bush Administration. I am a staunch opponent of the so-called "enhanced" techniques used in questioning of al-Qaeda detainees. I have interrogated a large number of terrorist captives. None of them was ever harmed in any fashion. They all talked.

This is an argument that we need to accept, that we are—whether we like it or not—in a struggle with a very brutal, fanatical foe. This foe is not Islam. It is a group of fanatics who seek to drag that great faith and the entire Islamic world back into a dark, fantasy version of the Seventh Century If anything, on some level, it is a war for Islam to preserve it from those who would hijack it and destroy it.

We would like to hope that we could find a way to combat this menace in some clean, antiseptic fashion. We would prefer that we could throw money at the problem, create a few new agencies and promulgate some regulations and that it would all be better. It will not, and the cost of not coming to grips with the problem will only increase. Someday, in the near future, when a nuclear weapon goes off in New Jersey or the bubonic plague sweeps London, it may become unbearable.

Human intelligence (HUMINT) is, of course, only one facet of the intelligence world. That said, it always has been and always will be the only form of intelligence which will definitively tell you the enemy's intentions. Signals intelligence and imagery may alert you to the fact that the Russians are massing troops on their border with Georgia. Only HUMINT will tell you what was discussed in yesterday's late-night meeting in the Kremlin and whether the deployment is intended to make a political point or is, in fact, a precursor to invasion.

The impact of HUMINT is all that much greater in regard to terrorism and the emerging threats associated with it. A small al-Qaeda cell operating with discipline and exercising good tradecraft will leave almost no traces detectable by other means. They will deal in cash. They will stay off the phones. Their logistical requirements will be minimal. In short, absent source reporting, there will be little if anything for you to see via other intelligence means.

Even a cell working on a WMD attack will produce a profile far below that which many people expect. Biological weapons can be made and biological agents mass produced in a small apartment using commonly available materials. There are no technologies for remotely detecting such operations. You may well be able to use technical means to confirm what was being developed once you raid the apartment, but only after someone has told you where it is and alerted you to its significance.

In short, as noted above, there is no magic, antiseptic solution to problem with which we are faced. We need better human intelligence. Despite their obvious value, other forms of intelligence will not compensate for our failure to collect it. We have suffered grievous losses already as the consequence of our failure to address this issue. The losses we suffer in the future may make what has gone before seem inconsequential.

We need to undertake real intelligence reform, not changes calculated to satisfy bureaucrats and staff aides, but changes which produce real, tangible results. We need to fashion human intelligence collection mechanisms which can go out into the dark places of the world and bring back the critical information we need to defeat terrorist organizations and prevent attacks.

It is all well and good to talk about connecting dots, but we need to remember a simple truth: You cannot connect the dots until you first collect them.

RUSSIA'S COUNTERTERRORISM POLICY: VARIATIONS ON AN IMPERIAL THEME

For over a decade, Russia has struggled with persistent domestic insurgency and terrorism. The country has experienced a multitude of terrorist and militant attacks, and the turn of the century was marked by a series of high-profile terrorist incidents involving a large number of civilian casualties. In response to this threat, Russian authorities adopted extensive counterterrorism legislation, established and modified institutions responsible for combating terrorism, and streamlined the leadership and conduct of counterterrorist operations. According to recent statements by the present Kremlin administration, the terrorist problem in Russia has finally receded, and the war on separatism had been definitively won. Yet, the daily reports on the shoot-outs and clashes between insurgents and Russia's security forces cast serious doubts on these official claims. Despite the signs of a slow normalization of life in Chechnya, the security situation remains tense there, and terrorist incidents and guerilla attacks have spread into the broader Southern region previously unaffected by terrorism.

Much ink has been spilled criticizing deficiencies of Russia's forceful, excessive, and poorly-coordinated responses. The state has been blamed for the lack of a comprehensive counterterrorism strategy encompassing socio-economic approaches and an effective system of prevention and protection from terrorism. Yet, judging the Russian campaign's excesses and failures does not improve our general understanding of why it has always favored the tactic of force and suppression as the most appropriate methods of fighting terrorism. Stressing the futility of a short-term reactive approach does not explain Russia's choice of the military approach over the long-term socio-economic solutions for resolving complex security concerns.

It is my conviction that many aspects of Russia's counterterrorism policy can be explained from the position of Russia's imperial tradition. The latter had considerable impact on the policies and security measures adopted by the Tsarist and Soviet regimes. Rekindled recently by the fear of disintegration and reduced international standing, it has been shaping security policies and perceptions of the modern Russian state. In the essay that follows, I briefly delineate the contours of Russia's contemporary counterterrorism policy and demonstrate the continuity of Russian counterterrorism from pre-Soviet and Soviet, to post-Soviet regimes.

Next, I define and demonstrate the endurance of the imperial tradition throughout the Tsarist, Soviet, and modern epochs, and apply the "imperial lens" for the analysis and interpretation of Russia's measures aimed at combating terrorism.

A BRIEF ON RUSSIA'S COUNTERTERRORISM POLICY

In the context of Russia, terrorism has been tightly associated with activities of Islamic militants in Chechnya and the broader North Caucasus region. The latter has been an area with the highest concentration of terrorist attacks, and Chechen guerilla fighters have been implicated in the vast majority of hostage-taking incidents and terrorist crimes in Russia. The development of Russia's counterterrorism legislation and institutional framework has trailed the government's experiences with fighting the Chechen resistance and coping with the threat of terrorism in the North Caucasus.

As a result of the developments in Chechnya, the Russian government adopted the Federal Law "On Combating Terrorism" in 1998, which became the main legal pillar of Russian anti-terrorist efforts. The law attempted to define terrorist activity omitting political motivation as one of the defining characteristics of the crime. It also sketched out the legal regime of the counterterrorist operation, and defined organizational basis of counterterrorism placing Russia's Federal Security Service (FSB), and the Ministry of Interior (MVD) at the top of the list of agencies responsible for combating terrorism.

The troops of the FSB, MVD, and military units from other "power" ministries - the Defense Ministry, the Ministry of Emergency Situations, and the Border Service – were used in counterterrorism and "mop-up" operations in Chechnya as part of the Combined Group of Forces. *To assist the military battalions in carrying out counterterrorism tasks, the FSB, the Interior Ministry, and the Main Intelligence Service of Russia created special task teams for the liquidation of terrorists and militants without trial.* With a lack of oversight and the virtual impunity of the military and special task forces, the counterterrorism operation in Chechnya has degenerated into the indiscriminate use of overwhelming military force, characterized by deplorable patterns of brutalizing the local population. Frequent abductions, summary executions, and torture have had a radicalizing effect on the population.

In 1999, Russia entered the second Chechen military campaign, and a new wave of terrorist violence and insurgency engulfed the country in the early 2000s. The government's reaction to a new wave of terrorism was similar to earlier policy responses. President Putin pledged to overhaul the system of Russia's security services and develop procedures for coordinating the activities of counterterrorism agencies. The Russian government vowed to re-assert its influence in the North Caucasus and restore order in the volatile Southern region. The military strategies were expanded outside of the Chechen republic, and the presence of military troops in the rest of the North Caucasus was substantially increased. Under the pretext of combating terrorism, the Kremlin increased the powers of its security services, strengthened the "power vertical," and expanded controls over mass media and political life. To streamline the changes in the leadership and conduct of counterterrorist operations, the Russian government adopted a new Federal Law "On Counteraction to Terrorism", which replaced the earlier version. Entered into force in 2006, the law legalizes the application of armed forces for counterterrorism operations inside and outside of the country, but provides only scant description of prophylactic measures aimed at defending the Russian people and infrastructure against the threat of terrorism. As the 1998 act "On Combating Terrorism," the 2006 counterterrorism law allows for suspension of certain individual liberties and media freedoms in the zone of counterterrorist operations, and authorizes counterterrorism units to carry out searches and demolition of suspicious airplanes and ships.

Extensive legislative measures and institutional reforms all *point to the Russian desire to learn from its experiences of managing horrific acts of terrorism.* Notwithstanding *the changes at the* tactical level of counterterrorist operations and development of new means for combating terrorism, the basic principles of tackling security threats in Russia have remained essentially the same. The striking similarities of the current views on the most effective and appropriate ways of combating terrorism to those of the Soviet and Tsarist regimes suggest the palpable continuity of Russian counterterrorism. The resemblance of contemporary measures to Soviet and pre-Soviet responses is indicative of an age-old understanding of the terrorist threat that Russia inherited from the previous regimes.

THE CONTINUITY OF RUSSIA'S COUNTERTERRORISM

Since the first terrorist campaign set up by the Russian revolutionaries in the late 19th century, terrorism in Russia has been regarded as an assault against the state personified by the Tsar, the communist party, or the central government and leadership of the modern state, respectively. In the epoch of Tsars, terrorism was coterminous with the revolutionary movement against absolutism. During the early years of the Bolshevik rule, it was tantamount to counter-revolutionary anti-Communist actions. Two decades later, terrorism was viewed as subversive activities of foreign intelligence services, or acts of resistance to the Soviet government orchestrated by secret services from Western states. Neither the Soviet Union nor contemporary Russia has clearly defined terrorism or distinguished it from other crimes of a violent or political nature. This ill-defined legal construct allowed the government full discretion to bring forth charges of alleged terrorist crimes. The vague definitions created uncertainty in the application of law, which allowed for politically motivated enforcement of the criminal legislative provisions.

The scope of Russia's counterterrorism measures has been traditionally confined to military operations and security services' efforts. This follows from Russia's understanding of terrorism as an attack on the state rather than an assault on individual rights. Subsequently, in Russia, concerns over human rights have always receded to the background of counterterrorism planning and operations. The very first counterterrorist campaign launched by the Tsarist regime was exemplar in this regard. The extent of oppression and violations of individual freedoms was incommensurable to the revolutionaries' attacks that the Tsarist government sought to deter and combat. Hundreds of "politically untrustworthy" people were sent to exile, placed under strict surveillance, or kept in the long-term pre-trial detention for having "intent" to commit terrorist crimes. The secret police monitored societal "moods," and exercised control over the theater, literature, and print media. It was also responsible for surveillance of intelligentsia in Tsarist Russia.

The Bolsheviks, who replaced Tsarist agents, employed terror tactics to counter bourgeois terrorism. Since the latter was viewed as a bi-product of class struggle, the annihilation of the bourgeoisie was deemed essential for eradicating terrorism. For the Soviet government, terrorism became a continuation of struggle launched by the capitalist governments against the communist regime. Subsequently, neutralization of "enemies" suspected in collaboration with the Western nations was considered a necessary dimension of counteraction to terrorism. In modern Russia, the ruthlessness of the Russian security forces and impunity with which its troops committed their crimes against ethnic Chechens were tantamount to the brutal practices employed against the peoples of the Russian Empire, whether under Tsarist or Soviet rule.

The "security departments" ["okhrannye otdeleniya," known in the West as Okhrana) that carried out counter-revolutionary and counterterrorism functions in the Tsarist administration became a prototype for the Soviet-era secret police. The "All-Russian Emergency Commission" ("Vserossiiskaya Chrezvychainaya Komissiya"), or VChK, became the main tool of the Bolshevik terror and a precursor of the Committee of State Security (KGB) created in 1954. Modern *Russia* has largely inherited the Soviet-era structure of counterterrorism institutions, and the FSB's anti-terrorism office was a direct successor of the KGB's department for the fight against terrorism. Many officers of the contemporary security organs continue to rely on Soviet-style work methods, and believe in the effectiveness of a security model emphasizing short-term, reactive, and coercive responses instead of exploring alternative long-term measures for preventing the threat of terrorism. A long-term strategy integrating preventive, prophylactic and reactive measures *had not been developed in the Soviet Union and is in a rudimentary stage in Russia. In 2006, the FSB chief, Nicholai Patrushev, evaluated Russia's system of terrorist attack prevention as very poor, giving it a score of "2" on a 5-point scale, which is a failing grade in the Russian educational system.*

The reason for this lack of a comprehensive preventive strategy is that in each regime neither the secret services nor the law-enforcement agencies of Russia have systematically *examined their counterterrorism experiences for preparing recommendations regarding improvements of methods and tactics of combating terrorism. The Russian security agencies, like their Tsarist and Soviet counterparts, carry out little analytical work and have a minimal understanding of complex scientific and methodological tools for the systematic processing and evaluation of data with the purpose of assessing strategic situations in the region, identifying patterns of crimes, as well as the causes and consequences of criminalization.*

RUSSIA'S IMPERIAL TRADITION AND ITS IMPACT ON STATE'S RESPONSES TO TERRORISM

It is my conviction that the continuity of the Russian counterterrorism program can be explained from the position of Russia's imperial tradition. The latter refers to a practice of extension and retention of the state authority over culturally, linguistically, and ethnically diverse populations by means of force and accompanying this practice with a set of beliefs regarding the greatness and inviolability of the empire.

Tsarist Russia and the Soviet Union were both imperial states formed by conquest and military force, retained by power and centralized control, and ruled by a Moscow-based bureaucracy. Geographical expansion was the essence of imperial existence in the epoch of the Tsars. In the Soviet time, territorial aggrandizement became commensurate with the extension of the Soviet Union's national power. Both the USSR and its predecessor were multi-national states in which ethnic cultures and indigenous traditions were subordinated to "high" Russian culture and language. Although, neither entity had succeeded in building a nation, both undertook measures to develop a sense of "Russianness" in the diverse population. The Russian settlers colonized the vast territories inhabited by the non-Slavs, and occupied the key military, security, political, and economic posts in the non-Russian regions. Russian language and traditions were imposed on other ethnic groups, and myths about Russia's leading role in their present and past were actively disseminated.

Contemporary Russia has all of the trappings of an imperial state. It encompasses most of the territory of Soviet and Tsarist Russia, and many regions located on its territorial fringes still bear the scars of the colonial past. In this multi-ethnic state, a predominantly Slavic political elite rule over a multitude of disempowered ethnic cultures and groups. The Russian government, elite, and general public perceive their country as the successor of both the USSR and the Russian empire. Vladimir Putin, upon assuming his post as a Russian president, attempted to build a historical bridge from the present to the past including the Soviet time. The ideas of Russia's greatness and its destined superpower status have been used as a centerpiece of the seemingly continuous Russian identity. The notions of "gosudarstvennost'" and "derzhava," associated with strong statehood and great power, have firmly entered public discourse and have become a staple of the ruling United Russia party's platform.

Thus, the history of Russia has been that of an imperial state. Yet, it has also been an empire with a different tradition. It has never evolved into a national empire with a strong sense of national consciousness. On the contrary, Russia's nationhood has always been bound with *imperium*, Tsarist or Soviet, and citizens — regardless of their nationality — owed allegiance to the Tsar, the Communist party, or the state. Contemporary Russia reveres this tradition. "For the Russian, a strong state is not an anomaly, not something with which he has to struggle, but, on the contrary, a source and a guarantee of order, as well as the initiator and main moving force of any change," declared Putin. A strong state with direct and decisive command over the people has been viewed as a key to resolving Russia's mounting economic and political concerns.

Strengthening the state through centralization and the erection of the "power vertical" has become a marker of Putin's eight-year rule.

The imperial tradition and myths about Russia's preordained status of super power have had considerable impact on its perceptions of the threats to security and the ensuing security policies. The decline and collapse of the USSR struck a severe blow to Russian status internationally and its image as a super-power. The loss of the former Soviet Republics not only reduced the size of Russian territory, but also significantly damaged its strategic position with regard to access to the high seas and strategic resources. The deteriorating military-industrial capabilities that could not compete with the military and economic performance of the West were a source of significant unease. Like imperial Russia and the Soviet Union before, contemporary Russia has been insecure about the openness and indefensibility of its new borders as well as encirclement by what it perceives to be, at least moderately hostile states. Internally, a wave of nationalist and separatist claims that threaten a further disintegration of Russian territory have exacerbated this post-imperial frustration.

Faced with imminent decay, Russia was in no position to perform its imperial function of continual geopolitical expansion. It only sought to preserve its landmass and retain the state on a vast area of land that was in danger of shrinking away. Russia's handling of the Chechen conflict has been a product of its imperial policy, a "test of Russia's imperial will." The Chechen war and concomitant counterterrorism operations have been used to preserve the Russian "imperial body" against all odds of further degeneration. The policy toward Chechnya has been invigorated by several elements: the archaic views on the backwardness of the Chechen people; primordial beliefs in the historical enmity of the Chechen toward Russians and their supposed propensity for violence; and Russia's "calling" to protect the Slavs, Orthodoxy, and the West from the grip of Islamic radicalism. According to Putin, Chechnya was an "irresponsible quasi-state" that became a "gangster enclave while the ideological vacuum was quickly filled by fundamentalist organizations". This kind of rationalization employed by Russian leadership is not unique to the Chechen conflict. It is a frame commonly used by imperial incumbents to justify their fight against anti-colonialism.

It should be noted, however, that the Chechen resistance forces have always posed variable levels of threat to security of the Russian state. The first Chechen President Dzhokhar Dudaev let various armed groups to carry out attacks on the Russian security forces and engage in a range of criminal activities under his watch. Aslan Maskhadov, elected as a President of Chechnya in 1997, had limited success in curbing the growth of radical Islamic groups, which continued insurgency campaign against Moscow. Yet, the first military campaign in Chechnya was instigated by fear of the Chechen precedent for other discontent republics, and the primary motive for the Chechen war was to prevent disintegration of Russia. The second Chechen war was launched in response to insurgents' operations in Dagestan and a series of bombings in the heartland of Russia. The latter attacks were blamed on the Chechen resistance groups, a fact that has never been fully confirmed, and many analysts pondered over the role of the second war in boosting legitimacy and support for Putin. Furthermore, no level of threat can justify the extent of atrocities committed by the Russian military against the Chechen, official tolerance, if not outright support for, their discrimination, and demonization of the entire Chechen population in statements of some politicians and Russian mass media. Not only did these practices expand the support base for guerilla fighters and terrorists, they also prompted the change in the tactics of the Chechen insurgents who resorted increasingly to terrorist attacks inside and outside of Chechnya.

The Tsarist and Soviet empires were held together by strong authoritarian rule. The preservation of Russia's territory by means of the war and counterterrorism also revived authoritarianism. Against the backdrop of the military and counterterrorism operations in the North Caucasus, the government launched extensive political and administrative reforms carried out under the guise of restoring order, reducing lawlessness, and combating terrorism.

The first in a series of the state-wide transformations was aimed at eliminating dysfunctional features of Yeltsin-style federalism. Russia was divided into seven federal districts likened to the six Governorate Generals established by Alexander II in the wake of an assassination attempt in 1879. The presidential envoys, heading each federal district and accountable directly to president, have been tasked with the restoration of the preeminence of federal law and order, and coordination of federal agencies' activities in the districts they head. Yet, their unofficial assignment – to monitor the threats to state security and assist in the consolidation of Putin's regime – was similar to the tasks of the Governorate General formed in the epoch of the Tsars.

The 1866 assassination attempt by a young Russian revolutionary, Karakozov, gave the Tsar an excuse to take away certain municipal freedoms, and clamp down on the democratic press. The Dubrovka theater crisis of 2002 and the 2004 Beslan tragedy supplied the Russian government with a pretext for abolishing direct popular elections of regional leaders. The curtailment of media and political freedoms, and establishment of barriers for electoral competition have further strengthened the powers of the ruling regime.

The reliance on repressive and simplistic military-bureaucratic solutions to complex security problems falls in line with the imperial practices of coercion and the related belief regarding the effectiveness of the use of force. The Russian government has traditionally had a low threshold for the use of violence and few scruples about using coercion over negotiation as a policy tool. The Russian security agencies have frequently been on par with the "terrorists" in terms of their indifference for human lives and disdain for individual freedom. The impunity with which crimes were committed by the Russian troops and security services' units over the course of the war and counterterrorist operations resembled the measures of the Soviet security forces and practices of the Tsarist secret police, which also operated unchecked by any law. In modern Russia, as in Soviet or Tsarist times, Russian citizens have rarely had legal protection if pressure was exerted to force their collaboration, confession was extracted under duress, or arrests were made on the basis of false information.

To conclude, in the context of Russia's counterterrorism policy, the imperial tradition manifested itself in the notion of terrorism as an attack on the state, its interests and territory. Further, the protection of the state required the resurrection of sophisticated forms of authoritarianism. The forceful means of control is the essence of authoritarian rule. This explains the primacy of coercive, retaliatory, short-term counterterrorism responses that have been adopted by the Russian regime. The unrestricted expansion of the state's repressive powers for protection and preservation of state interests has rarely yielded good results. Instead of resolving security problems, the imperial tradition calls for their suppression. Inevitably, they re-emerge.

10

SUICIDE TERRORISM AS A TOOL OF INSURGENCY CAMPAIGNS

INTRODUCTION

Suicide attacks are offensive operations where success depends upon the death of the perpetrator. In most cases, the practice of suicide bombings represents the highest point of escalation towards a maximum level of destructiveness promoted by terrorist or insurgent campaigns. On the other hand, suicide operations are methods of growing application among insurgent groups. We have only to remember the most significant armed conflicts and terrorist episodes of the last three decades: for instance, the conflicts and attacks in Lebanon, Israel, Sri Lanka, Iraq, United States, Spain, United Kingdom, Afghanistan, Pakistan, India, Algeria, Morocco, Turkey, Chechnya, Uzbekistan, etc.

This paper offers a short review of the recent scientific literature about three main issues related to suicide violence. First, the strategic objectives as well as tactical and operational advantages of suicide attacks in the context of asymmetric conflicts. This will help to understand the rationale underlying the use of this tactic as well its instrumental utility following a plan designed by the leaders of an organization.

Nevertheless, suicide operations are not choices that are implemented by an organization, initially. As we explain later, usually these operations are the consequence of strategic shifts that follow strategic, tactical and operative criteria. Second, we interpret several scientific hypotheses about the socio-political causes of suicide terrorism in terms of risk factors. This could be useful to understand the conditions that might increase the probability of organizations opting for suicide methods rather than other tools of violence; whether alone or in combination with other political initiatives. Furthermore, this approach could help to design measures and policies to counter and prevent these kinds of attacks, an issue that will be addressed in the final section of this article.

STRATEGIC GOALS WITH TACTICAL AND OPERATIONAL ADVANTAGES

Contrary to some stereotypes, suicide attacks involve an instrumental logic. Rather, violent organizations chose suicide attacks from among a variety of tactical options in order to achieve certain strategic, tactical, and operational goals.

The strategic goals most often associated with suicide operations are the following:

1. Expulsion of foreign occupying forces;
2. Obtaining national independence;
3. Destabilization or replacement of a political regime;
4. Intensification of a violent conflict in progress;
5. Interruption of some process of peaceful solutions for a political, ethnic or religious conflict.

It can be observed through the study of suicide campaigns conducted in Israel and Iraq that the above objectives are not necessarily contradictory. Suicide operations against Israeli targets share the same goal with other forms of violence from Palestinian radical groups: the foundation of a new state in Palestine. However, all suicide campaigns undertaken by Palestinian groups have entailed a significant increase of violence and, on more than one occasion; have been utilized to interrupt peace negotiations between Israel and the Palestine Liberation Organization (PLO). In the case of Iraq, jihadi insurgent groups have directed their suicide operations against quite different targets with different purposes. Some operations are directed against Coalition Forces to expel them from the country and others against the Shiite population of Iraq in order to promote a civil war. It should be noted that each of those strategic goals could be pursued using conventional terrorist and insurgent methodologies. For this reason, qualifications for suicide terrorism as a choice above other tactics should be evaluated by exploring the tactic's potential advantages over other types of violent actions. From a tactical and operational point of view, these advantages are:

High lethality. Suicide operations cause much more casualties and material damage than any other typical insurgent method, especially when they are conducted against civilians. Suicide attacks have caused nearly 50% of victims registered since 1968, despite the fact that they represent a minority of the total number of terrorist incidents during that period. This makes suicide campaigns a very attractive option for the weaker contenders involved in asymmetrical conflicts.

Intense psychological and social impact. Because of the high number of causalities that are produced and the spectacular and illustrate the fanatical determination of its perpetrators, suicide attacks generate more anxiety, sense of helplessness, fear, and social disturbance than any other conventional violent method. Furthermore, these effects usually involve intensive media coverage.

Facilitates access to certain well-protected and high value political, military or symbolic targets. For example, political leaders or public buildings.

Precision guaranteed by means of the attacks. The use of suicide volunteers to activate explosive devices decreases dependence on remote controlled systems. The ability of the suicide bomber to decide the exact time and location of detonation provides the opportunity to adapt to any unforeseen change, such as an unexpected increase in protection arrangements of the target. Even if the suicide bomber would be stopped by a security force, he/she could still activate the explosive and cause some damage.

Simplification of the attacks and risk reduction. The death of the suicide bombers eliminates the need to design an escape plan as well as the risk of being captured and subsequently leaking sensitive information to the adversaries.

RISK FACTORS OF SUICIDE CAMPAIGNS

The data and studies accumulated over the last years make it possible to identify several conditions that correlate with suicide campaigns. We interpret these conditions as factors that could contribute to on increase in the risk that an insurgent or extremist group will resort to suicide violence.

At least, three main conditions are associated to the emergence of a suicide campaign. According to a theoretical model recently proposed by De la Corte and Giménez-Salinas, the satisfaction of those conditions occurs in two successive periods. A first phase involves the activation of collective deliberation and instrumental calculations inside an insurgent group (more specifically within its apex and its elite leadership). The ultimate outcome of this deliberation is a tactical shift in favour of promoting the use of suicide attacks. But the implementation of those operations requires two more conditions that should be simultaneously satisfied during a second phase. On one hand, the political or religious attitudes of the insurgent passive supporters must be polarized to the point that the organization favours or, at the very least, excuses the use of suicide violence. Moreover, this condition should be complemented by a radicalisation process that must be extreme enough so that the members of the organization are willing to participate in suicide operations (volunteerism is an almost universal feature of suicide attacks). In the following section some risk factors are addressed to understand the conditions increasing the risk of a tactical shift to suicide methods and the risk of a process of polarization and radicalization.

Risk Factors related to Tactical Shifts

According to available academic studies, the choice to promote a suicide campaign becomes more likely with the intervention of one or more of the three following factors :

1. *Feeling of stagnation, crisis or failure in the use of other insurgent methods*: suicide operations may be perceived as an effective method to accelerate the resolution of certain conflicts.
2. *Coexistence of several insurgent groups pursuing equivalent goals*: one of those groups may use suicide attacks to capitalize attention on their community of reference. According to several analyses, that has been a key factor in explaining the increasing periods of suicide terrorism in places like Israel and Sri Lanka.
3. *Pre-existence of suicidal activity*: the adoption of suicide methods by an insurgent group can result in a contagion effect encouraging other groups to introduce this method into their operational repertoire. This effect can be reproduced by two types of insurgent groups: those who are involved in the same conflict and those who participate in different or distant confrontations.

Risk factors related to the processes of polarization and radicalization

The polarization and radicalization processes that fuel suicide campaigns are closely related phenomena. After all, both processes are based on very similar psychosocial effects which include an attitudinal change coherent with certain political or religious arguments and a belief set that justifies suicide campaigns. Those changes could be facilitated by the subsequent factors:

1. *Dissemination of a subculture of martyrdom.* As pointed out by Gill, the concept of a "subculture of martyrdom" refers to a set of beliefs and symbolic resources that have been extracted from the political culture or the religion that insurgent groups who perpetrate suicide attacks share with a constituent community. These beliefs and symbolic resources are adapted in order to build a moral interpretation of suicide attacks as a legitimate and heroic sacrifice in favour of a certain community or social collective, or as a response to a sacred obligation (in the case of suicide violence

promoted by religious groups). Obviously, the spreading of a subculture of martyrdom is frequently connected with religious indoctrination and generally speaking should be understood as the result of several activities developed to attain that goal: proselytizing, preaching, charismatic leadership, propaganda, intensive indoctrination of future suicide bombers, etc. The subculture of martyrdom that promotes jihadi suicide violence adds two frequent and strong motivations for "martyrdom operations": as a way of atoning for the previous sins, or as an action that would be compensated with a rewards after death and/or some benefits to the suicide bomber's family in life (from cash bonuses to free apartments.

2. *Implementation of bloody counterinsurgent strategies.* Although a universal pattern cannot be set out, the correlation between overreactions to terrorism and the increase of terrorist activity has been noted on several occasions. That premise can also be applied to suicide terrorism. The polls show that the percentages of support for "martyrdom operations" are higher in countries or regions where potential sympathizers of the insurgent groups have suffered severe repression perpetrated by institutional or foreign security forces. Nevertheless, it should be noted that this is a controversial topic. For instance, the study of Pape shows that this condition does not always manifest itself in the same way. Generally speaking, there exist numerous examples of counterproductive counterinsurgent operations, in terms of how such operations contribute to an increase in suicide terrorism. Further, we can also find cases where suicide campaigns have occurred during periods of relatively lax counterinsurgent operations.

3. *Higher contrast of identities between insurgents and their adversaries and targets.* Usually, the larger the perceived differences between aggressors and their enemies are, the greater the levels of violence observed. In the same way, it seems more likely for

suicide campaigns to receive significant social support when the perpetrators of suicide attacks are perceived as members of a wider social community and there exists a clear contrast of identities between that community and the targets or victims of the attacks. Such contrasts may be based on any perceived difference, ranging from religion to nationality, political ideology to social status and profession (indeed, that is the reason why suicide attacks against military personnel or senior officials gain a stronger social support that those attacks carried out against civilians), etc.

SOME OPERATIONAL ASPECTS

The success of suicide operations is dependent on several conditions: a maximum level of secrecy, reconnaissance of the scene, the procurement of materials and the acquisition of information about the target. Secrecy ensures the preservation of the surprise factor, which is crucial for most operations. Familiarity with the attack's location, and information about the target, facilitates the anticipation of actions just before the attack and the planning of the suicide operation itself. Ordinarily, suicide bombers are supported by a cell whose members provide the attackers information on the target, safe accommodation, food, materials, explosive devices, and clothing, etc. Generally, just before the attack one of those members perform a final reconnaissance of the scene before engaging the suicide bomber.

There are different procedures for carrying out a suicide operation. The choice depends on the resources available to the group, the level of damage that is intended, and the identity of the target. Focusing on recent trends, the use of an explosive vest or belt rapped around the body and hidden under heavier clothing (SBBIEDs or Suicide Borne Improvised Explosive Devices) has become typical. The preparation of SBBIEDs is easy and cheap. The type of material used for these kinds of suicide attacks are often among the most powerful explosives, such as TNT or C4 (typical in Iraq), usually supplemented with shrapnel, ball bearings or nails.

Some vests contain a radio transmitter which allows for remote detonation from a cell phone. This allows the planning cell to ensure that the operation goes through as planed regardless of whether or not the 'martyr' suffers from second thoughts, or if he suffers a heart attack, or is intercepted by security forces. If the attack seeks to cause civilian casualties, suicide volunteers are trained to detonate themselves in crowded places, such as bazaars or public spaces.

In other cases, suicide bombers load their explosives in vehicles to crash them against their targets (VBIEDs, Vehicle Borne Improvised Explosive Devices). The use of VBIEDs increases the damage caused by the insurgents, but is a much more expensive and more complex mode of attack. The explosives used could be fuel, TNT, PE4, mortar ammunition, rockets or other artillery material. The most commonly used vehicles are motorbikes, sedans, or trucks. When cars are used several vehicles could participate in the same operation. The first car is sometimes used to distract people and break some door or barrier. Less often, suicide bombers utilize boats or airplanes to carry out their attacks, i.e. 2001 9/11 attacks.

SOME NEW TRENDS

There are other important trends not related with the technology of an attack. Two are the most significant: the implementation of suicide operations by small and isolated home-grown terrorist networks and suicide attacks which are carried out by women.

Until the end of the Twentieth Century well structured organizations used to have a near monopoly on the use of collective violence. This was also the pattern with respect to suicide terrorism; e.g., groups like Hezbollah, the Liberation Tigers of Tamil Eelam, Hamas, Palestinian Islamic Jihad, or Kurdistan Workers Party. The violence (suicide or not) promoted by those groups with insurgent goals traditionally fulfilled two conditions: it was a violence almost exclusively carried out inside a specific country or territory, and it was a violence that generated large amounts of support from a particular constituency. However, this classical pattern is no longer the case. Terrorist attacks (including suicide operations) are increasingly perpetrated by small, less structured and isolated networks, such as al-Qaeda and other groups integrated into the global jihadi movement. Those networks do not need to emerge within a broader constituency, who support suicide attacks, or if they do, their supporters could be a virtual constituency.

The March 11th attack, whose perpetrators finally committed suicide some days after the operation in the Madrid trains, is an example of suicide violence carried out by a home-grown jihadi network. Those attacks were planned and executed in order to help insurgent movements operating in far territories by forcing the withdrawal of Spanish troops in Iraq and Afghanistan. Suicide operations conducted by networks like the Madrid 3/11 group also have shown that a total differentiation among trainers and executers, which is common in other suicide insurgent organizations, is not an essential condition for suicide violence.

Although some nationalist groups like the Liberation Tigers of Tamil Eelam or the Kurdistan Workers Party have used women as suicide bombers, until recently it did seem likely that jihadi salafists would use them. There are precedents in Lebanon, from the mid 1980s, and Sri Lanka during the 90s, but the participation of women in jihadi suicide attacks has increased significantly in the past few years with examples in Palestine, Iraq, Afghanistan or Chechnya. Sometimes, women who commit suicide attacks are motivated by specific reasons like the need for revenge, the death of some member of their families, the desire to prove their equality with male peers or the aspiration to escape the predestined life expected for them. There are several operative advantages in using women as suicide bombers. First of all, this avoids the profiling used against men. Secondly, by simulating pregnancy, women can carry more explosives than men. Finally, suicide attacks by women capture the attention of the media easily.

As well as the use of women as suicide bombers, there is also a new trend that consists of using suicide bombers with other (traditionally) non-aggressive profiles. For example, al-Qaeda in Iraq has been using children and mentally deficient people who either freely or unwittingly participate in suicide operations.

MEASURES TO COUNTER SUICIDE ATTACKS

It is possible to distinguish two basic types of countermeasures to suicide campaigns: defensive and offensive measures.

Defensive measures

Defensive measures try to keep suicide bombers from reaching their targets. These include the erection of physical barriers, the installation of cameras and surveillance systems, as well as the implementation of road blocks, border checkpoints, etc. Some restrictions can be imposed to block access to information needed for planning suicide attacks (i.e., information about key infrastructure and routes or information about targets).

Military units in conflict zones can apply further defensive measures: building perimeters, armouring light vehicles, using firearms to repel the approach of car-bombs, etc. It is not by coincidence that suicide operations recently carried out in Iraq have produced more civilian casualties than military ones, which does not mean that those operations have not damaged the work of allied counterinsurgency operations. However, by forcing military units to increase self-defense measures, suicide campaigns have contributed to the isolation of military units from the civilian population.

Offensive measures

Offensive measures are those that try to prevent or reduce the implementation of suicide attacks. A preliminary offensive measure could be pre-emptive attacks against groups that promote suicide bombings in order to reduce their resources and capabilities, i.e., destroying their training infrastructure, capturing their leaders and militants, cutting their sources of funding, etc. Nevertheless, such actions involve risks. Experiences like the Israeli-Palestinian conflict also suggest that offensive operations could help to increase the number of sympathizers willing to replace insurgents that have been arrested or killed. Collecting intelligence about radical organizations is a secondary offensive measure that cannot be underestimated. Access to sufficient and rigorous information about the intentions of radicals, their plans, resources, infrastructure, procedures, etc. is of vital importance to prevent further attacks.

Finally, it is also crucial to use any available resource to reduce the insurgent group's capabilities for recruitment. Above all, this goal requires the implementation of measures to decrease the risk factors that contribute to the radicalization and polarization processes. The following countermeasures, further this final goal.

1. Mollifying any political, cultural, or socioeconomic condition that could promote the sense of threat or feelings of humiliation, revenge or hate within the real or virtual collectives who can support suicide bombers and their insurgent organization.
2. Appling specific operative measures to reduce access to propaganda distributed for disseminating the subculture of martyrdom.
3. Implementing information and counterpropaganda activities to counteract the arguments and ideas used to legitimate suicide violence. It should be noted that the chance of counteracting jihadi suicide violence requires an intense cooperation with moderate leaders, institutions and members of the Muslim community.

Bibliography

Allison, Graham: *Nuclear Terrorism: The Ultimate Preventable Catastrophe*, New York: Times Books, 2004.

Basrur, Rajesh M., and Hasan-Askari Rizvi, *Nuclear Terrorism and South Asia*, Albuquerque, NM: Sandia National Laboratories, February 2003.

Ben Wisner : *At Risk, Natural Hazards, People's Vulnerability, and Disasters*, London, Routledge, 1994.

Bhat, Chandrashekhar: *Ethnicity and mobility. Emerging ethnic identity and social mobility among the Waddars of South India*, New Delhi, Concept Publishing Company, 1984.

Fox, Lisa L. : *Management Strategies for Disaster Preparedness*, Chicago, American Library Association, 1989.

Greene, Mott : *Natural Knowledge in Preclassical Antiquity*, Baltimore, Johns Hopkins University Press, 1992.

Hoffman, Bruce, *Inside Terrorism*, New York: Columbia University Press, 1998.

Laquer, Walter, *The New Terrorism: Fanaticism and the Arms of Mass Destruction*, Oxford: Oxford University Press, 1999.

Odum, Howard T. : *Environment, Power and Society*, New York, Wiley-Interscience, 1971.

Potter, William C., Nikolai Sokov, Harold Müller, and Annette Schaper, *Tactical Nuclear Weapons: Options for Control*, Geneva: United Nations Institute for Disarmament Research, 2002.

Spector, Leonard S., Going Nuclear, Cambridge, MA: Ballinger Publishing Company, 1987.

Worster, Donald : *Dust Bowl: The Southern Plains in the 1930s*, New York, Oxford University Press, 1979.

Index

A

Al-Qaeda, 23, 53, 56, 64, 68, 86, 87, 230, 231, 239, 260.
Atmosphere, 46, 104, 175, 207.

C

Capitalism, 184, 192, 196.
Critical Information, 240.

D

Departments, 230, 245.
Developments, 165, 242.

E

Evidence, 15, 67, 77, 78, 79, 80, 81, 82, 97, 98, 99, 115, 118, 174, 181, 194, 225.

F

Foundation, 43, 111, 121, 127, 196, 253.

G

Governments, 7, 10, 16, 17, 21, 29, 32, 34, 45, 64, 74, 89, 188, 213, 236, 245.

I

Infrastructure, 42, 57, 110, 116, 200, 201, 243, 261, 262.
Insurgency Campaigns, 252.
Internet, 91, 113, 194.

M

Management, 27, 32, 52, 98, 204, 229.

N

National Development, 50, 52, 53, 55, 56, 58, 59, 60.

O

Organizations, 10, 11, 19, 32, 33, 38, 43, 106, 260, 262.

P

Psychological Dimensions, 220, 222.

R

Relationship, 38, 39, 64, 87, 88, 99, 129, 130.

S

Satellite, 64, 72.
Suicide Terrorism, 13, 23, 253, 254, 256, 257, 259.

T

Technology, 64, 109, 113, 114, 171, 184, 200, 202, 204, 205, 206, 210, 214, 217, 222, 226, 228, 259.

W

Wisdom, 33, 130, 140, 159, 166, 170, 171, 218.